THE BOOK UNBOUND
Editing and Reading Medieval Manuscripts and Texts

The Book Unbound

Editing and Reading Medieval Manuscripts and Texts

edited by

Siân Echard and Stephen Partridge

UNIVERSITY OF TORONTO PRESS
Toronto Buffalo London

Toronto Buffalo London
Printed in Canada

ISBN 0-8020-8756-6

Printed on acid-free paper

National Library of Canada Cataloguing in Publication

The book unbound : editing and reading medieval manuscripts and texts / [edited by] Siân Echard and Stephen Partridge.

(Studies in book and print culture)
Includes bibliographical references and index.
ISBN 0-8020-8756-6

1. Manuscripts, Medieval – Editing. 2. Literature, Medieval – Criticism, Textual. I. Echard, Siân, 1961– II. Partridge, Stephen III. Series.

PN162.B66 2004 809′.02 C2003-906540-5

University of Toronto Press acknowledges the financial assistance to its publishing program of the Canada Council for the Arts and the Ontario Arts Council.

This book has been published with the help of a grant from the Canadian Federation for the Humanities and Social Sciences, through the Aid to Scholarly Publications Programme, using funds provided by the Social Sciences and Humanities Research Council of Canada.

University of Toronto Press acknowledges the financial support for its publishing activities of the Government of Canada through the Book Publishing Industry Development Program (BPIDP).

For our parents

Contents

Acknowledgments

This collection had its beginnings in the 29th UBC Medieval Workshop, 'The Book Unbound: Manuscript Studies and Editorial Theory for the Twenty-first Century,' held at the University of British Columbia on 17–18 September 1999, and so our first thanks must go to the organizations and individuals who supported that workshop. Financial assistance was provided by the Social Sciences and Humanities Research Council of Canada, and by the following at UBC: the Leon and Thea Koerner Foundation; the Office of the Dean, Faculty of Arts; the Department of English; the Committee on Medieval Studies; and Green College, which hosted the workshop. We are grateful to Mary Carruthers, who gave the keynote talk, and to all who participated. Many of the arrangements which made 'The Book Unbound' such a pleasant experience were the work of Camilla Silzer McCabe, and Richard Unger helped guide us through the process of organizing the workshop.

We thank the Vice-President Academic of Memorial University for a subvention toward publication of the images in William Schipper's chapter. Irina Fainberg assisted in the preparation of the book; her work and other aspects of manuscript preparation were supported by a grant to Stephen Partridge from the Hampton Research Fund. This complicated project benefited from the care and patience of Barbara Porter and Jill McConkey of the University of Toronto Press. Elise Partridge assisted with proofreading and copyediting at crucial stages. We are both grateful to our families for their continued support.

Introduction
Varieties of Editing: History, Theory, and Technology

SIÂN ECHARD AND STEPHEN PARTRIDGE

> Texts and their editions are produced for particular purposes by particular people and institutions, and they may be used (and reused) in multiple ways, many of which run counter to uses otherwise or elsewhere imagined. To edit a text is to be situated in a historical relation to the work's transmissions, but it is also to be placed in an immediate relation to contemporary cultural and conceptual goals.[1]
>
> Jerome McGann, *The Textual Condition*

The essays in this collection grew out of papers delivered at the University of British Columbia's twenty-ninth annual Medieval Workshop, 'The Book Unbound: Manuscript Studies and Editorial Theory for the 21st Century,' organized by the editors and held in September 1999. When we issued the call for papers, we hoped to assemble a program concerned with codicology, particularly as this has produced evidence for the reception of medieval texts; with the technologies that are allowing increasing amounts of medieval textual and manuscript evidence to be represented and analysed electronically; and with the newly sophisticated awareness of the editing and printing of medieval texts as a historically situated practice. In this we succeeded beyond our expectations, as scholars from several generations working in all of these areas brought their learning, energy, and generosity to an engaging and productive workshop.

As the workshop progressed, however, and as we reflected on it afterward, we recognized several patterns among the array of papers. A significant number of them brought together, in varying proportions, all three major themes of the workshop. Many of these papers, moreover, were delivered by scholars who had completed their PhDs since 1985, and particularly since 1990. For them, therefore, the New Philology, proclaimed in the 1990 special issue of *Speculum* bearing the same title, represented neither a liberating departure from, nor a threatening challenge to, their established methods and assumptions, but rather a formative influence.[2] Thus, in their essays here, these scholars take for granted the *mouvance* of medieval literary culture and the *variance* of medieval textual culture – so much so that explicit citation of such fathers of new philology as Paul Zumthor and Bernard Cerquiglini is sparse. This shift in the status of *variance*, from a methodological disruption demanding primary attention, to an enabling assumption, frees some of their energy for a more nuanced view of the history of philology than was sometimes espoused by Cerquiglini and his earliest partisans. While some of these essays, therefore, focus on the shortcomings of certain nineteenth- and twentieth-century editions, others argue that some such editions still have much to offer by way of example. As several contributors also emphasize, these modern editions deserve continuing, sympathetic attention at precisely this juncture, when such theorists as D.F. McKenzie have redefined bibliography as the sociology of texts.[3] Moreover, the writers readily accept that editing of medieval texts now must be informed by a codicology which considers the many kinds of evidence, beyond the textual, that manuscripts and early printed books contain.

The papers reflect, in some cases overtly and in others obliquely, the ways in which various philologies – old, new, material – have been combined into a mainstream awareness of the medieval and modern text as a social phenomenon. How widespread this awareness has become is made clear, for example, by David Wallace in his introduction to the new *Cambridge History of Medieval English Literature*: 'Medieval literature cannot be understood (does not survive) except as part of transmissive processes – moving through the hands of copyists, owners, readers and institutional authorities – that form part of other and greater histories (social, political, religious and economic).'[4] All of these essays, therefore, are informed by a sense of the history of the artifacts they examine: concerns with readership, post-medieval reception, and editorial history weave through many of our essays. In addition, many of our contributors are only too aware of the effects of a particular moment on the transmission of a medieval text: author after author returns to the themes of economics, national and institutional ideologies, and class politics in their assessments of the fate of medieval textual objects. What makes these reflections linked and new is their determination to use new tools to render all these textual *processes* – the processes by which texts are created, read, and passed on – visible.

Although their historical approach makes the authors of these essays aware that no editorial practice can be neutral, they do not, as some have accused New Philologists of doing, refuse to edit. Many of the contributors to this collection are in fact presently engaged in producing editions, and in this work they move beyond purely theoretical contestations and into questions of how to present medieval texts – questions that they understand to have both theoretical and practical elements. In doing this work, they take for granted the possibilities offered by the computer; many of the pieces explore the relationships between digital technology and the characteristics of medieval manuscript culture. Some of the experiments recorded in these pages are thought experiments only, as the authors of the various essays use the availability of digital technology to revisit traditional editorial theory. Others are pragmatic, as editors currently engaged in projects involving digital media record their experiences with these new methods of delivering medieval texts to our own historical moment. But what is most striking is the extent to which all the contributors, whether or not they explore particular new technologies, deliberately engage with the practicalities of editing a wide range of medieval texts – a process that they understand to include reflection on past and current contexts, as well as past and current methods and technologies.

The essays that make up this collection thus respond critically to Cerquiglini himself and to his reception by showing what happens when new philology is modified by encounters with current editorial practice, including technological and institutional constraints, and by close scrutiny of the history of medieval editing.[5] These papers can be characterized by the varying degrees to which they are concerned with common issues: the history and practice of editing, the theory of editing, and textual and editorial technologies. The essays move in a continuum from those emphasizing history and practice through to those primarily concerned with theory and technology. We begin with essays which examine editorial projects of the past, sometimes in order to imagine editorial projects of the future. Anne Klinck, writing from her unique position as the heir to Sarah Horrall's edition of the southern version of the *Cursor Mundi*, begun in 1978, comments on the changes that have taken place in editorial assumptions and practice over the last few decades. She compares Horrall's essentially conservative approach with the more radical theory presented in John Thompson's 1998 study of the work's transmission, but her conclusions are surprising: it is the conservative Horrall who grants the southern version of the *Cursor Mundi* the kind of status that contemporary theory would seem to assign it, while Thompson's positing of an 'open' text in practice gives way to pejorative comments about scribal meddling which suggest a far more conservative attitude. She concludes, 'It is Horrall, not Thompson, who faces up to the implications of the 'open' text, not by refusing to chart manuscript relations or make editorial choices, but by selecting a stage in the poem's evolution which marks a significant departure from the author's intent.' Klinck's essay points to a tension between theory and practice, a tension that several of our contributors argue we may now begin to resolve with the new opportunities offered by digital technology.

Julia Marvin's essay on F.W. Maitland and the editing of Anglo-Norman is an instructive one in a collection such as ours, for her delineation of Maitland's 'unassuming' stance in relation to his Anglo-Norman legal texts – his separation of observation from interpretation – clarifies the extent to which current developments in editorial theory and practice have at times been anticipated by previous generations.[6] Long before the re-evaluations of Lachmannian procedures which are now commonplace in discussions of the editing of medieval texts, Maitland 'devoted his attention to how the language actually worked in his manuscripts, not to how it should have worked, or how it worked in relation to a putative continental norm.' But Marvin goes on to point out that Maitland is the exception; dismissive attitudes towards Anglo-Norman have conditioned and continue to affect the editing of Anglo-Norman texts. A significant thread in Marvin's argument is that historical and national factors played a role in the history of Anglo-Norman editing; like Meg Roland in the next essay, Marvin is sensitive to the role of ideologies, national and institutional, in the history of textual editing. Because Anglo-Norman was seen as barbarous, either it was not edited at all, or it was edited in diplomatic transcriptions at a time when critical reconstruction was the state of the editorial art. Thus Anglo-Norman was by implication relegated to the status of linguistic curiosity. Anglo-Norman fits poorly with normal assumptions about dialect: it was a status and a written language, and it adapted by mingling with English to transform the latter into a hybrid. Thus Anglo-Norman should lead us, Marvin argues, to reconsider not only the editorial methods that have been applied to it, but also the 'normal' assumptions about the operation of language. She closes by arguing for facing-page translations of Anglo-Norman texts, because such editions display most clearly the decisions made by editors. Like many of the contributors to this volume, Marvin does not so much advocate a new approach, as call for the open and honest display of the effects of our own particular ideologies and assumptions.

Meg Roland traces a similar path to Marvin with respect to the famous battle over the relative status of the Winchester manuscript and Caxton's edition in establishing the text of Thomas Malory's *Morte Darthur*. She points out that this split has (with a few notable exceptions) been an Anglo-American divide, and she devotes extended attention to the class, institutional, and national politics that contributed to the drawing of the battle lines. But she also argues that the two camps share the same central desire: to identify the genuine Malory. By contrast, Roland advocates a parallel-text edition of one of the most obviously variant sections of the text, the Roman War episode, *not* so that we may finally settle on Caxton or Winchester, but rather so that we may explore 'the intertwined textual history of the two witnesses as a rich source for understanding what has come to be known as *Le Morte Darthur*.' The verb of becoming is crucial here; Roland argues for an edition that shifts the site of inquiry from authorial intent to textual transmission. Like Klinck, then, she advocates truly accepting the challenge of *variance* and charting the stages in a text's development, *without* making a final ruling about correctness or intent. But is this approach a refusal to edit? Tim William Machan, for example, has argued that to produce a properly historical document, one must attempt to recover what lies behind the individual manuscript; it is not enough to reproduce what one medieval reader actually read, because that reader inevitably supplemented his or her copy with a variety of literary and cultural contexts.[7] The essays that follow from these first pieces frequently discuss the ways in which new technologies might allow editors to present such material (and make visible their own assumptions) more clearly than has hitherto been possible. Some of the authors speculate about how their essentially theoretical concerns could be translated into practice, while others, even as they report on practical applications of editorial technique, use these reports to speculate on questions of editorial theory.

Peter Diehl's essay, like many in this collection, begins from a gap in editorial history and practice: despite its acknowledged importance and comprehensiveness, there is no modern edition of Zanchino Ugolini's manual of inquisitorial practice, as is the case for most medieval inquisitorial manuals more generally. But Diehl has made a virtue of necessity;

because Ugolini can only be studied in manuscript and in early printed editions, Diehl has had the opportunity to trace the use and evolution of this text, and has thus drawn some conclusions about what an edition *should* look like. Unlike most of our contributors, Diehl is a historian, but he takes up a position against the historian's traditional Lachmannian analysis: inquisitorial manuals are, he argues, living texts, and the record of their use in the glosses, commentaries, and additions that characterize such manuscripts are far more important to the historian than a hypothetical *Ur-text.* Thus he calls for a hypertext edition of Ugolini, one which would facilitate a study of the reception and use of his manual in the medieval and early modern periods.

Thus far, all our contributors have dealt, in theory or in practice, with text editing. Andrew Taylor's essay points out that the word 'text' is insufficiently considered, even in our most theoretical discussions of the practice of editing. His concern is with acoustic objects, and he argues that we have yet to reckon with sound: 'As editors we pick up at the point where a text ceases to be an acoustic score and silent reading begins.' Here the imagined solution is not in new technologies. We have long had the ability to make sound part of our editions of works such as the *Chanson de Roland*, but by and large we have chosen not to do so – apparently from a conviction that editions are acoustically neutral. On the contrary, Taylor argues that the fact that the *Roland* has always been understood as a song – although it is never called that in the manuscript – has had a fundamental effect on how it has been edited, even as editors have refused to grapple with the question of how it might have been performed. Like other contributors to this volume, Taylor is aware of the role of national ideology in the promulgation of medieval texts; here, he argues that nineteenth-century France needed an oral chivalric epic, so that was what editors found in Digby 23. He echoes Marvin's comments about the denigration of Anglo-Norman by pointing to critics' discomfort with the *Roland's* dialect: the France conjured by this oral, chivalric epic is an elite and international place, in which there is no room for the local dialect in which the poem is preserved. Taylor closes his essay with an analysis of the few recordings that exist of the *Roland*, and despite his concerns about all of them, he insists that we cannot label medieval texts as songs while refusing to think about how they might have sounded. His argument – that a state of frustrated uncertainty is better than a state of false assurance – runs along with William Robins and Roland in their calls for *visible* editorial practice: the point for all of these writers is not somehow to get things 'right,' but rather to advocate for a method that makes clear what we are actually doing, thus forcing us to recognize and question our own procedures and the assumptions underlying them. We may not be able to hear a medieval text at the end of this procedure, but we will at least know that we are missing something.

Taylor's paper is about the desire to make an originary text of a certain kind out of the poem found in Digby 23 – to provide France with its own Homeric epic. Carol Symes's analysis of the editorial history of the French play *The Boy and the Blind Man* is similarly about the desire to make an ambiguous manuscript survival into something that its editors need and want it to be. She points out that the complicated paleographical evidence in the manuscript shows that this piece, identified as one of the oldest vernacular plays, has in fact been through five main stages of transmission, and that those elements which to us most clearly signal that the text *is* a play – as opposed to a fabliau or a verse story – are not part of the first copying. She argues that there is little contemporary manuscript evidence to suggest that medieval scribes and/or performers were interested in defining texts as 'plays,' while the further subdivisions and categorizations used by modern critics – even such broad ones as secular and religious drama – are even less attested. The manuscript of *The Boy and the Blind Man* shows a history of several hundred years of use, during which later generations understood – or failed to understand – the text and markings before them. Yet the practices of traditional editing have all but effaced this history, have all but hidden the *process* on which so many of our contributors insist. Symes's essay includes samples of transcriptions that show, more clearly than the available editions do, the stages of transmission: she makes clear how scholarly editions of early plays, driven as they are by anachronistic assumptions about what a play script looks like, place 'restraints on the unruly manuscript remnants of medieval theatre.'

The next essay is perhaps the most purely theoretical in the collection, for although William Robins offers various specific possibilities for editing particular texts, his main purpose is to outline a new method of editing, which he calls 'disjunctive philology.' Like Roland in her essay on Malory, Robins is aware of the impact of national institutional structures on editorial practice: he begins by noting that 'philology' has historically meant different things to different academies. Here the Anglo-American academy has been united in regarding philology as the science that understands textual objects within the contexts of recognized linguistic and material practice. Continental academics, however, in concert with developments in hermeneutics, have tended to see philology partly in terms of an object's resistance to classification. Like Klinck, Robins notes that there is often a disjunction between contemporary editorial theory and the edited texts actually produced; his 'disjunctive philology,' a practice which could be made visible through new technologies, would involve consciously modelling different editorial strategies. In *Changing Places*, David Lodge's irascible Morris Zapp imagines writing a series of books on Jane Austen, each using a different theoretical method, in order to silence writing on Austen forever. Robins does not advocate exhaustiveness, nor does he imagine that disjunctive editing would foreclose debate. Instead, 'Disjunctive text-editing ... brings contrasting editorial methods into juxtaposition in order to generate usable models, and also in order to interrogate those models for the partialities and falsifications they effect.' He praises in particular the possibilities of parallel-text editions, thus confirming Roland's thinking. But while Roland had only two versions of Malory with which to deal, Robins imagines the effect of parallel-text editing in a more varied corpus, and suggests the advantages of an edition that would present a 'best' text next to a 'worst' one, or of an edition that set an eclectic text next to one or more diplomatic ones. Such editions make clear that the work is still in process, and invite and confirm the role of readers as producers of meaning. Like Roland and Marvin, Robins points out that editors partake in many discursive practices; a disjunctive edition has the advantage of laying at least some of those practices bare.

The last three essays in the collection concern themselves with specific applications of digital technology to the editing of medieval texts. William Schipper records his experiences with commercial image-enhancing software and manuscripts that have until recently been classified as unreadable. He recounts how a fragment of Cyprian's letters that spent nine centuries as part of a binding can be read more easily once it has been scanned and enhanced with common photo-editing software. In the next essay, Stephen Reimer describes his design for a hypertext edition of John Lydgate's *Lives of Ss. Fremund and Edmund*. Where Schipper uses technology to make parts of his *manuscript* visible, Reimer proposes using digital technology to make visible the context for his manuscript, a context that includes not only the actual pages of the manuscript itself, but also images of sites in East Anglia associated, in the Middle Ages and even today, with the life of St Edmund. His argument is that the overlaying of sacred geography onto the geopolitical map of East Anglia created a 'geography of power' the impact of which can be suggested to a modern reader through photographs and accounts of persistent local legends associated with the saint. Reimer argues that by restoring some of the non-textual contexts for medieval texts, we can begin to move away from an exclusive focus on the word, an exclusivity imposed by a combination of disciplinarity and economics.

Like Reimer, Joan Grenier-Winther is aware of the economic advantages of web-based editions; it is now economically feasible to include far more information in an edition than ever before. However, she points out that this opportunity brings with it its own burdens: 'This abundance of data presents a whole new set of choices to the editor regarding which aspects of the text to present to readers who undoubtedly have different purposes for viewing the text.' She sees in digital editions the possibility for enabling the kind of reader participation envisioned by Robins in his disjunctive editions. The bulk of her essay lays out the choices she has made in designing her database-driven web edition of *La Belle dame qui eut mercy*. Like Reimer, she is concerned to rehabilitate a neglected text, and in so doing, to enrich the context in which we read more canonical works (in this case, the poem on the same subject by Alain Chartier). Her relational database is designed to facilitate linguistic and structural studies. Her decision to include an 'Editor's Choice' text answers the call to keep editing issued by critics of new philology; at the same time, however, provisions in her design that allow readers to compare individual witnesses with the 'Editor's Choice' encourage the kind of readerly response imagined by Roland and Robins. Her database will include audio clips, thus accepting the challenge issued by Taylor. This essay is well-positioned then, as the conclusion to our collection, because it offers a theoretically informed, pragmatic response to today's editorial possibilities.

Ivan Illich identifies the twelfth century as a turning-point 'in the history of that technology which has shaped western reality in a most profound way ... the alphabet.'[8] He argues that in the middle of the century, elements that the Middle Ages had inherited from the past – Roman letters, tools for writing, the materials of the book – were 'integrated into a new set of techniques, conventions, and materials,' and he sets out to explore, through a reading of Hugh of St Victor's *Didascalion*, the 'habits and meanings' resulting from the interplay of these technologies and their associated practices.[9] Illich's argument is a salutary reminder that technological revolution is not to be found only beyond the Middle Ages (for example, with the advent of the printing press or the television age).[10] It is tempting to see the digital age as a new frontier, to assert the uniqueness of our own technological moment. But the essays in this collection are not simply about bringing new technologies to bear on old problems. Certainly the technologies available to contemporary editors of medieval texts present us with undreamed-of opportunities, but these can be taken advantage of only if we keep in mind what all our contributors stress: editors are themselves historically and socially located readers – super-readers, perhaps, to borrow a term from Grenier-Winther – but no less subject to the prejudices and assumptions of their day than any other reader. Even as new editorial theory and practice revise our reception of medieval texts, we create new reading contexts, participating in the ongoing processes of the textual condition. Cerquiglini foresaw a new millennium in which the computer's power to store and present vast amounts of data in a non-sequential way would allow editors and readers to evade the choices that had constrained print editions of medieval works. Ten years later, the participants at the workshop tested this power, and those essays in this collection which directly address the promises and pitfalls of the digital world are one result. And all of the essays, whether their concerns are technological or not, manifest the awareness of our own current moment in textual studies: a time when we begin to wonder what might be after the 'new' and to explore what our present offers us – what new set of habits and meanings might be waiting to be discovered and to be made manifest.

NOTES

1 Jerome McGann, *The Textual Condition* (Princeton: Princeton University Press, 1991), p. 47.

2 The special issue of *Speculum* – 65:1 (1990) – was edited by Stephen G. Nichols. Bernard Cerquiglini, *Eloge de la variante: Histoire critique de la philologie* (Paris: Seuil, 1989), might reasonably be considered a foundation of this approach, and Nichols quotes Cerquiglini's famous remark – 'Or l'écriture médiévale ne produit pas des variants, elle est variance' (p. 111) – in the introduction to the special issue (Stephen G. Nichols, 'Introduction: Philology in a Manuscript Culture,' *Speculum* 65:1 [1990]: p. 1, quoted in translation; the line appears in French in Suzanne Fleischman's essay in the same volume: 'Philology, Linguistics, and the Discourse of the Medieval Text,' p. 25). Cerquiglini's emphasis on *variance*, of course, consciously builds on Paul Zumthor's discussion of the *mouvance* characteristic of medieval literary culture, as articulated in *Essai de poétique médiévale* (Paris: Seuil, 1972). Thus, while the phenomenon of the new philology may be identi-

fied with the late 1980s and early 1990s, its roots are considerably older. A recent translation of Cerquiglini into English (*In Praise of the Variant: A Critical History of Philology*, trans. Betsy Wing [Baltimore and London: Johns Hopkins, 1999]) suggests that the currency of *variance* will continue to grow.

3 The title of his 1986 Panizzi lectures: D.F. McKenzie, *Bibliography and the Sociology of Texts* (London: The British Museum, 1986; reprint, Cambridge: Cambridge University Press, 1999). McKenzie prefaced this new definition by arguing that 'bibliography is the discipline that studies texts as recorded forms, and the processes of their transmission, including their production and reception,' p. 4.

4 David Wallace, ed., *The Cambridge History of Medieval English Literature* (Cambridge: Cambridge University Press, 1999), pp. xx–xxi.

5 For a recent attempt to use new technologies to explain and, in a limited way, to enact *mouvance* for a student audience, as well as some reflections on the process, see Bella Millet's 'What is *mouvance*,' on the site *Wessex Parallel Web Texts*, http://www.soton.ac.uk/~wpwt/mouvance/mouvance.htm#Conclusions (last updated 6 November 2003; accessed 22 March 2004). The appearance of this essay on a site aimed at undergraduate students of medieval literature is a fair indication of the extent to which the idea of *mouvance* has become common currency in medieval studies.

6 R. Howard Bloch puts 'new philology' in quotation marks throughout his contribution to the *Speculum* special issue ('New Philology and Old French,' pp. 38–58), remarking on the pejorative undercurrents in such labels: 'Use of the labels "new" and "old," applied to the dialectical development of a discipline, is a gesture sufficiently charged ideologically as to have little meaning in the absolute terms – before and after, bad and good – that it affixes. On the contrary, to the extent that calling oneself "new" is a value-laden gesture which implies that something else is "old" and therefore less worthy, it constitutes a rhetorical strategy of autolegitimation – with little recognition, of course, that the process itself is indeed very old' (p. 38).

7 Tim William Machan, *Textual Criticism and Middle English Texts* (Charlottesville and London: University Press of Virginia, 1994), p. 184.

8 Ivan Illich, *In the Vineyard of the Text: A Commentary to Hugh's Didascalion* (Chicago: The University of Chicago Press, 1993), p. 93.

9 Illich, pp. 94–5.

10 We are thinking here of other moments famously declared revolutionary, as in Elizabeth Eisenstein's delineation of *The Printing Press as an Agent of Change* (Cambridge: Cambridge University Press, 1979); and Marshall McLuhan's description of the electronic age in *The Gutenberg Galaxy* (Toronto: University of Toronto Press, 1962).

THE BOOK UNBOUND
Editing and Reading Medieval Manuscripts and Texts

1

Editing *Cursor Mundi*: Stemmata and the 'Open' Text

ANNE L. KLINCK

A comparison between two approaches to editing and textual criticism, John J. Thompson's *Cursor Mundi: Poem, Texts and Contexts*, and Sarah M. Horrall's newly completed *Southern Version of Cursor Mundi*, sheds some interesting light on the implications of postmodern and traditional attitudes – and throws up some significant paradoxes. *Cursor Mundi* is a very long Middle English biblical paraphrase, a history of the world from the Creation to the Apocalypse that runs to 29,547 lines in its longest version. Composed somewhere in the north of England between 1275 and 1325, it survives in nine manuscripts, the contents of which vary significantly from one to another:

E	Edinburgh, Royal College of Physicians
C	London, British Library, MS Cotton Vespasian A.iii
G	Göttingen, Göttingen University theol. MS 107r
F	Oxford, Bodleian Library, MS Fairfax 14
Add	London, British Library, MS Additional 31042
H	London, College of Arms, MS Arundel LVII
T	Cambridge, Trinity College, MS R.3.8
L	Oxford, Bodleian Library, MS Laud Misc 416
B	London, British Library, MS Additional 36983 (earlier in the Bedfordshire General Library).[1]

The poem was edited for the Early English Text Society (EETS) over a hundred years ago by Richard Morris, and this edition remains standard. Though he printed several parallel texts,[2] Morris regarded the Cotton

(C) manuscript as the most authoritative, since this appeared to him to correspond the most closely to the original version.

Some thirty years ago, the late Alphonsus Campbell of the University of Ottawa envisaged another edition, based on the poem as it exists in a group of manuscripts from the south Midlands: Arundel (H, in the keeping of the Heralds of Arms), Trinity (T), Laud (L), and Bedford (B). This version takes the poem only up to line 23,898 – the Marian and devotional material that follows the Apocalypse in C is not present. A collective edition of the southern version, with manuscript H as the base text, began to emerge, under the editorship of Campbell's doctoral students, especially Sarah (Sally) Horrall, who undertook the general editorship. Volume 1, edited by Horrall, appeared in 1978; volumes 2, 3, and 4 were published over the next twelve years.[3] But Sally Horrall died prematurely in 1988, and the project fell into abeyance.

Several years ago, Laurence Eldredge, retired from the University of Ottawa, was asked to take over the project, and invited me to join him. Before she died, Sally had completed a good deal of work on the fifth and final volume; she left Text, Explanatory Notes, General Introduction, and some material for Appendices. I had prepared a Glossary and an Index. Larry Eldredge now undertook the task of writing the Textual Notes, updating the Explanatory Notes, and completing the Appendices. It fell to me to bring the General Introduction into a presentable condition. This had been left with no references, no stemma diagram – although one was obviously intended – and gaps in the typescript where Greek letters denoting hypothetical manuscripts were to be inserted. In trying to fulfil Sally Horrall's intentions, I was led to a re-evaluation of her work and its relation to current scholarship.

As Sally Horrall's Introduction to Volume 1 makes clear, she envisages her new edition as complementary to Morris's rather than superseding it. She chooses to edit the southern version because Morris did not do it justice. The manuscripts printed in his edition are all northern except one, T. Horrall's choice of her own base manuscript, H, which she admits is only 'very slightly better than' T, and which she has to supplement from T,[4] is determined by Morris's earlier printing of T. 'The present volume,' she says, 'constantly invites the reader to compare the readings of the southern version of *CM* with those of the northern MSS as printed by Morris.'[5] Horrall supposes that the southern version was someone's deliberate adaptation of *Cursor Mundi*: 'Systematically this person revised the poem he found in the MS or MSS, changing phonology, morphology, rhymes, vocabulary and ideas, and completely revising the ending of the poem. As a result, southern England acquired not a corrupt copy of a northern poem, but a new poem, substantially changed in language and scope from its original.'[6]

Her editorial policy with regard to the manuscript is highly conservative. Unattested readings are sometimes suggested in the Notes but never allowed into the Text. Manuscript H is followed faithfully except for 'obvious scribal blunders.'[7] Thus, she prints *souned* instead of *sonderd* (Morris's suggestion) in connection with God's separation of the upper and lower waters (line 378); *thonder fyre* and *thonder eyer* instead of C's *þe ouer fir* and *þat ouer air* (lines 539–40), the reading confirmed by the Latin source, 'ex caelesti igne'; and *nyȝe* instead of B's *neuere* in '... þe world shall nyȝe han ende / Ar ...' ('the world shall never have an end until ...,' lines 1393–4). All three readings, as Horrall admits, are clearly wrong. She does, however, take errors like these into account when considering the relationships between manuscripts. For her, the establishment of correct readings is prior to any hypothesis about genetic relationships. The stemma she constructs is merely a diagram of these relationships, and not an important stage in a process of stemmatic recension.

In an article published in *Text* (1985), a paper which in many ways anticipates the Manuscript Relations section of her General Introduction, Horrall takes issue with Max Kaluza's stemma, which he had produced at the time of the EETS edition, and which had never really been superseded. Horrall notes that this stemma, 'constructed in classical fashion by an examination of minute verbal similarities and differences among the manuscripts ... involved him in difficulties, as he had to account for apparent manuscript contamination among E, F, and the four south Midland manuscripts derived from δ.'[8] Basing her own theory on the preservation of 'original' readings in the southern group, Horrall argues that the scribe of the exemplar of this group (i.e., δ) 'may have collated two different copies of *Cursor Mundi*, one of them related to CG, and one whose descent from the archetype [of all the extant manuscripts] we will never know.'[9] This other, shadowy, ancestor is indicated by a broken line and a question mark, left floating in the *Text* article, indicating Horrall's unwillingness to speculate about its derivation.

On page 6 is my reconstruction of the similar stemma diagram Horrall devised for her edition. This diagram and the associated discussion are influenced by the stemmatic analysis of C.V. Ross as well as that of Kaluza, and trace a somewhat more complicated relationship between

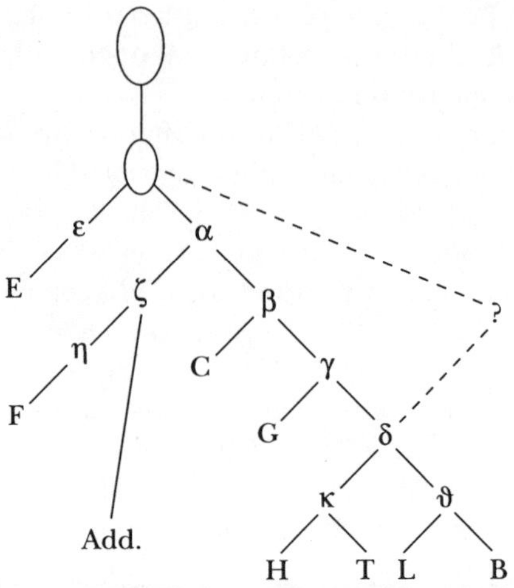

HTLB (in the *Text* article, HTLB all descend directly from δ, and there is no mention of Ross's work). Her grappling with manuscript relations is also reflected in a pencilled stemma diagram left among her notes. In the pencil sketch, the arrangement of FAdd and of HTLB is slightly different, there is no question mark, and both C and the ancestor of FAdd descend directly from O^1.

Horrall's explanation in her General Introduction of the rationale behind the southern version reflects a more complex situation than the above diagram can actually show – and illustrates the typical problems with classical stemmatics. She believes one of the ancestors of the southern group to be the south Lincolnshire exemplar from which the first 11,000 lines or so of manuscript G were copied. G, in fact, shows evidence of being copied from two distinct exemplars: the first south Midland, the second Northern. Thus the sigil γ in Horrall's stemma denotes two distinct entities; the southern group is descended from only one of these.[10] Again, the possibility of lateral as well as vertical influence, indicated by her broken line and question mark, raises another stock problem with stemmatic tree-diagrams, dependent as they are on indications of vertical descent. Her view of the relationship between the *Cursor Mundi* manuscripts is based not just on agreement in error, as in classical recension, but also on the preservation of original readings from the Latin or French source texts. Her treatment of the subject, then, is eclectic in its methodology, and although she proposes a new stemma, she is well aware that no diagram can adequately convey the complex relationships which she perceives.

Sally Horrall's handling of textual criticism and manuscript relations was not simplistic, but in the twenty-five years since she began her edition, the subject has been increasingly problematized, to the point where scholars hesitate to postulate a text at all. In 1998, John Thompson's study of *Cursor Mundi* appeared. While Horrall questions the use of classical stemmatics at the time of the EETS edition of *Cursor Mundi* and tends to favour a best-text approach, her attitude towards textual criticism remains traditional. Thompson, however, rejects the view of variant manuscripts as more and less faithful representations of 'an authorial final text' that has been 'mutilated by a succession of wretched scribes,' as Larry Eldredge puts it in the Preface to volume 5.[11] Instead, Thompson proposes an 'open' or 'unstable' text, the changing of which over time is to be regarded as evolution, not corruption.

Like Morris, Thompson treats C as his base version, but he is 'particularly anxious *not* to argue that the choice of C ... should be based on the classical methods of textual recension that have ... proved so troublesome for modern editors since the time of Morris and Hupe.'[12] At no point in time does the text possess an especially authoritative status. In Thompson's view, the author himself envisaged the poem in different ways at different times, and his successors merely continued this process.[13] Not surprisingly, Thompson offers neither stemma nor text, though he does provide an extremely detailed and careful account of the poem's relationship to its sources at various stages in its evolution.[14] In doing so, he is led to critique Horrall's analysis. He puts his finger on some weak spots in her exposition – notably her assumption that accurate rendering of *Cursor Mundi*'s sources proves preservation of an original reading. Thompson rightly points out that it would have been easy for scribes to correct mistakes in translating well-known sources – like the Bible.[15] And he notes that a traditional stemma cannot trace polygenesis, the dissemination of different 'authorized' versions of *Cursor Mundi* which he postulates.[16]

John Thompson's assumption of a fluid text is entirely reasonable. His attempt to sort out the various chronological layers of 'authorized' additions – a scheme summarized in tabular form in his Appendix II[17] – is less persuasive, and essentially very speculative. Also, interestingly, as soon as Thompson comments on specifics he abandons his theoretical position and begins to speak in the terms that he claims to reject. He criticizes Horrall because she has failed to solve the problem of manuscript inter-relations.[18] He notes, 'F frequently agrees with CG, and sometimes E, in preserving readings that seem to reflect a more *faithful* [my emphasis] Middle English rendering of the *Cursor*-poet's sources than Add. or THLB.'[19] Although he believes that 'the case for the so-called "Southern version" has been overstated,' he thinks the southern texts 'mark an ill-defined but crucial transitional period in the textual history of the *Cursor Mundi* compilation.'[20] Most strikingly, he declares that 'THLB can ... be said to represent an inglorious textual tradition where readings have been introduced that weaken or distort our sense of the *Cursor*-poet's narrative presence.'[21] Here, Thompson seems to want to have it both ways: (a) the southern version is not an identifiable entity, and (b) the southern version is a corruption of the author's text. All his criticisms of the southern manuscripts – and they are quite persuasive – reflect his view of them as a debased rendering and the traditional mindset such a view implies: 'these texts probably represent a relatively inept attempt to partially revise the poem'; readings are 'more consistently suspect' in the 'non-northern texts'; 'the authority of the first person singular voice ... [is] diluted in ... THLB.'[22] He attempts to reconcile his two positions by suggesting that the source of the southern group may have been an *avant-texte,* a draft of 'work in progress' which did not yet contain the material on the Sorrows of the Virgin and her Immaculate Conception with which the poem's prologue proposes to end (*CM* 217–20), but his position remains rather unclear.[23]

Questioning of traditional editing practices has become one of the standard themes of medievalist discourse, and has usefully raised questions about the unexamined assumptions that have informed medieval studies. Computer technology has made the hypertext possible – Hoyt Duggan's *Piers Plowman Archive,* Kevin Kiernan's *Electronic Beowulf,* for example – so that readers can survey the materials on which editorial choices are based. But the practical difficulties of making these choices remain. Thus, Tim Machan's *Textual Criticism and Middle English Texts* criticizes editorial assumptions about an author's authority as unmedieval,[24] and by way of illustration offers a variety of historically sensitive ways in which the *Boece* might be edited – but no specific examples.[25] When, for the sake of his argument about Henryson's *Moral Fables of Aesop,* Machan needs to posit a specific order of the material, he makes textual choices of a traditional kind and buries this anomaly in an endnote.[26] Though Machan denies that a refusal to apply traditional editorial techniques means a refusal to edit, he never demonstrates other ways in which the textual choices editors are faced with might be made.[27] David Greetham argues for the network-form of the rhizome rather than the lineal descent of the tree as a stemmatic model, averring that 'the hypertextual model of free-floating links is a better simulacrum of medieval textuality than the fixed critical text of the codex ever was,' only to end up by conceding that new editors will still first look for the right tree to hang their witnesses on.[28] Both Machan and Greetham stop short of taking their proposals beyond the theoretical level. Ultimately, neither dispels the anxieties of Lee Patterson, who in his essay on the Kane-Donaldson edition of the B version of *Piers Plowman*,[29] notes that poststructuralist thought rejects the assumption that there is an original which can be recovered, and asks, 'are we prepared ... to ... accept ... medieval literature ... as by definition incapable of yielding to editorial ministrations?'[30] Patterson's argument is not that this position is untenable, but that it is impractical. It can be maintained only on a theoretical, abstract level.

Thompson, also, remains attached to the traditional thinking he questions. In fact, his whole attitude to *Cursor Mundi* as an open, unstable compilation is curiously equivocal. On the one hand, he speaks critically of the notion of bad readings and the way 'mistrust of texts'[31] has influenced stemmatics and other approaches to textual criticism.[32] On the other, he deplores the dilution of the authorial presence in the southern version, and notes that its readings often have to be corrected from northern texts. His view of the author's authority and 'authorized' versions can thus be seen to be precisely that which Machan criticizes. Thompson repeatedly uses the term 'meddling' to refer to later revisions.[33]

Horrall's and Thompson's accounts of the evidence presented by the various *Cursor Mundi* manuscripts do not actually differ that much. What differs is their interpretation and their emphases. Both point out that the versified table of contents at the beginning of the poem specifies that it will end with the Immaculate Conception of the Virgin, that this must have been the poet's original intention, and that among the extant manuscripts this intention is only followed in E, 'arguably the oldest of the surviving manuscripts.'[34] The main thrust of Thompson's book is that the poet himself made additions to *Cursor Mundi* at various points in time. For example, Thompson regards interpolations from a supplementary source into a section based on another main source as an indication that these interpolations represent a later stage. Horrall thinks this technique shows the poet worked with several sources at once. It seems to me there is absolutely no way of knowing which of these theories is correct. Very likely there is truth in both of them. Again, Horrall comments that 'there is a very stable core to the poem, although at certain recognized places additions and deletions could be made.'[35] Thompson investigates the unstable sections, notably the Passion and the supplements at the end of the poem.[36] Thus, both of them perceive *Cursor*

Mundi as consisting of more and less stable sections, but Horrall chooses to emphasize the former, Thompson the latter. And both of them see the southern texts as significantly different from the 'authorized' version. Thompson, rather inconsistently, regards this departure as a deterioration which makes the southern group less worthy, Horrall as a new rendition which makes the southern group interesting. She sees this version as 'an attempt to tailor an older text to a changed market,' points out that 'the southern version retains almost nothing but the chronological narrative portions of *CM*,' and suggests that this version was adapted for a series of relatively short reading sessions.[37]

As for my own position, I suspect that most readers will find in manuscript C, edited by Richard Morris between 1874 and 1893, a more distinctive and thematically more coherent poem than in manuscript H, edited by Sally Horrall et al., between 1978 and 2000. I am sceptical as to whether the four manuscripts preserved in a south Midland dialect, partly, actually reflect a new poem. They do reflect another version. Thompson's repeated criticisms of it confirm this.[38] Perhaps the principal problem in presenting this southern version is to decide whether troubling readings are to be regarded as simple error on the part of the redactor or as part of his systematic revision.[39] The Ottawa University Press edition rounds out our knowledge of the poem and its evolution, restoring what was previously regarded as a debased version to its rightful place. Curiously, it is the traditionalist Horrall who does this, rather than the postmodernist Thompson. It is Horrall, not Thompson, who faces up to the implications of the 'open' text, not by refusing to chart manuscript relations or make editorial choices, but by selecting a stage in the poem's evolution that marks a significant departure from the author's intent.

NOTES

1 For the date, see Sarah Horrall, ed., *The Southern Version of Cursor Mundi*, 5 vols (Ottawa: Univerity of Ottawa Press, 1978–2000), 5:13 and 17–18. Horrall suggests York as a possible place of composition; Thompson notes that the three earliest manuscripts – E, C, and G – 'preserve dialect features associated with the West Riding of Yorkshire'; John J. Thompson, *The Cursor Mundi: Poem, Texts and Contexts* (Oxford: Society for the Study of Medieval Languages and Literature, 1998), p. 14.

2 Principally C, G, F (of Lancashire provenance), and T (non-northern). Morris resorts to other manuscripts to supplement the gaps in his main texts: *Cursor mundi (The Cursur o the world). A Northumbrian poem of the XIVth century*

in four versions, ed. Richard Morris et al. EETS, o.s., nos. 57, 59, 62, 66, 68, 99, 101 (1874–93).

3 Edited by Roger Fowler, Henry Stauffenberg, and Peter Mous, respectively.

4 Horrall, *Southern Version*, 1:23–4.

5 Horrall, *Southern Version*, 1:13.

6 Horrall, *Southern Version*, I.12.

7 Horrall, *Southern Version*, 1:25. The only justification I can find for Thompson's statement that subsequent editors have diverged from this policy (*Poem, Texts and Contexts*, p. 17) is Fowler's importation of *two* readings from the northern version into his text, at lines 11,191 and 11,941. See *Southern Version*, 2:66 and 91; 133 and 138 (Explanatory Notes).

8 Sarah Horrall, 'The Manuscripts of *Cursor Mundi*,' *Text* 2 (1985): 71.

9 Horrall, 'Manuscripts,' 79.

10 Cf. Hanna's stemmatic analysis of *The Siege of Jerusalem*, in which he diagrams and comments on the descent of manuscript C from two separate exemplars (Ralph Hanna III, *Pursuing History: Middle English Manuscripts and Their Texts* [Stanford: Stanford University Press, 1996], p. 91).

11 Larry Eldredge in Horrall, *Southern Version*, 5:x.

12 Thompson, *Poem, Texts and Contexts*, p. 20. Hupe worked on the stemma for Morris's edition, and neither of his two efforts was satisfactory. For these two stemmata, as well as the two others proposed by Kaluza and Ross respectively, which are more convincing, see *Southern Version*, 5:42–3. See also Max Kaluza, 'Zum Handschriftenverhältniss des *Cursor Mundi*,' *Englische Studien* 11 (1888): 235–75, and Charles C.V. Ross, 'An Edition of Part of the Edinburgh Fragment of the Cursor Mundi,' B. Litt. thesis, Oxford University, 1971.

13 See Thompson's summary of his views in his introduction: 'Taken as a whole, the evidence assembled in this study suggests that much of ... [the *CM* poet's] not inconsiderable creative talent was taken up with the task of expanding and revising his own pre-existing collection of biblical stories with newly translated extracts from other sources. Before a single *Cursor Mundi* text had been released, the *Cursor*-poet's working version had probably already outgrown the fossilised form of the monumental work described in the prologue. A number of different late medieval readers, book-producers, editors and copyists then took a continuing and active interest in reworking parts of the *Cursor Mundi* compilation for their own purposes' (pp. 21–2).

14 Especially valuable is Thompson's detailed account of the surviving manuscripts, which points out the errors in the standard guides, and enumerates very precisely the main features of the nine principal witnesses (ECGFTHLBAdd). See chapter 1 (pp. 23–46).

15 Thompson, pp. 48–9. Horrall admits that 'a particularly alert scribe' might

correct his exemplar from his own knowledge of scripture (*Southern Version*, 5:45). But the other examples she cites where a less reliable manuscript has apparently preserved a particular source reading – from the *Elucidarium* of Honorius Augustodunensis, the *Bible* of Herman of Valenciennes, and the *Traduction anonyme de la Bible entière* – also involve well-known and widely disseminated sources. On *CM*'s relationship to these works, see Thompson, pp. 109 ff. (on Herman), 121 ff. (on *Trad. anon.*), 159 ff. (on *Eluc.*).

16 Thompson, pp. 61–3.

17 Thompson, pp. 183–4.

18 Thompson, pp. 47–8, n. 3.

19 Thompson, p. 48.

20 Thompson, pp. 17, 49.

21 Thompson, p. 49.

22 Thompson, pp. 51, 52 n. 7.

23 See Thompson, p. 61. Thompson finds in lines 23,905–8, preserved in ECGF but not in the southern texts, evidence that the poet plans to speak in praise of Mary in a later redaction. In these lines he promises to tell of her 'worship' 'elsewhere,' when he comes to a 'better space.' However, earlier on Thompson seems to be thinking in terms of deliberate deletion rather than an early stage of composition: 'the texts in THL *fail to preserve* [my emphasis] the Marian additions' (p. 54). MS B also lacks the Marian material, but instead has Chaucer's *ABC to the Virgin.*

24 Vernacular texts not being regarded as the work of 'auctores' or having 'auctoritas' in the Middle Ages; see Tim William Machan, *Textual Criticism and Middle English Texts* (Charlottesville: University Press of Virginia, 1994). Machan is strongly influenced by the work of Alastair J. Minnis, especially his *Medieval Theory of Authorship*, 2nd ed. (London: Scolar, 1988).

25 Machan does point out that one historical option 'would be to edit the *Boece* so as to recover *for historical interest* the actual text Chaucer wrote, regardless of how this text was received and processed in the Middle Ages. Such an edition would be of *Chaucer's Boece*, not of the *Boece* itself' (p. 186). He adds, 'Minnis and I have attempted just such a recovery in *The Boece*' (p. 220, n. 2), referring to their variorum edition. Machan's actual editorial enterprise, then, is of a perfectly traditional kind.

26 Machan's demonstration of the way a well-known vernacular author usurps the authority of his Latin source depends upon a central position for the *Lion and the Mouse* fable. See *Textual Criticism*, pp. 126 and 130. He supports this arrangement on the basis of 'thematic coherence and symmetrical patterning' – while acknowledging the awkward possibility that the arrangement may be attributable to a later redactor (p. 212, n. 62).

27 As Hoyt N. Duggan observes, 'Much of what Machan has to say about conceptions of vernacular writing in late Middle English is true and important. But it is not at all clear that the differences in attitude toward authority and textuality ... have any relevance to the issues facing textual critics of late Middle English works' (Review of *Textual Criticism* in *Text* 10 [1997]: 385).

28 See David Greetham, 'Phylum-Tree-Rhizome,' in *Reading from the Margins: Textual Studies, Chaucer, and Medieval Literature*, ed. Seth Lerer (San Marino, California: Huntington Library, 1996), pp. 123 and 126, respectively.

29 An essay that Patterson first presented as a conference paper in 1982, published as 'The Logic of Textual Criticism and the Way of Genius: The Kane-Donaldson *Piers Plowman* in Historical Perspective,' in *Textual Criticism and Literary Interpretation*, ed. Jerome McGann (Chicago: University of Chicago Press, 1985), pp. 55–91 and finally incorporated into his *Negotiating the Past* (Madison: University of Wisconsin Press, 1987).

30 Patterson, p. 112.

31 The phrase is Eugène Vinaver's. See his 'Principles of Textual Emendation,' in *Studies in French Language and Medieval Literature Presented to Professor M.K. Pope* (Manchester: University of Manchester Press, 1930), p. 352.

32 Thompson, p. 47.

33 While actually commenting on a passage where the poet invites others to 'amend' his story of the Cross, Thompson observes that 'the *Cursor*-poet's words ... suggest that he would not have been entirely surprised with the later textual *meddling* that this part of his narrative has had to *endure*' (p. 135, my emphases). See also the subheadings of sections vi, vii, and viii in chapter 2, all entitled 'Scribal meddling.'

34 Thompson, p. 14.

35 Horrall, *Southern Version*, 5:11.

36 For the instability of the Passion section, see Thompson, pp. 63 and 66 (Fig. 1).

37 Horrall, *Southern Version*, 5:11, 11–12, and 12.

38 Thompson illustrates well the way in which the deletion of direct address in the first person, from the poet to his audience, weakens the sense of a controlling authorial presence and agenda. See especially pp. 51–5.

39 Greetham refers to the need to distinguish among 'a) linear, parentally derived features, b) the effects of immediate environment, and c) idiosyncratic aberrations' (p. 111). Cf. also Seth Lerer and Joseph A. Dane: 'where do we draw the line between a 'variant' and an 'error'? ... how can we distinguish between a lapse and an intrusion – and, in the case of what appear to be intelligent and meaningful intrusions, how do we distinguish between the variant and wholesale rewriting?' (*Reading from the Margins*, Introduction, p. 3).

2

The Unassuming Reader: F.W. Maitland and the Editing of Anglo-Norman

JULIA MARVIN

F.W. Maitland was so zealous a champion of primary sources that he devoted his 1888 inaugural lecture as Downing Professor of the Laws of England at Cambridge to these sources and their promulgation: 'hoarded wealth yields no interest.' Arguing that 'legal documents, documents of the most technical kind, are the best, often the only evidence that we have for social and economic history, for the history of morality, for the history of religion,' he urged legally trained scholars to study and publish 'the most glorious store of material for legal history that has ever been collected in one place ... free to all like the air and the sunlight.' And at the self-promotional opportunity of a lifetime, the day he was entitled and expected to strike a magisterial pose, he concluded, 'Copy-books there ought to be and I would gladly spend much time in ruling them, if I thought that they were to be filled to the greater glory of the history of English law.' The lecture is entitled 'Why the History of English Law Is Not Written.'[1]

When, two years before, Maitland had agreed to edit the Anglo-Norman Year Books of Edward II, he took them on in avocation rather than duty.[2] The Year Books contain what are in effect reports of cases argued in the King's Court in London; Maitland loved them not least for their immediacy, for their representation of particular cases and real speech, and for what they hint about the interests of those who took the cases down. As he says in the introduction to the first volume of the Year Books, which appeared for the Selden Society in 1903, what their writers 'desired was not a copy of the chilly record, cut and dried ... What they desired was the debate with the life-blood in it.'[3] Maitland chose to excavate this part of the documentary trove because he saw in it the development of English law in practice, through 'the play of those moral and economic forces of which legal logic is the instrument,' as 'logic yields to life, protesting all the while that it is only becoming more logical' (pp. xviii, xix).

Maitland's interest in the volatile relationship of logic and life, as well as the primacy he here assigns to life, are consistent with his general habit of working from known specifics toward unknown generalities. So described, his approach sounds obvious and commonsensical.[4] How are we to start with what we do not know, after all? But in both theory and practice the particulars offered by the past are constantly subjected to the authority of the general and the preconceived. And in no area of medieval studies has this tendency been more pronounced than in the study of the dialect of the Year Books, Anglo-Norman.

The language brought to England by its Norman conquerors and in use for some centuries afterwards has met with scorn for a long time.[5] Maitland points out that as early as the thirteenth century continental French speakers were making fun of the English inclination to turn all verbs into the first conjugation.[6] And it may not be too much to say that Chaucer's jibe at the Prioress's French after the school of Stratford atte Bowe has given generations of scholars license to ignore at best and ridicule at worst the language and literary milieu of some of the most important vernacular literary innovations in England or France: the first drama, the first scientific treatises, the first poetry known to be written by women, the first complete national histories, and, as Maitland points out, the first contemporary records of live conversation.[7]

Part of the difficulty with Anglo-Norman is that, as a variety of French used in England, it fits so poorly within standard boundaries of language and nation: it confounds the generic and disciplinary expectations of modern audiences. In the early days of the institutionalization of medieval studies, Anglo-Norman could be something of an embarrassment for all parties concerned. For a French academy that located its literary peak and linguistic norm in the romances of the twelfth century, Anglo-Norman was a degenerate byblow. For the English academy, Anglo-Norman was far from providing evidence of an authentic native past: instead, it was a reminder of past colonization, and of the mongrel nature of the language, culture, and government of England. It evinced not God's plenty, but William the Bastard's. The peculiarity of this remarkable cultural phenomenon tended to repel rather than attract scholarly attention. After the first generation to take an interest in Anglo-

Norman, that of the 1830s, the dialect was viewed and edited as a debased version of Old French, insular in all the worst senses of the word.[8]

Keith Busby, William Rothwell, and D.A. Trotter have written compellingly and even passionately on the history of Anglo-Norman studies, and in particular, on the dominance of narrowly philological and morphological habits of mind on the perception of the dialect. As Busby puts it, by the 1870s, 'The French attitude to Anglo-Norman ... can basically be summed up as follows: during the twelfth century, insular authors wrote passably correct French and are worthy of our attention, but as time progresses Anglo-Norman simply becomes bad French; the impurity of the language is generally measured by the degree to which versification diverges from the continental norm; later works are generally only interesting as curiosities.'[9] French scholars of the period describe Anglo-Norman writers as unable to preserve the language brought over by the Normans and the dialect as being 'français dégénéré'; anomalies in the texts – that is, differences from the continental French given normative status – are attributed to scribal and authorial illiteracy, incompetence, and metrical tone-deafness.[10] Paul Meyer, the most prolific editor of Anglo-Norman of the day, freely refers to the dialect as 'barbare' and 'mauvais.'[11]

Meyer, along with Gaston Paris, was one of the initial proponents of critical text reconstruction, but he himself made best-manuscript editions of Anglo-Norman works, perhaps because there could by definition be no way to recreate the pristine original of a work in a language defective by nature: a 'good' Anglo-Norman text would no longer be Anglo-Norman at all.[12] Meyer's experience with the insusceptibility of Anglo-Norman to critical reconstruction may have contributed to his loss of enthusiasm for the method, although if such was the case he did not acknowledge it, as far as I know. The challenges that Anglo-Norman poses to traditional conceptions of linguistic and literary development have more often than not led to the dismissal of the dialect, not to the reconsideration of preconceptions.

It has become increasingly clear over the years that the notion of a linguistic norm is not an especially meaningful, much less fruitful, one for Anglo-Norman. As a vernacular of status that became largely a written phenomenon, it cannot be expected to have operated or developed in ways directly analogous to either Latin or the other vernaculars of Britain or France (which of course present complications of their own). Even during its lifetime, Anglo-Norman held a peculiar and constantly changing status as a dialect falling out of ordinary spoken use: it picked up English syntax and was apt to lose distinctions such as those of grammatical gender, as English rather than French became the mother-tongue of its users.[13] At the same time, those who continued to use Anglo-Norman did so in large part because it was not English. Its value resided in its difference, so that in one respect at least it remained linguistically conservative. It adopted relatively little English vocabulary at a time when English itself was taking in Anglo-Norman words wholesale.[14] Of course, Anglo-Norman looks so outlandish to modern eyes because it did not survive as French of Paris did: Anglo-Norman survived by infiltrating English, helping to transform the prevailing vernacular of England into a truly hybrid language.[15] The question now may be not what traditional approaches to language reveal about Anglo-Norman, but rather what Anglo-Norman may reveal about traditional approaches to language, and also what other approaches the distinctive realities of Anglo-Norman may suggest and reward.

The understanding of Anglo-Norman is certainly improving, especially with the publication of the *Anglo-Norman Dictionary*, itself a case study in the development of thought on the dialect.[16] In the general preface to the dictionary, Rothwell quotes the minutes of the 1945 meeting at which the project was first proposed: L.W. Stone, who was to become its first chief editor, 'raised the question of the need for a glossary of Anglo-Norman, suggesting that the compilation of such a work would avoid the need for printing texts of which the only interest lay in the vocabulary.'[17] The proposal speaks volumes about the governing assumptions of even those who presumably took Anglo-Norman most seriously. The glossary's purpose, as Rothwell describes it, would be to 'obviate difficulties caused to readers of Anglo-Norman by strange spellings and abnormal verb forms,' in an approach he characterizes as 'entirely in line with the intellectual climate of the age.'[18] Over the next forty-odd years, the project both reflected and promoted the development of a better understanding of Anglo-Norman. The first fascicles, governed by the choice of words and spellings not found in continental French, and based for the most part on purely literary sources, present the dialect eccentrically and are none too easy to use; the later ones, which draw on the increasing variety of sources coming into print and aim to represent general Anglo-Norman usage, give the dictionary's users occasion to see that, in Rothwell's phrase, 'Anglo-French was far from being merely Old French as used by ignorant islanders who could neither spell nor conjugate correctly.'[19]

But Anglo-Norman's early pariah status has had its consequences. For the past century, scholars have been crying in the wilderness for more respect and attention to Anglo-Norman culture, language, and literature: examples include Maitland in 1903, Paul Studer in 1920, Ruth Dean and Dominica Legge in mid-century, and Rothwell and Busby from the 1970s until now.[20] The titles of works in Anglo-Norman studies incline towards the wistful: to name a few, 'What Is Anglo-Norman?' 'A Fair Field Needing Folk,' 'Glimpses into Our Ignorance of the Anglo-Norman Lexis,' and 'Neither Flesh nor Fish, nor Good Red Herring.'[21] A tendency towards Shakespearean, Langlandian, and also Biblical allusion is notable: characteristic, I suspect, of a bid not for borrowed status but for the comfort of a shared frame of reference that the field itself cannot provide, since the only common catchphrases for Anglo-Norman are the ones denigrating it as 'faus francais.'[22] And the laborers in the vineyard are still lamentably few. The cycle of contempt and neglect is difficult to break.[23] Two series alone, the Selden Society and the Anglo-Norman Text Society, still account for the majority of Anglo-Norman editions produced. The debris of outdated ways of thinking litters available texts and established editorial habits and so quietly continues to influence ideas of the language.[24] It helps perpetuate the impression of Anglo-Norman as a deviant form of something else rather than a thing in itself.

Such was of course received opinion when Maitland began his work on the Year Books: Anglo-Norman was a bad language, and legal French was the worst kind of Anglo-Norman.

Maitland acknowledged these views. 'Badish French it may be,' he concedes, in some badish English of his own (p. xvii). He then proceeds with tongue even more firmly in cheek to quote Hippolyte Taine's description in his *Histoire de la littérature anglaise*: 'un français colonial, avarié, prononcé les dents serrées, avec une contorsion de gosier' (a colonial, spoiled French, pronounced with clenched teeth and convulsed throat), 'à la mode, non de Paris, mais de' – of course – 'Stratford-atte-Bowe.'[25] To this characterization Maitland responds, 'Is not the very rudeness of the French that we find in these legal manuscripts ... a quality which its best judges would not willingly miss? Is it not a guarantee of genuineness? No one has tried to polish or prune, or to make what is written better than what was heard. We fancy that learned men who explore the history of the French of Paris would sacrifice many a *chanson de geste* for a few reports of conversation that were as true to nature, as true to sound, as are our Year Books' (p. xvii). What Maitland did in the face of the obstacles to the unprejudiced representation of this rude French was start from scratch: since there were no editorial standards for Anglo-Norman as such, he devised ones for the project, working out a grammar of Anglo-Norman from his set of manuscripts.[26] He presented the results of his thinking in the introduction to the first volume of the Year Books, for the years 1307–9: 'Observations of an empirical kind have been accumulating in the course of our task, and the publication of some of them, though they cannot pretend to phonological or grammatical science, may perhaps ease the labour of other students and transcribers' (p. xxxiii).

This material, by the way, might well never have made it into print. It is tempting to think of the great older editions as products of palmier days, when publishers had plenty of money and scholars plenty of time, but such was not the case either for the Selden Society, which almost ceased to be when its treasurer embezzled its funds and then killed himself, or for Maitland himself, who was overworked at Cambridge and chronically ill.[27] He worked on the Year Books from photographs of the manuscripts that he took along to rest cures in the Canary Islands: he died in 1906, at the age of 56, with the fourth volume of the series still in progress. In order to save the Selden Society money, Maitland offered to omit the first volume's discussion of Anglo-Norman, but the Secretary declined, and so the introduction survives.[28] It is a testament of a kind: towards the end of the introduction, while characteristically soliciting criticism from his readers, Maitland acknowledges that the work of publishing the Year Books 'will soon pass out of the hands that are endeavoring to begin it; but if members of the Society will speak their minds, every volume of the Year Books may be better than the last' (p. lxxxix).

That expression of hope bespeaks Maitland's understanding of his task as an editor: he knew that the most he could hope for his work on Anglo-Norman in general and the Year Books in particular was to make a good start; he did not harbor delusions of completeness or perfection.[29] He knew that his skills, and especially his time, had limits, as did the resources of the Selden Society. But he still hoped that the Society might 'redeem the Year Books from that kingdom of darkness in which they are captives, and ... hasten the day when they will once more be readable, intelligible, and – we do not fear to say it – enjoyable books' (p. ix). The kingdom of darkness in question was not the manuscripts, but the seventeenth-century blackletter edition known as *Maynard's Edward II*, which Maitland precisely calls 'incorrigibly bad.'[30] Even as he condemns it, he cannot keep himself from considering the possible effects of circumstance on editorial practice: 'Of the nameless editor, or rather copyist, whom they employed we will say no hard words. We do not know how few months were allowed him for a task that demanded years; we do not know how small was his recompense; we do not know what opportunity he had of consulting any manuscripts beyond the one that belonged to Maynard' (p. xxiii). Within the constraints that he himself faced, Maitland devised editorial principles in service to both text and reader, as far as he could reconcile the requirements of the two.

Some examples will afford a sense of Maitland's thinking about the Anglo-Norman dialect. On orthography, he begins, 'No word was so short that it could not be spelt in at least two ways' (p. xlii). And he concludes, 'The spelling of Anglo-French in the fourteenth century was probably less variegated than was the spelling of English in the days of Henry VIII; but it was variegated enough' (p. xliii). On the declension of nouns, and in specific the decay of the two-case system, he says, 'The French of England hurried rapidly along a path which the French of France was to tread with slower steps' (pp. xlv–vi). Later, he observes that 'what we see will almost entitle us to say that the passive participle does not "decline for gender"' (p. l). He discusses the varied 'good and normal' Anglo-Norman uses of the word *qe* in terms of mastering the editorial 'temptation which assails us when we see the *q* with a tittle' – namely the temptation to expand it into forms that seem like good French to modern readers but are not attested in the manuscripts (p. xlviii).

The novelty of these descriptions lies in their temper rather than their content. Maitland devoted his attention to how the language actually worked in his manuscripts, not to how it should have worked, or how it worked in relation to a putative continental norm. 'Consistency is not to be expected,' he cheerfully concedes (p. xlii). When he pokes fun, it is at his own expectations rather than the dialect's failure to meet them.

Maitland thinks about the ways in which the character of the texts as legal transcripts might affect the language to be found in them. He wonders whether the rarity of the imperfect indicative 'was a peculiarity of Anglo-French conversation or a peculiarity of our legal vocabulary,' since it might stem from the legal tendency to assign past events specificity and singularity (p. lxi). He notes, perhaps with a glance at French as spoken by the English of his own day, that 'our ancestors had no dread of the subjunctive,' but he also speculates that its commonness in these texts might have to do with the chronically hypothetical state of legal argument (p. lxvii). He points out that the rampant isolated use of the term 'd'autrepart' (on the other hand) may only signal that 'an advocate is often desirous of apparently introducing a new argument when really he is only going to repeat what he has already said' (p. xxviii).

This alertness to the particulars of the manuscripts led Maitland to a clearer understanding of the nature of the Year Books, which until then had been considered official records. He made sense of elements that another sort of editor might have chalked up to scribal laxity or supererogation: the omission in different manuscripts of cases and parts of cases, the elimination or garbling of proper names, and what he calls 'the outcome of private enterprise': 'Mixed up with the words attributed to judges and counsel we see notes and comments, criticisms and speculations which a writer who speaks of himself as "I" (*jeo*) gives us as his own. If all these be mere accretions, then we must deal with our manuscripts in an heroic style, cutting and carving right and left in pursuance of a preconceived theory' (p. xiii). Maitland concludes that these comments are not corruptions of an official record but a fundamental part of the thing itself: 'We may strongly suspect that what was wanted was instruction, and that these books were made by learners for learners, by apprentices for apprentices' (p. xiii). That is, the users of the Year Books adapted them for their own purposes, and that adaptation is part of their basic character: 'We are provisionally inclining to the belief that brief notes were taken in court and that divers lawyers expanded or "wrote up" these notes in different ways, so that no one archetypal text ever existed, or, to put it in other words, so that the archetype was a grammarless string of abbreviated words' (p. xc).

The manuscripts of the Year Books themselves are thus works without archetypes, fabulously indeterminate, but with as specific a genesis as can be imagined, not in the intention of a single author but in an event, in the words uttered in the court that day. Maitland knew that those precise words were irrevocably lost, and that their recovery was not the goal. To try to make the Year Books yield a court transcript would not realize their true nature but vitiate it.

As historian, editor, and philologist pro tem, Maitland sought to recover and, as far as was feasible, to reenter the mentality of the world of the Year Books, through their reportage and commentary as well as their attempt 'to get down on paper or parchment the shifting argument, the retort, the quip, the expletive' (p. xvii). In the closing sentences of *Domesday Book and Beyond*, such reanimation is literally his ultimate hope for early English historical studies 'a century hence' (that is, by 1997): 'Above all, by slow degrees the thoughts of our forefathers, their common thoughts about common things, will have become thinkable once more. There are discoveries to be made; but there are also habits to be formed.'[31] Maitland's sense of the language and nature of his texts and his sense of how to represent them as an editor were inseparable, born of his effort to understand the Year Books on their own terms and informed by his awareness that he could never completely do so.

First and foremost, he wanted to give his audience a readable book while making his own editing apparent: he endeavored to make his interventions obvious, so that his mistakes would be accessible to – and therefore correctable by – later, better readers.[32] He represented as much of the variation among the manuscripts as he practically could, in the variants, in brackets in the text, and by the occasional side-by-side printing of different versions (p. lxxxiii). Eclectic, but effective. Or perhaps effective because eclectic. He explains,

> Our primary rule must be to choose a manuscript and to copy it letter by letter, though *u* and *v* and *i* and *j* will be dealt with in conformity with modern practice, and the punctuation and use of capital letters will be our own. Then as regards mere matters of spelling we shall leave our text as it stands, even though we think that the shape which it gives to a word is a distinctly bad shape and one that hardly fell within the limits of permissible variation ... For aught we know it may be an interesting form, and if we once began to amend bad spelling we should not know where to stop. When, on the other hand, there seems to be a danger that a reader will take one word to be another, then, giving express notice, we make a correction ... Then when our manuscript gives, not an ill-spelt word, but what we take to be a wrong word, we shall give both right and wrong ... But we shall not even in our notes endeavour to amend bad accidence, still less bad syntax, unless it is unintelligible. We have twice seen *la pape* (the pope): it is needless to express our opinion that *le pape* would be better. (p. lxxxi)

He does not allow his own sense of what is right and what is interesting to deprive readers of the opportunity to form independent judgments.

Maitland regrets that the expansion of abbreviations may not be shown ('from the scientific but expensive process of distinguishing those letters by italic type we are compelled to shrink'), but he tries to minimize the possible damage: 'Real danger begins when the editor must conjugate a verb. Whenever we are conscious of a danger of anything that is worse than bad spelling – in particular of a wrong tense – our added letters will be placed within brackets. Fidelity with a leaning towards correctness should be our aim. We must not strain the stenographic signs in order to obtain pleasant results ... The correctness should be an Anglo-French correctness' (pp. lxxxii, lxxxiii). He also has qualms about the introduction of graphic accents. He uncharacteristically first justifies such intervention on the basis of common practice, saying that he will follow 'the example that is set by French medievalists of repute,' specifically Paul Meyer (pp. lxxxiii–iv). But he cannot prevent himself from thinking about the issue:

> It need hardly be said that graphic accents are not to be found in our manuscripts, and there seem to be ample reasons why no attempt should be made to impose upon medieval materials all or nearly all the accentual signs which were introduced by grammarians of the sixteenth and later centuries. But the accent placed upon a final *e* or final *es* stands by itself. In our reading of French books we have learned to rely upon it so strongly, and to take such heed of its presence or absence, that our apprehension of the meaning of a word is appreciably retarded if we fail to receive our ordinary guidance. (p. lxxxiv)

That is, accents are defensible only as a crutch for modern readers, the equivalent of the marked vowels in a student edition of the *Aeneid.* Maitland decides to use other accents as needed, on a case-by-case basis, not to improve on the manuscripts before him, or to illuminate their phonology, but to help the reader. Utility is everything. He includes the occasional accent grave, 'for it helps us in our reading' (p. lxxxvii). On similar grounds, he uses the apostrophe that, for example, distinguishes *cest,* 'this,' from *cest,* 'that is.' 'The introduction of the apostrophe needs, so we think, no apology,' he says, before embarking on a paragraph of apologetics (pp. lxxxvii–viii). He uses the cedilla only as 'every now and then an occasion will arise when this modern sign will be useful,' and he forgoes the tréma entirely, thereby anticipating the recent trend in Old French editing.[33] As he says, 'No doubt the use that we propose to make of the graphic accent gives an editor one more chance of disgracing himself; but this seems to be a risk which the convenience of his readers requires him to run ... the reader will know that accents, like commas, come from him' (p. lxxxvii).

Maitland keeps reminding the reader of what in an edition comes from whom exactly because it is all too easy to forget. His approach could be considered conservative or radical, but in any case it permits less intervention in the text than is presented as a matter of course in works such as the Foulet and Speer handbook widely used today. It offers a sympathetic understanding of Anglo-Norman unmatched until recently – and still not matched universally.[34] Maitland also anticipates later questions about manuscript culture, textual transmission, the trilingual nature of medieval English culture, and the relationship of language to thought itself. (Of the Norman Conquest he elsewhere writes, 'Among the most momentous and permanent effects of that great event was its effect on the language of English lawyers, for language is no mere instrument which we can control at will; it controls us.')[35] And Maitland did all these things ten years before Joseph Bédier published his revolutionary second edition of the *Lai de l'ombre*, which broke the spell that critical text reconstruction had cast on the editing of French texts.[36]

Maitland developed his editorial method not by subordinating his texts to 'a preconceived theory' but by closely observing and considering the particulars of the manuscripts to be edited in relation to the practical constraints on the edition to be produced. The success of this inductive approach raises the question of how many of the current standard and potentially unconsidered interventions remain truly helpful, much less necessary, today.

Facing-page translation is becoming increasingly common (and Maitland does, by the way, provide one for the Year Books). Even with its considerable attendant risks and limitations, such translation not only aids those who cannot read the language (or read it well), or who may benefit from occasional guidance (which means virtually all of us), it also performs many of the same interpretive functions as editorial interventions in untranslated editions. And, as anyone who has made one knows, translation helps to keep editors honest, not to mention humble.[37] In the editing of Anglo-Norman with facing-page translation, especially in prose, there may remain little compelling justification for the anachronistic introduction of accents and apostrophes or the alteration of *i*, *j*, *u*, and *v* to conform to modern practice. The latter habit has the peculiar effect of effacing the medieval graphic distinction of *u* and *v* in favor of its own distinction, based on the notion of sound values, a notion that also entails an editorial distinction between vocalic *i* and consonantal *j*, and therefore the introduction of what amounts to a new grapheme to the medieval writing system. Such emendation has already become far less common in Middle English editing.[38]

One modernizing change often necessitates more changes. Alterations in word division in particular seem to require serial emendation. For instance, the usual Anglo-Norman phrase meaning 'of England' is 'Dengleterre,' with the capital signaling a proper name at the beginning of the sequence of letters. Either the introduction of the apostrophe alone ('D'engleterre') or the transposition of the capital alone ('dEngleterre') makes for a construction alien by the standards of either time. Both anachronistic changes must be made to produce results ('d'Engleterre') that work as well as the original. And what has been gained is the delineation of a simple preposition, intelligible in context to any reader of French who has spent a few minutes getting acclimated to the text.

Foulet and Speer say that in punctuation 'the medieval scribe's practice is usually so far removed from today's usage that it provides no guide to the syntactical structuring of the text.'[39] I am not so confident. In my own experience with many manuscripts of one work, the Anglo-Norman prose *Brut* chronicle, punctuation and capitalization assuredly fail to conform to modern usage, and are sparing by comparison. But they nevertheless provide much guidance. For instance, a scribe may signal a transition with either punctuation marking the end of one sentence or a capital letter marking the beginning of the other: modern practice could seem redundant by comparison. A scribe may embellish the page and save himself a lift of the pen by elaborating the final stroke of a word into something like a punctus; such a gesture reads well but is not easy to translate into type. A sentence concluding at the end of a line may be deemed to require no other graphic signal, or it may provide the occasion for a flourish.[40] Little in medieval scribal practice is so contingent upon the discretion of the individual writing and the particulars of the page being written, and therefore so little transferrable into other contexts. I hesitate to generalize further from my own experience, and editions that replace punctuation wholesale offer little opportunity for judgment.[41] But the conspicuous consistency of scribal habits of abbreviation alone – especially compared to modern haphazardness – should give the lie to the notion that Anglo-Norman scribes were incapable of methodical or rigorous work.

'Toilette du texte' sounds harmless enough, but like all kinds of artistic restoration it runs the risk of disguising, rather than merely tidying up, its original. The advantages of expanding abbreviations, for example, are obvious, as is the visual clutter of representing expansions by means of italics (inexpensive as doing so now may be). It is common and reasonable practice to expand a word spelled different ways (say, 'cheualer,' 'cheualier,' 'chiualer,' or 'chiualier') into the full form most often found in the text. But when this shift is made, the chosen form may vastly and artificially predominate in the edition, potentially affecting linguistic studies and even subsequent dictionaries, which in turn influence future editors. Unusual word forms that are in fact an editor's transcription errors do the same, and there are no doubt many of them in dictionaries of all medieval languages. The correction – and certainly the silent correction – of supposed scribal errors, particularly when they are not comprehensible on mechanical grounds, may be ill-advised, in part because the understanding of Anglo-Norman correctness is still compromised by its critical history.[42] The emendation of homonyms may be imprudent, since it may misrepresent the range of contemporary usage and understanding.[43] Naturally, editors of verse have more ways of noticing that something has gone awry than do editors of prose, and they face more complicated dilemmas as to what, if anything, to do about it.

Editors are, of course, themselves scribes and must make scribal judgments suited to the medium in which they are working, even as they concern themselves with anachronism in a way medieval scribes did not have to. Distinctions in manuscript that cannot be practically maintained on the printed page may as well be represented by means of modern conventions as by some equally foreign hybrid. For the majority of editions, modern syntactic punctuation, and therefore capitalization at the beginning of sentences, and therefore other modern conventions of capitalization, may often be as good a solution as any.

But such a solution is not to be undertaken lightly, or in adherence to abstract editorial standards, for whenever an editor introduces something into a text that would not have been needed – or perhaps even conceived of – at the time of the work's writing, he or she is making interpretive decisions and generating increasing anachronism. Derek Pearsall offers the examples of systematic capitalization and quotation marks for direct speech, which he regards as imposing on the edition and editor, 'in the prison-house of modern typographical practice,' otherwise unnecessary choices, such as whether or not an abstraction is a personification or where a speech begins or ends.[44] Editorial decisions that are both interpretive and effectively invisible are of the most hazardous kind, particularly given the proclivity of even professional medievalists to treat an edition – often a canonical edition of a canonical text – as a transparent, unmitigated true text, not an editor's representation of one.[45] Whatever the theoretical celebration of variance, critics do not in practice engage with specific variants in a textual tradition as often as would be fruitful, in part because variants are so often minimized and relegated to endnotes, so that their use is discouraged, but also because the tendency to make a medieval text look as much as possible like a modern book disposes people to think of it as if it were a modern book and to conceive of Anglo-Norman (or any other language) in terms of later language and textual disposition they already know. It may also leave them less rather than more prepared to read in manuscript when the occasion arises.

That even the apparently simplest decisions can have far-reaching and unintended consequences does not imply that such decisions can or should be avoided. A potential infinitude of downloadable facsimiles available to those with the necessary training will not obviate the need or desire for editions, which are among the most vital and lasting work that scholars can perform and are in no danger of mass obsolescence. They are so dangerous precisely because they are so important, and because they are so much more than imitation manuscripts. Among many other things, they offer the readers the tremendous benefits of an editor's long consideration of a body of material; they do some of the work of synthesis that is necessary for any inquiry to advance; they provide an artifact that scholars can consider and discuss in common (even while recognizing it for the approximation that it is); they offer relatively inexpensive – and generally the only – access to texts that can be quickly read. And for good or for ill, they determine what will enter the scholarly mainstream and what will not.

Given the responsibility that editors incur, and the inevitability and necessity of editorial intervention, it is essential for them to assess as a matter of course why they do what they do, to consider what degree of intervention is necessary in any editorial venture (given the texts involved, the audience to be served, the medium, and the material constraints on the project), and to evaluate rigorously the costs and benefits of doing more than is necessary.[46] And in the case of Anglo-Norman at least, simply by abandoning habits of standardization governed by the scholarly assumptions, tastes, and desires of another time, and by minimizing distinctions unknown to Anglo-Norman readers and writers, editors may be able to produce substantially more revealing editions. Such editions may indeed be superficially and initially more challenging for modern readers. They may also avoid gratuitous, as well as disguised, error, offer an experience of reading closer to that of the original audience, and be less invisibly dominated by the editor's interpretive choices, much less the embalmed choices of past editors.[47]

For however drowsy the scribe, however little he cared about the work he was copying, I at least cannot really claim to know Anglo-Norman better than he did, not in the way that a classicist looking at a late copy of Cicero can. I may aspire to be a more patient, observant, and self-conscious reader. I may notice, or think I notice, mistakes in the scribe's writing, just as I notice typographical errors in printed books. Some readers may think in terms of the history of the language and the development of particular words, or they may take more interest in grammatical regularity and have a different notion of the allowable limits of syntax and spelling. But, as Maitland says, 'In matters of language the careless, the slovenly, the vulgar, are often the pioneers and ultimately the victors' (p. lii). It would be preposterous to claim that academic, systematizing ways of thinking, powerful as they can be, allow one to know a dialect such as Anglo-Norman more authentically than did a man who used it in daily life.

Editing is not an impersonal process, and editorial guidelines designed to assist in the modern presentation of medieval works can, when taken for granted, become editorial rules that subordinate at best and distort at worst the particulars of the works that editors labor to bring to light.[48] Maitland loved the particular and the concrete and found the value of the general and theoretical limited in comparison. His approach is far from reducing editors to timid transcribers: on the contrary, it admits editorial judgment fully and honestly and calls for constant discernment. Exercising restraint is, after all, part of exercising judgment.[49]

And in editing, at least editing of a language as nonconformist and incompletely understood as Anglo-Norman, I think we would do well to follow Maitland's model. Maitland is, paradoxically, exemplary for me in his very reluctance to prescribe and generalize. He earns my confidence by his modesty, his efforts to make his interventions apparent, his candid admissions of subjectivity, his willingness to build from the ground up rather than force the Year Books and their language into a poorly fitting but pre-existing mold, and the evidence pervading his introduction of the entire, judicious, and respectful attention he devoted to the manuscripts he was editing. When life and logic – or system – came into conflict, life won, and Maitland felt no compulsion to protest that he was only becoming more logical.

Toward the end of his introduction Maitland voices this hope for his readers' judgment of the Anglo-Norman of the Year Books: 'the more learned they are, the more lenient it will be' – that is, the less likely they will be to let superficial strangeness or prior expectations distract them from what is of greater interest (p. lxxix). He is invoking the flexibility of learnedness, the disinclination to demand one species of correctitude and devalue all else. Surely this is a sort of flexibility that should be encouraged among the makers and readers of editions of medieval texts, and it can be encouraged in simple, practical ways as well as sweeping theoretical ones.

In his work on Anglo-Norman, Maitland strove to notice and test his own assumptions, to extend his sympathy to the texts he was editing, to do no more or less than was necessary for his readers' ease of comprehension, and to keep those readers apprised of what he was doing. These may seem modest qualities to commend, but their powers are not to be underestimated. Maitland demonstrates how vital they are to the editorial process, for it was largely by means of them that, at a time when others found Anglo-Norman so frustrating that they declared the dialect itself – not their understanding of it – to be a failure, he succeeded with and even delighted in it. He found it, and helped it to become for others, readable, intelligible, and enjoyable.

NOTES

1 'Why the History of English Law Is Not Written,' in *The Collected Papers of Frederic William Maitland*, ed. H.A.L. Fisher, 3 vols (Cambridge: Cambridge University Press, 1911), 1:482; following quotations, 486, 496, 497.

2 G.R. Elton, *F.W. Maitland* (New Haven: Yale University Press, 1985), pp. 26–7.

3 F.W. Maitland, *The Year Books of Edward II*, vol. 1: *I and II Edward II, 1307–1309*, Selden Society, no. 17 (London: Quaritch, 1903), p. xv. All subsequent references to this volume will appear in parentheses in the text.

4 For a discussion of Maitland's historical method, its contemporary context, and its influence, see Elton, *Maitland*, pp. 19–34, 97–107.

5 Johan Vising's catalogue of disparaging commentary, which he dates to the thirteenth and fourteenth centuries, has influenced generations of scholars (*Anglo-Norman Language and Literature* [London: Oxford University Press, 1923], pp. 20–7). William Rothwell, however, argues that received opinion on thirteenth-century contempt for Anglo-Norman has been largely based on tendentious readings of possibly misdated sources, without consideration of context ('Playing "Follow My Leader" in Anglo-Norman Studies,' *French Language Studies* 6 (1996): 185–93).

6 Maitland, Introduction, p. lix, citing Paul Meyer on Philippe de Beaumanoir and *La pais aux Anglais* in the introduction to *Les contes moralisés de Nicole Bozon*, ed. Paul Meyer and Lucy Toulmin-Smith, Société des anciens textes français, vol. 50 (Paris: Firmin Didot, 1889).

7 Introduction, pp. xvi–xvii; Keith Busby discusses the first three items on this list, with consideration of Marie de France, in '"Neither Flesh nor Fish, nor Good Red Herring": The Case of Anglo-Norman Literature,' in *Studies in Honor of Hans-Erich Keller*, ed. Rupert T. Pickens (Kalamazoo: Medieval Institute Publications, 1993), pp. 399–400; Ruth J. Dean also discusses insular firsts, as well as the difficulties of assigning works or authors insular or continental status, in 'What Is Anglo-Norman?' *Annuale Medievale* 6 (1965): 33, 41–3. Dominica Legge offers the most complete account in 'La precocité de la littérature anglo-normande,' *Cahiers de civilisation médiévale* 8 (1965): 327–49. The women in question are Marie de France, Clemence of Barking, the anonymous nun of Barking, and Marie of Chatteris (Busby, 'Neither Flesh nor Fish,' p. 400).

8 For the first Anglo-Normanists, especially Gervais de la Rue, Francisque Michel, and Thomas Wright, see Busby, 'Neither Flesh nor Fish,' pp. 405–6.

9 Busby, 'Neither Flesh nor Fish,' p. 409. See also William Rothwell, 'Appearance and Reality in Anglo-Norman,' in *Studies in Medieval Literature and Languages in Memory of Frederick Whitehead*, ed. W. Rothwell et al. (Manchester: Manchester University Press, 1973), pp. 239, 248, 255–6, as well as his other works cited in this essay; and Trotter, 'Language Contact and Lexicography: The Case of Anglo-Norman,' in *The Origins and Development of Emigrant Languages*, ed. Hans F. Nielsen and Lene Schøsler (Odense: Odense University Press, 1996), pp. 23–4.

10 Busby, 'Neither Flesh nor Fish,' pp. 409–11; Busby offers many examples of such critical judgments. See also the discussion of Anglo-Norman versification and past judgments of it in David L. Jeffrey and Brian J. Levy, eds., *The Anglo-Norman Lyric: An Anthology*, Pontifical Institute of Medieval Studies, Studies and Texts, no. 93 (Toronto: Pontifical Institute of Medieval Studies, 1990), pp. 17–27; R.C. Johnston, 'On Scanning Anglo-Norman Verse,' *Anglo-Norman Studies* 5 (1983): 153–64; and Bernadette A. Masters, 'Anglo-Norman in Context: The Case for the Scribes,' *Exemplaria* 6 (1994): esp. 172–84 (a heated account).

11 'Notice et extraits d'un fragment de poème biblique composé en Angleterre,' *Romania* 36 (1907): 187; *Les contes moralisés de Nicole Bozon*, p. ii; cited by Busby, 'Neither Flesh nor Fish,' p. 411.

12 For Meyer's initial support of critical reconstruction, and his own editorial practice, see Mary B. Speer, 'Old French Literature,' in *Scholarly Editing: A Guide to Research*, ed. D.C. Greetham (New York: Modern Language Association, 1995), pp. 389, 392–3.

13 See Douglas A. Kibbee, 'Emigrant Languages and Acculturation: The Case of Anglo-French' in *The Origins and Development of Emigrant Languages*, ed.

Nielsen and Schøsler, pp. 7–12, for evidence of the influence of English on later Anglo-Norman. The question of how long Anglo-Norman remained a 'living' language remains a vexed one, as evidenced by Kibbee's essay, which places its demise as 'imminent' in the thirteenth century (pp. 15–17); for an argument for the longevity of spoken Anglo-Norman, see Dominica Legge, 'Anglo-Norman as a Spoken Language,' in *Proceedings of the Battle Conference on Anglo-Norman Studies*, vol. 2, ed. R. Allen Brown (Woodbridge: Boydell, 1980), pp. 108–117. See also, for example, Rothwell, 'The Legacy of Anglo-French: *Faux Amis* in French and English,' *Zeitschrift für romanische Philologie* 109 (1993): 20–8. (Much of Rothwell's recent work concerns the vigor of later Anglo-Norman; see the useful bibliography in the festschrift *De mot en mot: Aspects of Medieval Linguistics*, ed. Stewart Gregory and D.A. Trotter [Cardiff: University of Wales Press, 1997], pp. xi–xiv.) Much of the vexation seems to stem from differing definitions of language death, on the basis of evidence of use (in speech or writing) or evidence of linguistic development (or lack thereof); see Kibbee, 'Emigrant Languages,' p. 16.

14 But see also Trotter, 'Language Contact,' on Anglo-Norman borrowings from Latin and English.

15 As Rothwell says, unlike other peripheral dialects of French, Anglo-Norman became 'not a preserver of archaisms but a propagator of semantic innovation' ('Legacy,' 21).

16 William Rothwell, Louise W. Stone, and T.B.W. Reid, eds, *Anglo-Norman Dictionary* (London: Modern Humanities Research Association, 1977–92). For a general description and critique of the *Anglo-Norman Dictionary*, published before the last fascicle and general preface appeared, see Frankwalt Möhren, 'Theorie und Praxis in Stones Anglo-Norman Dictionary,' *Zeitschrift für romanische Philologie* 107 (1991): 418–42.

17 Rothwell, general preface, p. ix.

18 General preface, p. ix.

19 General preface, p. xi. The preface as a whole makes for moving and instructive reading about the history of a gigantic editorial project.

20 Maitland, introduction, pp. xxxii–iii, lxxx; Paul Studer, *The Study of Anglo-Norman* (Oxford: Clarendon, 1920), pp. 22–7; Ruth Dean, 'Anglo-Norman Studies,' *Romanic Review* 30 (1939): 3–14; 'A Fair Field Needing Folk: Anglo-Norman,' *PMLA* 69 (1954): 965–78; 'The Fair Field of Anglo-Norman: Recent Cultivation,' *Medievalia et Humanistica*, n.s. 3 (1972): 279–97; Dominica Legge, *Anglo-Norman in the Cloisters* (Edinburgh: Edinburgh University Press, 1950), esp. pp. 1–5; *Anglo-Norman Literature and Its Background* (Oxford: Clarendon, 1963), esp. pp. 1–2, 362–73; Rothwell, 'Anglo-Norman Perspectives,' *Modern Language Review* 70 (1975): 41–9; and Busby, 'Neither

Flesh nor Fish,' pp. 414–17. For a review of Anglo-Norman studies from the 1920s to 1965 and some unusual optimism ('Anglo-Norman now enjoys linguistic prestige and renown'), see K.V. Sinclair, 'Anglo-Norman Studies: The Last Twenty Years,' *Australian Journal of French Studies* 2 (1965–6): 113–55, 225–78, 113 quoted.

21 Rothwell, 'Glimpses into Our Ignorance of the Anglo-Norman Lexis,' in *Medieval Textual Studies in Memory of T.B.W. Reid*, ed. Ian Short (London: Anglo-Norman Text Society, 1984), pp. 167–79; other works cited above. To be precise, in his title Busby is citing Legge (*Anglo-Norman in the Cloisters*, p. 2) citing the long version of the proverb that Shakespeare cites in short in *Henry IV, Part 1*, 3.3.

22 This deathless phrase comes from the *Vie d'Édouard le Confesseur*, as part of the anonymous (and highly capable) translator's characterization of her own work: 'Un faus francais sai d'Angletere, / Ke ne n'alai ailure quere' (ll. 7–8). The poem's editor, Östen Södergärd, dates it to 1163–70 (Uppsala: Amqvist och Wiksells, 1948). Rothwell argues at length that the characterization is not really a slur but part of a modesty trope informing the nun's discussion of the difficulties of translating Latin: the lines immediately preceding read, 'Qu'en latin est nominatif, / Ço frai romanz acusatif' (ll. 5–6) ('Playing "Follow My Leader,"' 185–90). See also Legge, *Anglo-Norman Literature*, pp. 63–4, 369.

23 Susan Crane and William Calin have, however, led the way with full-length works addressing Anglo-Norman writings as worthy both of attention in themselves and as parts of English cultural history writ large: Crane, *Insular Romance: Politics, Faith, and Culture in Anglo-Norman and Middle English Romance* (Berkeley: University of California Press, 1986); Calin, *The French Tradition and the Literature of Medieval England* (Toronto: University of Toronto Press, 1994).

24 The rules proposed by M.M. Roques in 1926 in 'Etablissement de règles pratiques pour l'édition des anciens textes français et provençaux' (which, as the title indicates, establish a single approach to all varieties of medieval French) are still applied today (*Romania* 2 [1926]: 243–9).

25 Introduction, p. xvii, quoting *Histoire de la littérature anglaise*, 5 vols (Paris: Hachette, 1885), 1:103.

26 Some studies of dialectal features of different texts and periods were made in the 1870s and 1880s, particularly by Hermann Suchier, Paul Meyer, and Johan Vising. Louis Menger's synthetic grammar appeared in 1904. For details of this early work, see Dean, 'Anglo-Norman Studies,' 4–11. For Maitland's own reading, see his introduction, p. xliii, n. 2.

27 C.H.C. Fifoot describes the aftermath of the suicide of P. Edward Dove in

Frederic William Maitland: A Life (Cambridge, Massachusetts: Harvard University Press, 1971), pp. 113–14.

28 Fifoot, *Maitland*, p. 255.

29 Even when he tries to drum up nationalistic enthusiasm for the new edition, he does so with what I take to be self-consciously ironic bombast: 'What we want is a new and worthy edition of the Year Books undertaken as a national enterprise ... We must have it, or England, Selden's England, will stand disgraced among the nations. The tide of conquest is advancing. The Anglo-Saxon laws are already German property ... A French librarian shows us how a Year Book should be read ... Lo! they turn unto the gentiles' (pp. xxxii–xxxiii). See also 'Why the History of English Law Is Not Written,' 484–5.

30 *Les Reports des Cases argue & adjuge in le temps del' Roy Edward le Second ...* (London: Sawbridge, Rawlins, and Roycroft for Basset, 1678); introduction, p. xxi.

31 Maitland, *Domesday Book and Beyond: Three Essays in the Early History of England* (Cambridge: Cambridge University Press, 1897), p. 520.

32 See his discussion, pp. lxxxii–iii.

33 Introduction, p. lxxxviii. See Albert Foulet and Mary B. Speer, *On Editing Old French Texts* (Lawrence: Regents Press of Kansas, 1979), pp. 69–73, for the 'perplexing problem' of the tréma and their suggestions about its use.

34 Rothwell has returned to Maitland's territory to ask scholars to pay attention to context and to exercise caution in using phonology while editing Anglo-Norman (see especially 'Appearance and Reality in Anglo-Norman'). As recently as 1996, Kibbee has characterized fourteenth-century Anglo-French as suffering its 'death agony' and 'degenerating into a risible jargon' – loaded language for the historical description of linguistic change ('Emigrant Languages,' pp. 1, 16).

35 Frederick Pollock and F.W. Maitland, *The History of the English Law*, 2d ed., 2 vols (Cambridge: Cambridge University Press, 1898), 1:87. Maitland's discussion of the importance of the French language to the development of the English law falls on pp. 80–7; for an analysis of his sensitivity to contemporary language and his awareness of the perils of using anachronistic terminology, see John Hudson, 'Maitland and Anglo-Norman Law,' in *The History of English Law: Centenary Essays on 'Pollock and Maitland,'* ed. John Hudson, Proceedings of the British Academy, no. 89 (Oxford: Oxford University Press, 1996), pp. 32–4, which called my attention to the passage quoted, as well as to the conclusion of *Domesday Book and Beyond*, cited above. Maitland also argues in his last volume of the Year Books that a single manuscript may have multiple exemplars: 'The assumption that

every codex is the offspring of one other codex is a natural starting-point if we would draw a pedigree; but in such a case as ours it may well be fallacious' (*The Year Books of Edward II,* vol. 3, *III Edward II 1309–10,* Selden Society, no. 20 [London, Quaritch, 1905], p. xiii).

36 *Le lai de l'ombre,* by Jean Renart, Société des anciens textes français, vol. 15 (Paris: Firmin Didot, 1913), pp. i–xlv; for a general discussion of this famous edition and its consequences, see Speer, 'Old French Literature,' pp. 394–9.

37 As J.P. Collas, later Year Book editor and student of Anglo-Norman legal vocabulary, says in a lament on the deficiencies of translations of legal material, 'Only in most exceptional circumstances will we, in a critical footnote, acknowledge the doubts, misgivings and hesitations which lie behind a dozen renderings on any page' (*Year Books of Edward II,* vol. 24, *XII Edward II, 1319,* Selden Society, no. 81 (London: Quaritch, 1964), pp. xi–xii). His account of 'Problems of Language and Interpretation' (pp. xiv–cxxviii) is sobering for what it reveals about the nuances of Anglo-Norman usage and vocabulary and the immense effort and expertise required to achieve adequate appreciation of those nuances. Collas's unpublished work on Anglo-Norman legal language resides in the collection of the Anglo-Norman Research Centre at the John Rylands Library, University of Manchester (Rothwell, 'Legacy,' p. 46).

38 For thoughtful accounts of broader issues and trends in Old French editing, see Speer, 'Old French Literature,' pp. 382–416, and her 'Editing Old French Texts in the Eighties: Theory and Practice,' *Romance Philology* 45 (1991): 7–43.

39 Foulet and Speer, *On Editing,* p. 64.

40 Similarly, a careful scribe may choose a short or long spelling of a word (for example, 'granz' or 'grauntz') according to the amount of space he needs to fill to maintain an even block of text: orthography as an element of graphic design.

41 But see M.B. Parkes's pioneering study of punctuation 'according to the ways it has been used rather than the ways some have thought it ought to be used' (*Pause and Effect: An Introduction to the History of Punctuation in the West* [Berkeley: University of California Press, 1993], p. xi).

42 Rothwell considers what is lacking in Anglo-Norman linguistic studies and what might be done to improve the situation, with emphasis on progress from an 'atomistic' view (represented by the philological work of F.J. Tanquerey and Mildred Pope) to a more synthetic one, more attention to the historical and social context in which the language existed, further study and publication of material beyond the purely literary, and an orien-

tation of research 'towards comparison and contrast ... with a study of meaning paramount' ('Anglo-Norman Perspectives,' passim, pp. 42 and 49 quoted).

43 See Foulet and Speer, *On Editing*, pp. 58–73, 76–85, for discussion of the additions and alterations they advocate or disapprove. They do not suggest altering spelling or changing 'declensional solecisms' as a matter of course; they do, however, recommend altering homonyms and introducing other distinctions not found in manuscript. Rothwell is characteristically forthright on the issue: that a homonymic clash 'seriously incommodes twentieth century philologists to the extent of forcing them into errors of interpretation must not be taken as implying any similar difficulty for medieval Frenchmen on either side of the Channel' ('Appearance and Reality,' p. 255).

44 Derek Pearsall, 'Theory and Practice in Middle English Editing,' *Text* 7 (1994): 122.

45 For an example of this process, the reification of the Ellesmere arrangement of the *Canterbury Tales*, see Pearsall, 'Theory and Practice,' 112–15, and his 'Editing Medieval Texts: Some Developments and Some Problems,' in *Textual Criticism and Literary Interpretation*, ed. Jerome J. McGann (Chicago: University of Chicago Press, 1985), pp. 92–7.

46 Speer identifies four fundamental questions, with both theoretical and practical aspects: 'What is the text? For whom is it being edited? Why is it being edited? How can that particular text best be presented?' ('Editing Old French Texts,' p. 42).

47 For an example of an Anglo-Norman edition with less intervention than usual (it does not add accents or alter word division), see *The Anonimalle Chronicle, 1307–1334*, ed. Wendy Childs and John Taylor, Yorkshire Archaeological Society Record Series 147 (Leeds: Yorkshire Archaeological Society, 1991). Rothwell comments in his review on 'the considerable difficulties most readers will experience in trying to cope with this text in such a raw state,' but it is also clear that the 'raw state' aids him in identifying errors in transcription that might have otherwise been more difficult to catch (*Medium Aevum* 63 [1994]: 171–3).

48 Speer reaches similar conclusions on the role of general theory in particular editorial projects: good editing is 'skeptical – in an informed way – towards general theories of any kind'; good editors' 'primary allegiance is to the text, and they must devise for each text ways of presenting to the reader that text's textuality' ('Editing Old French Texts,' p. 24).

49 Much of G. Thomas Tanselle's objection to best-text editing, which he calls 'a confused combination of two incompatible procedures ... a critical

approach that embodies distrust of critical judgment,' rests on the view that it attempts, as a 'counsel of despair,' to eliminate subjectivity from editing ('The Varieties of Scholarly Editing,' in *Scholarly Editing: A Guide to Research*, ed. D.C. Greetham [New York: Modern Language Association, 1995], pp. 21–2).

3

'Alas! Who may truste thys world': The Malory Documents and a Parallel-text Edition

MEG ROLAND

In 1934, a scribal manuscript of Sir Thomas Malory's work was discovered in the Winchester College library. For over four hundred years, English printer William Caxton's 1485 edition *Le Morte Darthur* had been the sole witness to Malory's work. Since the manuscript's recovery, a primary focus of Malory scholarship has been the evaluation and assessment of the two witnesses to the work. Indeed, scholarly debate over the authority of the Caxton versus the Winchester has engendered a strong polarity between advocates of the Caxton text and those of the Winchester manuscript, in which both positions have sought to answer the same fundamental textual question – that is, which best represents the 'genuine Malory.'[1]

Questions of greater authority are based in an editorial theory of which the goals are to determine origin and to establish a unifying aesthetic. But first principles other than those based on theories of the author may be utilized as a means by which to conceive and represent a literary work. N.F. Blake of the University of Sheffield, despite long arguing that the Caxton text is an editorially corrupted version of the Winchester, acknowledges that 'the whole concept of a definitive version of a text based on the author's original or even final intentions may well be an anachronism for this period.'[2] Post-incunabula constructions of the author are fraught with complications when applied to Middle English writers, scribes, and early printers. The textual stance that seeks to recover an authorial version echoes the perspective of Sir Lancelot upon hearing of Arthur's death: 'Sir Lancelot's heart almost brast for sorrow, and Sir Lancelot threw his arms abroad, and said, "Alas, who may trust this world"'.[3] Or, as it appears in the Winchester: 'syr Launcelottes hert almost braste for sorowe, and sir Launcelot threwe hys armes abrode, and sayd, "Alas! Who may truste thys world?"'[4] Scholars interested in establishing an authorial work often adhere to what Eugène Vinaver termed a 'mistrust of texts,'[5] which is to ask, 'who may trust in this text?' If the object of study, however, is the 'activity of intelligence' of editors and readers,[6] a focus on the material artifacts and a dialogic relation between the texts can form the basis of a textual inquiry. This is not to say that the material text is to be accepted as an unquestioned authority, but rather that it can be understood, not as a site of error, but as a tool for inquiry into the social history of the work. I will argue that textual historicism forms a valid basis for parallel-text editing, both for the Malory texts and for Middle English works generally. This approach to editing is not intended to replace editions centered on the author, but to provide additional avenues of textual inquiry that study the uses, uncertainties, and appropriations of a given work. An over-reliance on the author as the primary organizing principle has produced editions whose claims for authority have obscured the continual re-representation of a literary work.

Through the lens of Malory texts and editions, I wish to consider the kinds of textual and theoretical questions that parallel-text editions, as distinct from eclectic (also called critical) editions[7] or single-text diplomatic editions, seek to propose and answer. Eclectic editions primarily seek to answer the question, What was the probable intent of the author? As a rhetorical construction, a parallel-text edition is based on the answers to two questions: What is the significance of difference? and How do parallel-text editions exploit the representation of difference? Parallel-text editions that represent the physical manifestations of two or more texts shift the site of inquiry from authorial intention to material production and the 'life' of a work. One of the primary aims of such an edition is to attempt to identify the 'transmission of discourse'[8] and the circumstances that produced the condition of alterity. As one way to represent the theories of material philology,[9] parallel-text editions highlight the indeterminacy of the editorial and transmission process. Though many editions do not explicitly state their situatedness in this nexus, scholars who claim that parallel-text editions are merely pragmatic responses to corrupted texts fail to see that, despite the assertion that social theories of texts have failed to provide corresponding editions, the parallel-text editorial format is in fact an embodiment of an approach to texts rooted in post-structuralist theory.

One of the greatest practical strengths of the parallel-text edition, clearly, is its function of bringing two texts into close proximity so as to foster a process of contrastive analysis. The two versions of Malory's Roman War account – found in the Winchester manuscript (London, British Library MS Additional 59678) and the Caxton printed edition respectively – are ideally suited to a parallel-text edition. Caxton's printed edition varies from the Winchester manuscript in three major ways: the chapter and book divisions, compressed or deleted *explicits*, and a substantially shorter account of the battle between Arthur and Lucius. Malory's account of the Roman War is derived from the English alliterative poem *Morte Arthure*, composed in the late fourteenth century, though the two documentary witnesses express that derivation in distinct ways. Because of the wide variation, the Roman War section draws particular attention from textual scholars engaged with Malory's work. This section, which occurs early in the work and establishes a conceptual framework for the figure of Arthur, displays the most significant variation from one version to the other. For fifteenth-century audiences, the well-known Roman War account and its emphasis on empire and models of kingship became a site of strong revision in order to carry the politics of the author/redactor and subsequent editor.[10] A highly politicized content is also found in Malory's final tale – the shadow-side of the successful Roman War campaign. The whole of Malory's Arthuriad would be a large parallel-text indeed, but because the Caxton and Winchester versions differ less dramatically in other parts of the text, a parallel-text edition of the whole work is not necessary. A reduction of the Caxton print to the status of an 'inferior' witness not only loses the re-readings of the Roman War narrative in the fifteenth century, but also effaces the print as a literary text that occupies the borderland of manuscript and print culture. A parallel-text edition of the Winchester and Caxton versions of the Roman War account explores the iconic nature of the two texts and contributes to our understanding of that borderland, a contribution that has been overlooked in the effort to establish a single, authoritative text. As Dan Embree and Elizabeth Urquhart argue in making their case for a parallel-text edition of *The Simonie*, the extant versions are 'quite distinct though closely related texts which need to be understood in relation to one another before they can be very seriously studied.'[11]

Intriguingly, the two documents have a shared physical history. The work of Lotte Hellinga has shown that the two witnesses to the work were – at one point – together in Caxton's printing house.[12] Hellinga

208

TLN

be beste and moste worshyp //The kyngis & knyghtis ga// rirde hem vnto counsayle & were condecended for to make .ij. chyfftaynes that was Sir Baudwen of Bre// tayne an Auncient & an honorable knyght for to councey// le and comforte Sir Cadore son of Cornuayle þ*at* was at þ*at* tyme called Sir Constantyne that aftir was kynge aftir Arthurs dayes//And þ*er* In the p*re*sence of all þ*e* lordis the kynge resceyved all þe rule vnto thes .ij. lordis and quene Gwenyvere And Sir Trystrams at þ*at* tyme he left with kynge Marke of Cornuayle for þe love of labeale Isode where fore Sir Launcelot was passyng wrothe //Than quene Gwenyu*er* made grete sorow that the kynge and all þe lordys sholde so be dep*ar*ted And þ*er* she fell doune on a swone and hir ladyes bare hir to her chambir //Than þe kynge com*ma*unded hem to god & be lefte þe quene In Sir Constantynes And sir Baudewens hondis And all Inglonde holy to rule as them selfe <u>75</u> seemed beste//And whan þe kynge was an horsebak he seyde In herynge of all þe lordis If þ*at* I dye In this Iurney here I make þe Sir Constantyne my trew Ayre for þou arte nexte of my kyn save Sir Cadore thy fadir And þ*er* fore if þ*at* I dey I woll þ*at* ye be crowned kynge // Ryght so he sought & his knyghtis towarde Sande// wyche. Where he founde be fore hym many galyard knyghtis. for þ*er* were þe moste p*ar*ty of all þe rounde ta// ble redy on þo bankes for to sayle whan þe kynge lyked Than In all haste þ*at* myght be they shypped þ*er* horsis & harneyse & all man*er* of ordynaunce þ*at* fallyth for þe werre & tentys and pavylyons many were trussed and so they shotte frome þe bankis many grete caryckis and many shyppes of forestage w*ith* coggis and galeyes & spynnesse full noble w*ith* galeyes & galyottys rowyng w*ith* many Ores. And thus they strekyn forth In to the stremys many sadde hunderthes.

:here Folowyth the dreme of Kynge Arthure .

As the kynge was In his Cog and lay In his Ca// ban he felle In a slu*m*beryng & dremed how a dredfull Dragon dud drenche muche of his peple & com fleyng one wynge oute of þe weste p*ar*tyes and his hede hym semed was enamyled w*ith* Asure and his shuldyrs shone as þe golde & his wombe was lyke may// les of a merveylous hew and his tayle was fulle of tatyrs & his feete were florysshed as hit were fyne

Figure 3.1 and 3.2 Two facing pages of a diplomatic, parallel-text edition of the Roman War account.

209

re he ordeyned two gouernours of this Royame that is to say
Syre Bawdewyn of Bretayne for to counceille to the best and

syr Constantyn sone to syre Cador of Cornewaylle/ whiche af

ter the dethe of Arthur was kyng of this Royamme/ And in
the presence of all his lordes he resyned the rule of the roya//
me and Gweneuer his quene to them/ wherfore syre launcelot
was wrothe/ for he lefte syre Trystram with kynge marke for
the loue of beal Isoulde/ Thenne the quene Gweneuer made gre
te sorowe for the departynge of her lord and other/ and swou
ned in suche wyse that the ladyes bare her in to her chambre

Thus the kyng with his grete armye departed leuyng the que
ne and Royamme in the gouernaunce of syre Bawduyn and
Constantyn/ And whan he was on his hors/ he sayd with an
hyhe voys yf I dye in this iourney I wyl that syre Constan
tyn be myn heyer and kyng crowned of this royame as next
of my blood/ And after departed and entred into the see atte

Sandwyche with alle his armye with a greete multitude of

shyppes/ galeyes/ Cogges /and dromoundes/ sayllynge on the
see/

__sig.i.ii__

C Capitulum iiii

And as the kyng laye in his caban in the shyp/ he fyll
in a slomerynge and dremed a merueyllous dreme /

hym semed that a dredeful dragon dyd drowne moche of his
peple/and he cam fleynge oute of the west/and his hede was
enameled with asure / and his sholders shone as gold / his be
ly lyke maylles of a merueyllous hewe / his taylle ful of tat

employed infrared photography to determine that the manuscript bore offsets which she identified as letter type from Caxton's print shop that was in use at the time that he printed *Le Morte Darthur.* However, the manuscript does not bear any of the marks used by compositors to ready a text for printing, leading to the conclusion that Caxton used a different, and now lost, manuscript as the marked-up copy for his edition.[13] Nevertheless, Hellinga's work assures us that the two documents share a close and intertwined history, further strengthening the usefulness of a parallel-text edition of the disputed section. A parallel-text edition of the Roman War account interrogates the two texts as integral to an understanding of the 'work,' that is, 'the global set of all the texts,'[14] and recognizes the intertwined textual history of the two witnesses as a rich source for understanding what has come to be known as *Le Morte Darthur.* In addition, a diplomatic parallel-text edition offers a text that eschews modernized punctuation, an editorial mediation that has altered syntactic cues and meanings of the earlier documents.[15]

While it is impossible for any edition – even a facsimile – to recreate a medieval reading experience, parallel-text editions that represent single-text versions (rather than eclectic texts) make a gesture toward facilitating an understanding of what that experience may have been like. A documentary edition, be it a parallel-text or single-text edition, provides a text that approximates, lexically though not visually, a historical document – that is, a text that was actually read. In the case of the Malory texts, the Caxton edition likely saw a printing of around 500 copies, whereas the Winchester manuscript had a relatively limited social history until its recovery in the 1930s. David Matthews has observed how manuscripts have tended to be privileged over printed texts and how they offer the illusion of putting the readers 'in contact with an original, medieval text.'[16] Matthews argues for the value and study of early printed editions of literary works, noting that while 'early editions [often] involve wild departures from the manuscripts, something is lost when they are ignored.'[17] The 'something' that Matthews laments is the cultural, political, and literary life of a work – the literary work in dynamic interaction with readers. In addition, the preference for manuscript witnesses, while an important emphasis, has had the effect of limiting study of the readers or the social history of texts. It is clear that a text presented in an earlier manuscript may represent a state of the text which is 'closer' to what the author wrote and 'intended,' if indeed such intent can ever be determined. Just how much closer, or what stages of intervention lie between the author's holograph and the manuscript, we cannot say with certainty as there is no direct link with Malory-as-author.

The Winchester version of the Roman War account consists of approximately 8,500 words, while the account in the Caxton version is about half that number.[18] Many scholars find this evidentiary of Caxton having edited the tale for publication by his printing house. Vinaver, who based his 1947 edition, *The Works of Sir Thomas Malory,* on the Winchester manuscript, had few kind words for Caxton, arguing that the printed version of the Roman War account was 'not only a drastic abridgement, but a new work ... Caxton "simple person," reduced it to less than half its size, and while doing so rewrote it from beginning to end.'[19] Vinaver chose a new title, *Works,* not only to emphasize the episodic or independent nature of the tales, but also to underscore Caxton's title as a 'misinterpretation, no doubt deliberate.'[20] As George Painter has humorously observed, Vinaver saw Caxton's title as a form of 'textual conspiracy.'[21] According to Vinaver, Malory's 'last explicit suggested to Caxton his most ingenious device – that of publishing the book under one title.'[22] Vinaver goes on to indict Caxton's use of the final explicit, while editing out the previous ones, asserting that '[t]his subterfuge proved successful.'[23] The weight of Vinaver's scholarly reputation served to cast the Caxton edition as a corrupted, compromised version of Malory's work: a low-culture print mutation of the high-culture manuscript. John Lawlor, in his introduction to Janet Cowen's Caxton-based edition, writes that the 'modern reader who is wholly intent on Malory, on seeing what he in fact wrote ... can now turn to Vinaver's irreproachable *Works of Sir Thomas Malory.* Those who wish to revisit the *Morte Darthur,* the book as Caxton shaped it, have their text in the present volume.'[24] Vinaver's edition was initially accepted as a transparent representation of Malory's intention; his reconception and re-titling of the work from *Le Morte Darthur* to *Works* privileged the manuscript over the early print version, a position that has dominated twentieth-century criticism. Despite the now general acknowledgement of the opacity of Vinaver's edition, itself a particular rhetorical representation,[25] the hierarchy of texts has remained.

Ideology of the Text

If reading and writing reflect sites of contestation for authority and privilege,[26] then the meta-text of mid-twentieth-century Malory editions and scholarship can be seen, in part, as a series of bids for ownership and authority. To date, little work has been done to excavate the ideologies that informed the making of Malory editions or the cultural work done by these editions.[27] The discovery of the Winchester manuscript in the early twentieth century coincided with the era of the eclectic, 'definitive' edition based on principles of nineteenth-century philology and stemmatics. Vinaver's edition of Malory embodies the debt of eclectic editing to the scientific principles of Darwin and the disciplines of natural science. As Jonathan Evans points out, botany and philology share a paradigmatic history in late nineteenth-century thought and the framework of taxonomy and the discipline of botany 'had a profound influence on both later 19th-century linguistics and textual editing.'[28] By revealing the ties between Malory's work and English verse,[29] the Winchester witness provided the basis for the claim that Malory's work was an instance of a national literature, not a mere borrowing from French sources. After its recovery in 1934, the Winchester manuscript, seen as the artifact of this previously under-recognized national literature, was subsequently championed as representing 'the real Malory.' Shadowed by the deep concerns of the Second World War, Vinaver saw his edition as connected to English national identity: 'To have seen a text of this magnitude through the press at a time of the greatest national emergency is in itself a unique achievement.'[30]

In addition to the practice of eclectic editing, including emending from Caxton and from source texts to produce a 'definitive edition,'[31] Vinaver overlaid a second major shape on the edition: he introduced modern paragraphing, punctuation, capitalization, genitive apostrophes, and the use of quotation marks for dialogue. Vinaver made these format decisions for two reasons. He wished to make the text accessible for twentieth-century readers, writing that 'an attempt has been made to give the work the appearance of a modern novel, not that of a learned treatise.'[32] But this remark makes it clear that he was also guided by his understanding of the place of Malory's work in the development of English literature. Vinaver saw Malory's work as a critical marker in the emergence of English literary prose. According to Vinaver, 'the aesthetic principle involved in such changes [from verse to prose] is fundamental for the transition from medieval to modern fiction.'[33] Vinaver remarks that what he finds 'surprising is a fifteenth-century author's instinctive understanding of the principle of 'singleness' which underlies the rhythmical structure of any modern work of fiction.'[34] The addition of dialogue markers by Vinaver, however, foregrounds a distinction between narrative and speech not apparent in either of the fifteenth-century texts. Thus, while Vinaver accused Caxton of imposing a false unity on the tales, Vinaver, too, was operating out of a literary and aesthetic principle of unity informed by philology and modernism. Like many of the great editors of the period, Vinaver had developed a strong sense of Malory's intentions and endeavored to produce a representation of those intentions. Jerome McGann chose Vinaver's editing of Malory as his case study for his chapter on 'The Problem of Literary Authority' in his 1983 landmark text, *A Critique of Modern Textual Criticism,* for the way in which Vinaver's methodology epitomized the 'predilection to believe that a text which shows no editorial intervention will be *prima facie* more sincere than one which exhibits intervention.'[35] McGann notes that Vinaver 'continually pushed the reader' toward the conclusion that the Winchester was more authoritative and that this predilection is 'deeply embedded in our textual criticism.'[36]

The choice of names used by British and American critics during the early work on the Winchester manuscript and its transfer to the British Library in the 1970s reflects a complex web of textual ideology, institutional affiliation, and nationality.[37] In 1983, the Caxton edition, which had fallen into a kind of textual disgrace after Vinaver's edition, received renewed interest when James Spisak (Virginia Polytechnic Institute) published an edition based on Caxton's text. Though it advocates a different base text, Spisak, like Vinaver, based his editorial work on the principles of eclectic editing. Spisak's edition sparked a critical debate in which scholars on both sides of the debate sought to establish textual authority for 'what Malory himself wrote'[38] or to establish the 'better text.'[39] Spisak entitled his edition *Caxton's Malory: A New Edition of Sir Thomas Malory's Le Morte Darthur based on the Pierpont Morgan Copy of William Caxton's Edition of 1485.* Spisak noted how Caxton had slipped from 'hero to whipping boy' (p. 618) since the publication of the Winchester-based *Works,* but proposed that the Caxton text stood in closer relation to Malory's lost original than the Winchester – thus his choice of 'Malory's *Le Morte Darthur.*'

Spisak's title, 'Caxton's Malory,' arose in part as a response to the 'Malorization' of the Winchester manuscript in which institutional affiliation played a strong role. In his introduction to the 1976 Early English Text Society's facsimile of the Winchester manuscript, N.R. Ker (Oxford University) refers to the manuscript as 'the Malory' and to the printed edition as 'Caxton's edition.' Similarly, in a *British Library Journal* article in 1976, 'The Malory Manuscript,' and in subsequent work, Hellinga (University of Amsterdam, British Library) uses the terms 'the Malory manuscript' and 'Caxton's edition.' The British Library catalogue, published for the Caxton quincentenary, also refers to the 'Malory manuscript' in its collection. Pairing Malory's name with the word 'manuscript' argues the greater authority of that version and almost implies that it is an author's holograph. Hellinga states that, once acquired by the British Library, 'it has been called the Malory Manuscript since.'[40] The British Library acquired the manuscript from Winchester College in 1976 for a controversial sum, generating letters of outrage in the daily papers for the spending of public funds on a transfer of the manuscript from Winchester to London. While the term can simply be a way of distinguishing the manuscript from other manuscripts held by the Library, it is also possible that the Library wished to assure its trustees, scholars, and the public that it had acquired 'the real Malory.'

Gabrielle Spiegel notes that the class and demographics of American medievalists radically changed in the 1960s and 1970s[41] when, not coincidentally, challenges to Vinaver's assumptions began to be raised. American editors and critics, in particular, began to champion the Caxton edition. R.M. Lumiansky (New York University) edited a 1964 collection of essays, *Malory's Originality*, in which the authors, American scholars, controversially countered Vinaver's view of the independent relation of the tales, arguing for 'our view of the unity of Malory's work.'[42] In the second edition of *Works*, Vinaver (University of Manchester) refutes the critique of his theory and mentions that the criticism is 'summarized in a book published in 1964 under the title of *Malory's Originality* by a group of American scholars who deny that "Malory wrote eight separate romances."'[43] Lumiansky's collection thus represented a kind of literary school of thought in regard to the Malory texts, a school that Vinaver saw as 'united in their rejection' of his theory of the eight tales.[44] Derek Brewer, a British scholar, had put together an influential critique of Vinaver's theory of the independence of the tales just a year earlier.[45] The collection, *Essays on Malory*, presented critiques by British scholars of Vinaver's theory and edition and included the well-known critique by C.S. Lewis.[46] In addition to the issue of unity, Lumiansky's volume initiated a wider divide between British and American scholars that began to separate into questions of which text – Caxton's or the Winchester – represented Malory's 'final intention.'[47] This divide was largely reflected in two volumes of essays on Malory published in the 1980s: the 1985 collection edited by Spisak, published in the United States and reflecting the 'American school's' espousal of the unity of the tales and the possibility that Malory was his own reviser; and the 1986 collection edited by

Toshiyuki Takamiya,[48] which included articles by British and Japanese scholars who argued, in part, against the theory of Malory as his own reviser. While British scholars such as Brewer disagreed with Vinaver about the unity or independence of the tales or books, few took up the argument advanced by several American scholars that the Caxton text best represented Malory's own revision. It may be noted as well that even the artifacts themselves ironically mirror this mid-century divide: the Caxton edition is held by the Pierpont Morgan Library in New York and the Winchester manuscript by the British Library.

In addition to nationality or institutional politics and their subtle effects on the positioning of the manuscript and printed versions of Malory's work, the scholarship of N.F. Blake (University of Sheffield) also raises the question of Caxton's class as another form of influence. According to Blake, although Caxton 'received gifts from members of the aristocracy this did not make him any different from a host of tradesmen at the time.'[49] In comparing Caxton to Lydgate, Blake notes how '[b]oth accepted commissions from aristocratic patrons and received rewards from them, but their friends and acquaintance and the bulk of their audience were to be found in their own class.'[50] Arguing against the portrayal of Caxton as a scholar, Blake concludes that '[i]t is still most acceptable to regard Caxton as a merchant, as a man that was interested in buying and selling.'[51] Blake avoids referring to Caxton as an editor or translator – activities Caxton clearly undertook – and refers to Caxton almost exclusively as a merchant or tradesman. By de-valuing the Caxton edition as non-authoritative, Blake exorcised the 'tradesman' in whose hands a literary icon had rested and condemned his work as a corrupting, even insidious, overlay – an overlay that had obscured the true identity of the high-culture manuscript.

One of the great contributions of Vinaver's *Works* was the intense scholarly research and discussion generated by his choice of the Winchester as his base text and the assumptions and conclusions he drew as a result of his work. The debate has provoked, at times, intense response, and points out the impossibility of a 'purely textual' edition. Of particular note is the exchange between Charles Moorman, of the University of Southern Mississippi, and P.J.C. Field, of the University of Wales.[52] Moorman's 1995 article, 'Desperately Defending Winchester,' broached the theory that the reception of William Matthews's theory of Malory as his own reviser, and the core of the Winchester-Caxton debate, lie in matters not found in either text:

> I, for one, am inclined to think it is because Matthews is perceived by his critics not simply as a scholar attempting to examine a literary problem, but as a genuine iconoclast, a breaker of idols. Think back to the discovery of W, of what was hailed from the moment of its dramatic discovery as one of the great literary finds of the century, the authoritative Malory, the genuine handwritten article, the real thing ... On that newly discovered manuscript old scholarly reputations were refurbished and new ones founded, new editions of it were published frequently at premium prices, the whole Arthurian industry bathed in its glory ... Then to have a California Cockney suddenly attempt, even indirectly by raising up its deposed rival, to discredit that fabulous manuscript, to reduce it to the status of first draft, of trial run, and to raise up Cinderella Caxton as Malory's finished product, why that would never do ... And so from desperation, out from the edge came the abacus and the grapeshot.[53]

Field's response to Moorman's allegation was to assert that academic debate, 'like civil life generally, depends on minimum assumptions of good faith. When a senior scholar comes to believe that those who disagree with him have colluded for twenty years in unprofessional practices, from ignoring evidence to ethnic prejudice against Cockneys, it is in everyone's interest to try to see if it is possible to generate less heat and more light.'[54] Matthews, a self-described 'London Cockney' and a professor at the University of California, Los Angeles, was a vigorous defender of the superiority of the Caxton version. His main argument in regard to his theory of Malory's revisions was published posthumously;[55] he asserts that the Caxton version is a 'much better text than that presented in the Winchester manuscript: more accurate, fuller, and, if our argument is correct, graced by Malory's own revision of the Roman War episode and possibly other small sections too.'[56] Robert Kindrick of the University of Montana supports Matthews's claim that Malory was his own reviser, arguing that the Winchester manuscript was an earlier and possibly more corrupt version that Caxton rejected in favor of a 'more authoritative text.'[57]

Field, editor of the third edition of Vinaver's *Works of Sir Thomas Malory* and the more recent *Malory: Texts and Sources*, refutes Matthews's conclusion and is supported by the linguistic analyses of Yuji Nakao and Shunichi Noguchi, both of whom argue that the evidence points to Caxton as the reviser.[58] Noguchi argues 'Caxtonian words and phrases' in the Caxton version of the Roman War account mark the text as edited by Caxton.[59] However, some aspects of the Caxton version defy a clear Caxton-revision explanation of the Roman War account. Field notes, for example, that the Caxton edition has 'northernisms' that 'do not appear in the same contexts either in *W* or in the alliterative poem.'[60]

Once the assertion that editions are ultimately rhetorical positions is accepted, then institutional affiliation, nationality, and class ideology can be productively assessed as having contributed to the dialectic of Caxton-based and Winchester-based editions. While critical work on Caxton's editions has moved past a binary perspective on the two texts, the residual influence of such responses to the Caxton edition has lingered long in the cultural work of Malory editions. Recent evidence of the continued polarization of the debate about which text best meets this criterion is the 1998 edition of the Winchester manuscript by Helen Cooper (Oxford University). The back cover blurb states that 'This modern spelling edition ... is based on the authoritative Winchester manuscript and represents what Malory wrote more closely than the version printed by William Caxton.'[61] Cooper's work is an excellent student edition, but the claim that it represents Malory more closely seems difficult to defend, at least for the Roman War account, when – like Caxton – Cooper edits the Roman War account for her audience: 'Few readers now are likely to share Malory's passionate interest in the details of battle tactics and tournaments, and I have cut these generously.'[62] After more than fifty years of scholarly debate, the title *Le Morte Darthur* has again gained favour over the title *Works* and scholars generally agree on the terms 'Winchester manuscript,' 'Caxton edition,' and the 'Vinaver/Field edition' or '*Works*.' Because the debate between the two camps has been a key aspect of Malory scholarship throughout the second half of the twentieth century, a parallel-text edition enables scholars and students to put the critical debate in context via a side-by-side analysis of the two texts. Such parallel-text editions can be profitably used in the classroom to disrupt singular readings of a work and to call attention to interpretive issues such as authorial revision, material culture, reception, and transmission.

A parallel-text edition of the Roman War account can promote further scholarship such as John Withrington's, in which the discrepancies inform our understanding of the role of the Roman War in the larger work.[63] Withrington points out, for example, that the Winchester version posits a politically frail kingdom and Arthur's foray against the Roman emperor as an attempt to solidify his domestic position. In the Caxton version, by contrast, Withrington notes that the compressed narrative establishes Arthur as secure in his realm and the challenge of the Romans as importing 'a sense of disturbed order.'[64] Similarly, the linking of the arrival of Lancelot and Tristan at Arthur's court – a pairing which only occurs in the Winchester – offers fertile ground for considering the representation of Lancelot as intimately linked with the Winchester's greater sense of internal fragility: 'Than sone aftir come Sir Launcelot de Lake vnto þe courte//And than Sir Trystrams come that tyme also.'

In both versions, upon embarking on the Roman campaign Arthur experiences a prophetic dream. In the Winchester, a 'dredfull Dragon' flies 'oute of þe weste p*ar*tyes' and fights a 'grymly Beare' that had come 'oute of þe oryent.'[65] In the Caxton edition the dragon fights a 'grymly bore,' and Field points out that 'the boar was the badge of King Richard III and the dragon that of Henry Tudor,' thus creating what Field has termed 'a bold political allusion.'[66] I have argued elsewhere that scribal transmission and/or confusion could account for this change: the animal described is a confused amalgam of paws and tusks,[67] but the recontextualization of the symbolism, be it political or textual, shows the potency of the narrative and its fluidity in the fifteenth century as a marker of meaning. Other discrepancies between the two narratives' positioning of the Eastern kings and dukes track emerging geographic knowledge in the mid-fifteenth century and the subtle changes in tenor of crusading rhetoric against the Islamic East.[68] Of course, such contrastive analysis can, and has, occurred without a parallel-text edition, but such an edition brings the dynamic interaction of the two versions to the forefront.

If parallel-texts offer a means by which to represent material production and the intervention of time, such an editorial representation is not without criticism. Nicholas Jacobs characterizes the argument for parallel-text editions as rooted in what he terms 'strong relativism,' the implications of which for an editor are that 'he or she should in effect cease to edit, and should merely reproduce ... as many versions of the chosen text as are to hand, and draw from each of them the appropriate conclusions regarding the contexts within which they were produced.'[69] But a parallel-text edition is more than an attempt merely to re-create or investigate the states of literary production: students and scholars, confronting what is alternately there in one text and not in another, must raise questions of how these additions or deletions change the narrative and its meaning. Kane and Donaldson once characterized 'any edition short of a fully reconstructed original' as little more than a 'poor-spirited and slothful undertaking.'[70] Parallel-text editions, I would argue, are not hopeless indications of overwhelming relativism, but rather representations of strong historicism, and the number of such editions of medieval texts continues to grow. To be sure, a parallel-text edition, like an eclectic edition, provides only a particular means by which to investigate a literary text. And, like the critical edition, it creates a text that never existed as represented. The facing pages, while individually representative of a particular document, create a new modality when joined together. And while A.V.C. Schmidt's parallel-text edition of *Piers Plowman* represents four versions of the work, it may well define the limit of the parallel-text form in terms of the printed page.[71] Furthermore, if parallel-text editions are to facilitate contrastive analysis, passages must be aligned, which creates the side effect of a fragmentary editorial form.

Critical inquiry based on a Foucauldian archeology currently dominates the shape and critical questions of much current scholarship and thus, in service to those questions, new editions of Malory, rooted in history and materiality, can be imagined as functioning in a 'post-Vinaver' world. Unlike the eclectic editions of the mid-twentieth century, a parallel-text edition of the Winchester and Caxton texts cannot be said to make a claim of 'definitiveness.' It is not an edition for posterity, but an edition useful for particular scholarly interests. Such 'small' editions, in contrast to the mammoth editorial endeavors, for example, of the Center for Editions of American Authors (now the Center for Scholarly Editions) may serve to loosen somewhat the hold of the 'tyrannical concept of the editorial function and the imperative need of editors and readers for unequivocal assertion concerning 'the author's text.'[72] There is a current emphasis on returning, not surprisingly, to a study of the Winchester manuscript, and a greater understanding that Vinaver's text was a particular representation that spoke to the interests of New Criticism, philology, and modernism. Cooper recently observed that her study of the manuscript yields 'the realization of just how far distant Vinaver's edition is from [the Winchester] itself.'[73] Cooper's evaluation represents a kind of watershed in the critical reception of Vinaver's edition. Despite the now tepid response to their theory, the work of the Malory-as-reviser scholars (Matthews, Kindrick, and Lumiansky) has had the effect of wearing away the impenetrable gloss of Vinaver's edition. While Caxton's edition bore the derision of the previous generation of textual and literary critics, *Works* – though undisputed as a scholarly endeavor of the highest caliber – is no longer univocally proclaimed 'the definitive edition': it is a version bound by the textual theories of its time and of its editor. Murray Evans (University of Winnipeg) calls for a diplomatic version of the Winchester manuscript to enable readers to go 'behind' Vinaver to discover the 'original landscape' of the Winchester.'[74] It is important, however, not to confuse this 'original landscape' of the Winchester with a conception of any ideal text attributed to Malory. Any medium by which the text is produced – be it script, typeface, or hypertext – alters, or more precisely defines, that ephemeral landscape and readers' perception of it, even if the editor strives to produce a diplomatic edition. All we have are two well-worn documents, and from these documents new editions are crafted.[75] The variety of recent editions of literary works reflects a growing capacity for reading variation within a literary work.[76] Particular or historical editions, which attend to the circumstances of production, circulation, and readership, are likely to emerge in greater numbers. Such editions of Malory will not negate Vinaver's work, but will propose alternative criteria to meet the interests and ideologies of a new century of Malory scholars.

I have endeavored to bring to bear the theoretical basis of a material philology while engaged in the task of traditional philology; that is, to make an edition which, as Chartier has argued, seeks to 'understand the appropriations and interpretations of a text in their full historicity' by identifying 'the effect, in terms of meaning, that its material forms produced.'[77] Two facing pages of a diplomatic, parallel-text edition of the Roman War account accompany this article (Figures 3.1 and 3.2). With increasing options for color printing, the red ink employed by the scribes of the Winchester manuscript for names and places might also be reproduced, allowing modern readers to experience the impact of that rhetorical decision. Punctuation has not been modernized, but the typescript makes the texts more accessible to students and general readers. A parallel-text edition of Malory's Roman War account provides evidence of the 'life of the work' as it existed in its primary manifestations in the fifteenth century and invites readers to participate in a discovery process that explicitly recognizes and utilizes the 'hermeneutic alterity'[78] of the two documents.

NOTES

1 R.H. Wilson, 'More Borrowings by Malory from Hardynge's *Chronicle,*' *Notes and Queries* 215 (1970): 209 n.

2 N.F. Blake, 'Reflections on the Editing of Middle English Texts,' in *A Guide to Editing Middle English*, ed. Vincent P. McCarren and Douglas Moffat (Ann Arbor: University of Michigan Press, 1998), p. 65.

3 Sir Thomas Malory, *Le Morte d'Arthur*, ed. Janet Cowen, 2 vols (Harmondsworth: Penguin, 1969), 2:524.

4 *The Works of Sir Thomas Malory*, ed. Eugène Vinaver, rev. P.J.C. Field, 3rd ed., 3 vols (Oxford: Clarendon Press, 1990), p. 1254. Hereafter: Malory, *Works*.

5 Eugène Vinaver, 'Principles of Textual Emendation,' in *Studies in French Language and Medieval Literature Presented to Professor M.K. Pope* (Manchester: University of Manchester Press, 1930), p. 352.

6 Derek Pearsall, 'Editing Medieval Texts: Some Developments and Some Problems,' in *Textual Criticism and Literary Interpretation*, ed. Jerome McGann (Chicago: University of Chicago Press, 1985), p. 95.

7 While eclectic editions are often referred to as critical editions or conflated editions, I reject the former term because it reserves the use of the term 'critical' for one particular kind of edition. All scholarly editions, I would argue, are 'critical' in that they result from critical scholarship. See Jerome McGann, *The Textual Condition* (Princeton, N.J.: Princeton University Press, 1991), pp. 48–50. The term 'conflative,' used by René Weis, ed., in *King Lear: A Parallel-Text Edition* (New York: Longman, 1993), refers to the practice of using several versions to create a single text. However, 'conflative' seems to imply a pejorative stance toward eclectic editing, for which reason I also reject this term.

8 Roger Chartier, *Forms and Meaning: Texts, Performances, and Audiences from Codex to Computer* (Philadelphia: University of Pennsylvania Press, 1995), p. 2.

9 See Bernard Cerquiglini, *In Praise of the Variant: A Critical History of Philology*, translation of *L'Eloge de la variante*, 1989, by Betsy Wing (Baltimore: Johns Hopkins University Press, 1999); Stephen G. Nichols, 'Philology and Its Discontents,' in *The Future of the Middle Ages: Medieval Literature in the 1990s*, ed. William D. Paden (Gainesville: University Press of Florida, 1994), pp. 113–41; Ivo Kamps, *Materialist Shakespeare: A History*, Foreword by Fredric Jameson (London: Verso, 1995); and Chartier, *Forms and Meaning*.

10 For studies of the Roman War as a narrative of empire, see Felicity Riddy, 'Contextualizing *Le Morte Darthur*: Empire and Civil War,' in *Companion to Malory*, ed. Elizabeth Archibald and A.S.G. Edwards (Cambridge: D.S. Brewer, 1996), pp. 55–73, and Fabienne L. Michelet, 'East and West in Malory's Roman War: The Implications of Arthur's Travels on the Continent,' *Multilingua* 18: 2–3 (1999): 209–225.

11 Dan Embree and Elizabeth Urquhart, '*The Simonie*: The Case for a Parallel-Text Edition,' in *Manuscripts and Texts: Editorial Problems in Later Middle English Literature*, ed. Derek Pearsall (Cambridge: D.S. Brewer, 1987), p. 58.

12 Lotte Hellinga, *Caxton in Focus* (London: The British Library, 1982); and Lotte Hellinga and Hilton Kelliher, 'The Malory Manuscript,' *The British Library Journal* 3.2 (Autumn 1977): 91–113.

13 Tsuyoshi Mukai, 'De Worde's 1498 *Morte Darthur* and Caxton's Copy-text,' *The Review of English Studies*, N.S., 51.201 (2000): 24–40.

14 McGann, *The Textual Condition*, p. 32.

15 See D. Thomas Hanks Jr and Jennifer L. Fish, 'Beside the Point: Medieval Meanings vs. Modern Impositions in Editing Malory's *Morte Darthur*,' *Neuphilologische Mitteilungen* (3rd Series) 98:3 (1997): 273–89.

16 David Matthews, *The Making of Middle English, 1765–1910*, Medieval Cultures, vol. 18 (Minneapolis: University of Minnesota Press, 1999), p. xv.

17 Matthews, *The Making of Middle English*, pp. xv–xvi.

18 P.J.C. Field, 'Caxton's Roman War,' *Arthuriana* 5.2 (1995): 37.

19 Malory, *Works*, p. xxx.

20 Malory, *Works*, p. xxi.

21 George Painter, *William Caxton: A Quincentenary Biography of England's First Printer* (London: Chatto and Windus, 1976; New York: Putnam, 1977), p. 17.

22 Malory, *Works*, p. xxxiii.

23 Malory, *Works*, p. xxxiii.

24 Malory, *Works*, p. xxx.

25 Murray J. Evans, 'The Explicits and Narrative Division in the Winchester MS: A Critique of Vinaver's Malory,' *Philological Quarterly* 58 (1979): 263–81; Helen Cooper, 'Opening up the Winchester,' in *The Malory Debate: Essays on the Texts of Le Morte Darthur*, Arthurian Studies 47, ed. Bonnie Wheeler, Robert L. Kindrick, and Michael N. Salda (Cambridge: D.S. Brewer, 2000), pp. 255–84. Murray Evans calls for a diplomatic edition of the Winchester manuscript while Helen Cooper has noted 'how far distant Vinaver's edition is from W itself,' p. 255.

26 Thomas Miller situates the role of class and political ideology in the formation of English literary studies in *The Formation of College English: Rhetoric and Belles Letters in the British Cultural Provinces* (Pittsburgh, Pa.: University of Pittsburgh Press, 1997). See especially p. 58.

27 Barry Gaines does provide many interesting details of the commercial transactions involving the early texts and a very useful discussion of the editors and the publication history of the various editions in *Sir Thomas Malory: An Anecdotal Bibliography of Editions, 1485–1985* (New York: AMS Press, 1990); Carol Meale considers the way in which the critical judgments of Malory editors shaped their editions as a 'hoole book' or as individual tales in '"The Hoole Book:" Editing and the Creation of Meaning in Malory's Text,' in *Companion to Malory*, ed. Elizabeth Archibald and A.S.G. Edwards (Cambridge: D.S. Brewer, 1996), pp. 3–17; and A.S.G. Edwards provides a reception history in 'The Reception of Malory's *Morte Darthur*,' in *Companion to Malory*, ed. Elizabeth Archibald and A.S.G. Edwards (Cambridge: D.S. Brewer, 1996), pp. 241–52.

28 Jonathan Evans, 'A Consideration of the Role of Semiotics in Redefining Medieval Manuscripts as Texts' in *New Approaches to Medieval Textuality*, ed. Mickle Dave Ledgerwood (New York: Peter Lang, 1998), p. 25.

29 Vinaver developed and affirmed the previously unrecognized dependence of Malory's Arthuriad on the alliterative *Morte Arthure* (as was far more evident in the Winchester manuscript). H. Oskar Sommer, editor of *Le Morte Darthur by Syr Thomas Malory, the original edition of William Caxton now reprinted and edited with an Introduction and Glossary*, 3 vols (London: Nutt, 1889–91) had earlier suggested this connection.

30 Malory, *Works*, p. xii.

31 Malory, *Works*, p. ix.

32 Malory, *Works*, p. x.

33 Malory, *Works*, p. ix.

34 Malory, *Works*, p. ix.

35 Jerome McGann, *A Critique of Modern Textual Criticism* (1983; Charlottesville: University Press of Virginia, 1992), p. 82.

36 McGann, *A Critique of Modern Textual Criticism*, p. 82.

37 Kamps has argued that the major contribution of materialist criticism has been its recognition of literary criticism as 'an activity inescapably replete with ideological values' in *Materialist Shakespeare: A History*, p. 2.

38 Field, 'Caxton's Roman War,' p. 31.

39 Robert Kindrick, 'William Matthews on Caxton and Malory,' *Arthuriana* 7.1 (1997): 18.

40 Hellinga, 'The Malory Manuscript,' 90.

41 Gabrielle Spiegel, *The Past as Text: The Theory and Practice of Medieval Historiography* (Baltimore: Johns Hopkins University Press, 1997). See especially chapter 4: 'In the Mirror's Eye: The Writing of Medieval History in North America.'

42 R.M. Lumiansky, 'Introduction,' in *Malory's Originality*, ed. Lumiansky (Baltimore: Johns Hopkins University Press, 1964), p. 4.

43 Vinaver's rebuttal is included in the introductory material of the second and third editions of *Works*; pp. xli–li in the third edition.

44 Malory, *Works*, p. xli.

45 D.S. Brewer offers his critique of Vinaver's theory in '"the hoole book,"' in *Essays on Malory*, ed. J.A.W. Bennett (Oxford: Clarendon Press, 1963), pp. 41–63.

46 C.S. Lewis, 'The English Prose Morte,' in *Essays on Malory*, ed. Bennett, pp. 7–28.

47 Lumiansky, *Malory's Originality*, p. 4.

48 Toshiyuki Takamiya, ed., *Aspects of Malory* (Woodbridge, Suffolk: D.S. Brewer, 1986).

49 N.F. Blake, 'William Caxton Again in Light of Recent Scholarship,' *Dutch Quarterly Review of Anglo-American Letters* 12 (1982): 169.
50 Blake, 'William Caxton Again in Light of Recent Scholarship,' 182.
51 N.F. Blake, *William Caxton and English Literary Culture* (London: Hambledon Press, 1991), p. 18.
52 See P.J.C. Field, 'Caxton's Roman War,' *Arthuriana* 5.2 (1995): 31–73 and Charles Moorman, 'Desperately Defending Winchester: Arguments from the Edge,' *Arthuriana* 5.2 (1995): 24–30; both articles are reprinted in *The Malory Debate*, ed. B. Wheeler, R.L. Kindrick, and M.N. Salda, pp. 127–67 and 109–16, respectively.
53 Moorman, 'Desperately Defending Winchester,' p. 114.
54 Field, 'Caxton's Roman War,' 31.
55 William Matthews, 'A Question of Texts,' *Arthuriana* 7.1 (Spring 1997): 93–133, and 'The Besieged Printer,' *Arthuriana* 7.1 (Spring 1997): 63– 92.
56 Matthews, 'A Question of Texts,' 130.
57 Kindrick, 'William Matthews on Caxton and Malory,' 18.
58 Sunichi Noguchi, 'Caxton's Malory,' *Poetica* 8 (1984): 33–8 and 'The Winchester Malory,' *Arthuriana* 5.2 (1995): 15–23; see also Yuji Nakao, 'Does Malory Really Revise His Vocabulary? – Some Negative Evidence,' *Poetica* 25–6 (1987): 93–109, and 'Musings on the Reviser of Book V in Caxton's Malory' in *The Malory Debate*, ed. Wheeler, Kindrick, and Salda (Cambridge: D.S. Brewer, 2000), pp. 191–216.
59 Noguchi, 'The Winchester Malory,' p. 18.
60 Field, 'Caxton's Roman War,' 40.
61 Helen Cooper, ed., *Sir Thomas Malory, Le Morte Darthur: the Winchester Manuscript* (Oxford: Oxford University Press, 1998), back cover.
62 Cooper, *Sir Thomas Malory*, p. xxv.
63 John Withrington, 'Caxton, Malory, and the Roman War in the *Morte Darthur*,' *Studies in Philology* 89:3 (1992): 350–66.
64 Withrington, 'Caxton, Malory, and the Roman War in the *Morte Darthur*,' 353.
65 All quotations from the Winchester and Caxton are my own transcriptions from the facsimiles: *The Winchester Malory: A Facsimile Edition*, intro. N.R. Ker, EETS Supplementary Series 4 (London: Oxford University Press, 1976); and *Sir Thomas Malory, Le Morte Darthur printed by William Caxton*, 1485, reproduced in facsimile from the copy in the Pierpont Morgan Library, New York, intro. Paul Needham (London: Scolar Press, 1976).
66 Field, 'Caxton's Roman War,' 37.
67 Meg Roland, 'Malory's Roman War Episode: An Argument for a Parallel Text' in *The Malory Debate*, ed. Wheeler, Kindrick, and Salda, pp. 315–22.

68 See chapter three, 'Mapping the Roman War,' of my PhD dissertation, 'Material Malory: the Caxton and Winchester Documents and a Parallel-Text Edition,' University of Washington, 2002.

69 Nicholas Jacobs, 'Kindly Light or Foxfire? The Authorial Text Reconsidered,' in *A Guide to Editing Middle English*, ed. McCarren and Moffat, p. 5.

70 George Kane and E. Talbot Donaldson, eds, *Piers Plowman: The B Version* (London: Athlone Press, 1975), p. 129

71 A.V.C. Schmidt, ed., *Piers Plowman: A Parallel-text Edition of the A, B, C and Z Versions*, 'William Langland,' Vol. 1 (London: Longman, 1995). While Schmidt's edition may test the constraints of the page, the opportunity for comparison of a greater number of versions exists with electronic editions and archives. Electronic media has influenced print forms by reinscribing the use of parallel-text editions within a post-structuralist context in which a single text is decentered, where material culture and previously discarded texts are excavated, and where uncertainty is the basis for new theories of textuality.

72 Pearsall, 'Editing Medieval Texts: Some Developments and Some Problems,' p. 97.

73 Cooper, 'Opening up the Winchester,' p. 256.

74 Evans, 'The Explicits and Narrative Division in the Winchester MS,' p. 263. A diplomatic, on-line edition of the entire manuscript, under the direction of D. Thomas Hanks of Baylor University, is currently underway. In addition, my recent dissertation includes a diplomatic, parallel-text edition of the Roman War account from both the Winchester and Caxton versions.

75 For example, Stephen H.A. Shepherd's recent Winchester-based edition, *Sir Thomas Malory: Le Morte Darthur* (New York: W.W. Norton, 2004), re-introduces several of the visual and organizational features of the manuscript.

76 For example, see Michael Rudick, ed., *The Poems of Sir Walter Ralegh: A Historical Edition* (Tempe, Arizona: Arizona Center for Medieval and Renaissance Studies in conjunction with the Renaissance English Text Society, 1999).

77 Chartier, *Forms and Meaning*, p. 2.

78 Spiegel, *The Past as Text*, p. 79.

4

An Inquisitor in Manuscript and in Print: The *Tractatus super materia hereticorum* of Zanchino Ugolini

PETER DIEHL

Medieval repression of religious dissent has fascinated generations of scholars. A great deal of what we know about heresy and its suppression comes from inquisitorial sources. While valuable historical evidence, such sources present numerous difficulties of interpretation.[1] The inquisitors' agendas rarely match the historian's, and one rarely hears the unmediated voices of accused heretics in medieval sources. Nevertheless, antiheretical polemics, inquistorial registers, and manuals of inquisitorial procedure remain indispensable sources. This essay will examine one such text, the *Tractatus super materia hereticorum* of Zanchino Ugolini, an inquisitorial manual from the early fourteenth century. The great nineteenth-century historian Henry Charles Lea described Ugolini's work as 'one of the clearest and best manuals of practice that we possess.'[2] Lea consulted a sixteenth-century edition of the text as well as a transcription of a fifteenth-century manuscript.[3] A century later, we must do the same. No modern edition exists. One can say the same about medieval inquisitorial manuals in general. Only a small number of texts are available in modern editions, and some of those editions do not reach an adequate standard.[4]

Despite the difficulty of gaining access to manuscripts or early printed editions, there are some advantages to this situation. One can learn a good deal about the practice of inquisition by studying the text as it appeared in these contexts. Ugolini's *Tractatus super materia hereticorum* presents an ideal opportunity to use an inquisitorial text to study the evolution of inquisitorial theory and practice from the later Middle Ages to the Counter Reformation. During the former period the text circulated in multiple manuscripts, while in the latter it was considered worthy of being put into print four times in less than twenty years. The present essay is a preliminary study of the text's reception in manuscript and print, based on close examination of one manuscript and one printed edition. This examination will lead to a number of suggestions on how best to present the text, and others like it, in a critical edition. I shall argue against the usual solution of historians as editors – a Lachmannian approach to the text. An attempt to privilege the hypothetical *Ur-text* of the *Tractatus* would minimize the historical usefulness of an edition. One can learn a great deal from the variations, additions, and glosses that accompany the text in its various presentations, though it is just these things that a Lachmannian edition would ignore or relegate to the obscurity of an *apparatus criticus*. Instead, the text should be presented in a form that conveys its meanings in its different medieval and early modern settings. I shall conclude this essay, therefore, with suggestions on how to do so using an electronic format rather than print.

The Treatise

Around 1330, a Franciscan, Frà Donato da Sant'Agata, was appointed as inquisitor for the Romagna. At his request, Zanchino Ugolini of Rimini, a lawyer trained at the University of Bologna, drew up a manual of inquisitorial procedure, the *Tractatus super materia hereticorum*. This treatise was neither the first such manual nor the longest, but it addressed a significant need. Ugolini noted the problems created by most inquisitors' lack of legal training: 'Since inquisitors very often are ignorant of the law and can thus easily be deceived in trials, so that they absolve one who should be condemned or perhaps condemn one who should be absolved, thus ... they should partake of the counsels of those learned in the law.'[5] His treatise provided inquisitors with an up-to-date manual of procedure, characterized by a legal rigor lacking in most previous inquisitorial manuals.[6] The work is divided into forty-one chapters, each replete with references to both canon and Roman law. Ugolini focused on issues of legal procedure almost to the exclusion of heresiology. Seven chapters deal with forms of proof, ten with penalties (five of these focusing on monetary penalties), and several more with other issues of procedure. Every chapter is well endowed with ample references to standard canon law texts ranging from Gratian's *Decretum* and the *Decretals of Gregory IX* (alias *Liber extra*) through the *Liber sextus* of Boniface VIII and the *Decretals of Clement V* (alias *Clementines*).[7]

Other than a passing mention of 'Patereni' (Cathars), Ugolini said little about what makes a person a heretic. He did, however, inform the reader that 'heresis' is derived from the word 'erro,' to err.[8] His lack of interest in specific heresies may reflect the circumstances of the early fourteenth century. The once-widespread heresies of the previous century that had inspired the development of inquisitorial procedure and inquisitions for heresy no longer posed much of a threat in Italy. Catharism was essentially defunct by 1330, and the Waldensians and the Poor Lombards now survived only in small groups in the Alps and in Apulia and Calabria.[9] The main challenges to orthodoxy in Ugolini's day came from the Spiritual wing of the Franciscans, many of whom were excommunicated in the pontificate of John XXII (d. 1334), and various individuals and small groups collectively labeled the 'Heresy of the Free Spirit.'[10] Most inquisitorial manuals of the thirteenth and early fourteenth centuries contained a more extensive discussion of the varieties of heresy an inquisitor might encounter. Some, such as the well-known manual of Bernard Gui, provided extensive guidelines on the interrogation of heretics and characteristic evasions used by different kinds of heretics.[11] The *Tractatus super materia hereticorum* stands out among inquisitorial manuals for its lack of heresiological material. Perhaps Ugolini felt that extensive theological discussion lay outside his competence, or that his patron, Frà Donato, would have the theological training necessary to detect heresy. Interestingly, he includes a somewhat fuller discussion of sorcery and magic than Bernard Gui, the anonymous *De officio inquisitionis*, or other contemporary inquisitorial writers.[12] Ugolini describes various sorts of diviners, enchanters, magicians, and *mathematici*, none of whom quite match later definitions of witchcraft. Most of these offenders fell not under the jurisdiction of inquisitors but rather of their local bishops.[13]

The *Tractatus* achieved some success during the later Middle Ages. It survives in six manuscripts dating from the fourteenth and fifteenth centuries:

Rome, Biblioteca Apostolica Vaticana, MS Vat. lat. 2648, fols. 1ra–28vb (fourteenth century)
Rome, Biblioteca Apostolica Vaticana, MS Vat. lat. 4031, fols. 1r–64r
Lyon, Bibliothèque Publique, MS 396, fols. 1r–57r

Milan, Biblioteca Trivulziana, cod. 404, fols. 9r–46r (mid-fifteenth century)
Paris, Bibliothèque Nationale, MS lat. 3373
Paris, Bibliothèque Nationale, MS lat. 12532 (fifteenth century)

In 1947, Antoine Dondaine suggested that a few more manuscripts might exist, but in the unsettled conditions of the immediate post-war period, he was unable to pursue his leads.[14] Any prospective editor of the text would have to investigate this possibility, as well as examining the known manuscripts carefully. Glosses, signs of wear, and other codicological details can reveal a great deal about how and how extensively a manuscript was used. Some examples of the sorts of information one may glean appear below in the discussion of Trivulziana 404.

The *Tractatus* attracted new interest during the Counter-Reformation. The first printed edition appeared at Rome in 1568, published at the expense of Pope Pius V. This edition included extensive annotations, additions, and corrections by the Dominican Camillo Campeggi, inquisitor in the duchy of Ferrara. Another edition, ascribed mistakenly to Giovanni Calderini, was published in Venice in 1571. In 1579 a third edition appeared at Rome, containing not only Campeggi's additions but also further remarks on Ugolini's text and Campeggi's notes by Diego de Simancas, Bishop of Zamora and a prominent spokesman for the Spanish Inquisition.[15] Finally, in the 1580s a massive compendium of legal texts published in Venice, the *Tractatus uniuersi iuris*, included a reprint of the first (1568) Roman edition.[16] The publishing history of the text hardly matches that of the most popular medieval inquisitorial manual, the *Directorium inquisitorum* of Nicholas Eymerich, which had appeared in twenty-one editions by 1607.[17] But Ugolini's text was evidently thought important enough to publish four times in two decades. It probably found use in some of the provinces of the Roman Inquisition, as no single inquisitorial manual ever gained recognition as the authoritative handbook of the Roman Inquisition.[18] In addition, compilers of newer inquisitorial manuals would have made use of it, as a manuscript in the Vatican Library demonstrates.[19]

Presentations of the Text

Especially in the absence of a modern critical edition, both manuscript and early modern printed exemplars of Ugolini's manual merit discussion as witnesses to the text. This discussion will show that the work remained relevant long after its composition, and that the ways in which the text was presented provide important clues to how its medieval and early modern readers received it and made use of it. The following analysis is based on examination of one manuscript and one printed edition.[20] It will show both that Ugolini's treatise had some value for later generations and that later generations saw a need to revise and augment the text to keep it relevant.

The *Tractatus super materia hereticorum* forms the centerpiece of manuscript 404 of the Biblioteca Trivulziana in Milan. This manuscript originally consisted of three independent sections, the first two on paper and the third on parchment. Paleographical evidence and the watermarks of the paper sections all suggest dates for the paper portion in the 1450s or 1460s.[21] These sections are written in a Gothic cursive using a brownish ink. The third section, on parchment, was bound with the paper sections at an early date, though I am unable to say exactly when this happened. The script is a heavy Gothic text script – *littera Bononiensis* – of the sort used frequently in the fourteenth and fifteenth centuries for legal texts, and difficult to date. It contains an elementary discussion of the legal rights and duties of bishops.[22] This last work is dedicated to bishop-elect Johannes of Vercelli (perhaps Giovanni Giliaco, elected in 1452). The author is not identified. This work does not have anything to do with inquisitorial procedure and may have been bound with the rest of the manuscript by chance. The parchment section does, however, contain a colophon in an early modern hand identifying the manuscript as the property of the Dominican convent of Saint Peter Martyr at Vigevano, a small city near Milan (fol. 89v).

The first two sections contain a number of texts that effectively comprise a working inquisitor's handbook. The first section, consisting of nine folios, and the second, of 56 folios, are in different hands and probably originated separately. The first section consists of one gathering of five sheets of paper, folded once to form ten folios. However, the text contained in this section ends at the bottom of folio 9v, and the tenth folio has been cut off, leaving only a thin, unnumbered strip between folios 9 and 10. The watermarks of the first section date to the 1450s, while those of the second are perhaps a decade later. The second section preserves its original foliation, numbered 1 to 56, suggesting that it was not originally bound to the first section. (I shall use the later foliation of the manuscript as it now exists.) Like the parchment section, both paper sections have colophons identifying them as belonging to the Dominican convent of Peter Martyr at Vigevano. A list of rubrics in the second section reveals, however, that the two paper sections were joined together by the later 1400s (fol. 53r). Both paper sections show considerable signs of wear. One quire of the second section, folios 45 to 52, is written in a different hand from the rest of the section, and on a different, thinner kind of paper. This quire contains a formulary for inquisitorial documents and a catalog of heresies, and it may be that these texts received particularly heavy use and had to be replaced.

The first section contains rules for a confraternity, the 'De institutione et origine Crucesignatorum.' The Crucesignati were organized as a lay auxiliary to support the work of inquisitors.[23] The version of the rule contained in this manuscript is a local adaptation at Vigevano of the Crucesignati statutes.[24] While originally separate from the inquisitorial handbook and other texts in the next section, this text had obvious relevance for an inquisitor.

The heart of the handbook, folios 10–52, is Ugolini's treatise. The scribe apparently worked carefully from a good exemplar. Trivulziana 404 contains fewer scribal errors and omissions than the other manuscript I have examined (Vat. lat. 2648). This is not to say, however, that the compiler of Trivulziana 404 attempted to adhere scrupulously to an *Ur-text* of the *Tractatus*. Ugolini's treatise lacked two important elements found in most other inquisitorial manuals: a collection of papal decretals relevant to inquisitors, and a catalog of specific heresies. In addition, the treatise provides only a limited number of model documents, fewer than in other manuals. The compiler tried to make good these omissions. First, he added several new model documents (summonses of witnesses and the like) to chapter 41 (fols. 44v–47v). He also added an entirely new chapter to the *Tractatus*, describing the varieties of heresy (fols. 48r–52v). This chapter is presented as part of Ugolini's treatise and numbered as chapter 42 in the list of rubrics, but the text of the chapter reveals that it was written in the mid-fifteenth century. After giving a brief description of the faithlessness of pagans and Jews, the bulk of the chapter addresses Christian heresies. The author of this text draws heavily on canon law, from Gratian's *Decretum* through the *Clementines* and some individual papal letters of later date. He begins (fols. 48v–50r) with an extensive though sometimes garbled paraphrase of a description of heretics in the *Decretum*. This portion was hardly up to date; Gratian compiled the *Decretum* about 1140 but drew this catalog of heretics from Isidore of Seville's *Etymologies*.[25] After this list the author describes the characteristics of heretics in terms of general principles, with citations of relevant passages in the *Decretum*. The rest of the chapter (fols. 50r–52v) discusses a variety of heresies of the High and Late Middle Ages, from Berengar of Tours (1080s) to the Fraticelli, and includes a notice that a number of Fraticelli were burned at Fabriano and Florence in 1440.[26] The date is probably a scribal slip for 1449; in the cursive Gothic used here, the Arabic numerals 0 and 9 are similar. A number of sources describe the burning of Fraticelli in 1449, and one, the *Summa theologica* of St Antonino, Archbishop of Florence (d. 1459), is probably the source of the notice about the Fraticelli in this chapter.[27]

Several heretical individuals and groups, though not all, are identified by glosses in the margin. Those identified include Berengar, Joachim of Fiore, and Amalric of Bène (fol. 50r); the Beghards (fol. 50v); Petrus de Corbaria (Pietro Rainalducci of Corvaro, the antipope Nicholas 'V,' 1327–30), the Pauperes (also Spirituals), the Fraticelli (fol. 51r); and 'maxime et grosse hereses' (three Italian Cathar sects, fol. 51v). The chapter also mentions the Waldensians (fol. 50v), Hussites (fol. 51v), and several other groups that do not receive marginal glosses. The author may have been a member of one of the mendicant orders, since he mentions the condemnation and punishment of William of Saint-Amour by Pope Alexander IV for his publication of a book against the mendicant orders (fol. 51v). A list of chapter headings on folio 53 identifies this text as chapter 42 of the *Tractatus*. One may conclude that the compiler wanted to update Ugolini and provide a fuller description of heretical doctrines than had appeared in the original version of the *Tractatus*.

Another supplement appears after Ugolini's treatise. It bears the title 'Capitulum constitutionum papalium editarum contra hereticam prauitatem' (Chapter of papal decrees published against heretical wickedness). Apparently written in the mid-thirteenth century, this text begins with a short narrative describing a visit to Como in 1255 by the inquisitor Rainerio Sacconi.[28] While there, Sacconi convened a meeting of the secular and religious authorities of the city and suggested urgently that they add a small collection of papal decretals against heresy to the city's statutes. The rest of this section contains the texts of the decretals. All of these decretals had been issued by Pope Innocent IV in the spring of 1254 as part of his reorganization of Italian inquisitions, and most were reissued by his successors.[29] The compiler of the manuscript no doubt felt that these decretals formed a useful supplement to Ugolini's treatise, which, unlike some other inquisitorial manuals, does not contain an appendix of papal decretals. The capitulum of decretals ends with a short colophon giving thanks to the Virgin Mary for the completion of the work.

The last few pages, folios 62 verso to 65, were left blank by the original scribe. A later hand made an intriguing addition to the collection of papal letters. This was a copy of the decretal *Summis desiderantes* by Pope Innocent VIII. In this letter, issued in 1484, Innocent authorized the Dominican inquisitor Heinrich Kramer to conduct a witch-hunt in southern Germany. Kramer (alias Institoris) is most famous, or infamous, as the principal author of the *Malleus maleficarum*, one of the most famous treatises on witchcraft. Indeed, *Summis desiderantes* also appears as a preface to the *Malleus*. Copies of the letter were also sent to other inquisitors, to authorize investigations into witchcraft in various regions. The version preserved here is not addressed to Kramer or any other person but rather 'ad futuram rei memoriam' (fol. 62v). I do not know how the Dominicans of Vigevano got a copy of this letter or why they wanted it, but its inclusion probably reflects rising anxieties about witchcraft in the later fifteenth century.[30] Relatively few witch trials took place in Italy during the second half of the fifteenth century, though quite a few took place not far away in Switzerland.[31] Northern Italy and adjacent Alpine regions of France and Switzerland had seen the development of extensive prosecutions for witchcraft in the later fourteenth and early fifteenth centuries.[32]

Having examined a manuscript exemplar, we should now address the *Tractatus super materia hereticorum* as it appeared in print. All of the printed editions of the treatise appeared during a great boom in the publishing of inquisitorial manuals during the second half of the sixteenth century. The Counter-Reformation saw not only the organization of new inquisitions and the writing of new manuals to combat the spread of Protestantism but also a revival of interest in older forms of religious dissent and older remedies for dissent. Several medieval inquisitorial manuals were thus put into print in the later 1500s. Ugolini's treatise was first published at Rome in 1568. Pope Pius V, himself a former inquisitor, funded the publication of the text as part of his stern campaign against Protestantism.[33] This edition included extensive additions and corrections by Camillo Campeggi, who brought considerable experience to the task.[34] A Dominican, he had served as an inquisitor in Pavia and later as general inquisitor of the duchy of Ferrara. He gained a reputation as a rigorous theologian and attended the third session of the Council of Trent in 1559 at the behest of Pope Pius IV. In 1563 he served as secretary to a commission appointed to revise the *Index Librorum Prohibitorum.* On 31 May 1567, he was nominated Inquisitor General of Mantua as part of Pope Pius V's stringent campaign against Protestant heresy in Italy. His vigorous campaign of inquisition there led to a breach with the secular authorities which required the intervention of Carlo Borromeo, Archbishop of Milan, to settle. In May 1568, Campeggi became bishop of Nepi and Sutri, dying in Sutri in late 1569.

I have examined a reprint of this edition from the 1580s, contained in a legal compendium called the *Tractatus uniuersi iuris.*[35] Campeggi aimed to bring Ugolini's work up to date, so that it might serve the Church in its current struggle against dissent. He added summaries of the main points in each chapter, immediately after the chapter headings. For example, in the fairly short chapter 6, entitled 'De receptatoribus haereticorum' (On the shelterers of heretics), Campeggi added three subheadings: '1. Receptatores haereticorum qui dicantur; 2. Semel tantum recipiens haereticum, receptator dicitur; 3. Consanguineam receptans mitiori pena mulctandus est.'[36] (1. Who may be called shelterers of heretics; 2. A person who shelters a heretic only once is called a shelterer; 3. A person sheltering a blood relative must be punished with a lighter penalty.) Roman numerals to the left of the column indicate the sections of the chapter to which each subheading applies. His most important contributions came in the form of notes at the end of each chapter in a section labeled 'additio.' These notes functioned like the marginal glosses found in manuscripts and printed editions of legal texts.[37] They were tied to specific lemmata in the text of the chapter by superscripted lower-case letters (a, b, c, and so forth) much like modern endnotes. The notes usually contained numerous references to legal and other texts as well as general comments on the passages being glossed. They were often extensive, and in some chapters, exceeded the length of the text of the treatise by a great deal. For example, chapter 8, on general issues of procedure in heresy trials, occupies a little over two columns, while Campeggi's notes fill six.[38]

The volume of the *Tractatus uniuersi iuris* containing Campeggi's edition was compiled by the Spanish jurist Francisco Peña and also contained several other inquisitorial manuals.[39] Educated in theology at Valencia and in Roman and canon law at Bologna, Peña spent most of his adult life in Rome as an official in the papal curia, holding the position of auditor of the Rota as well as advising the Congregation of the Holy Office of the Roman Inquisition.[40] He also had a prolific literary career, producing more than forty books, including an edition of

Nicolas Eymerich's *Directorium inquisitorum* and an original inquisitorial manual, the *Introductio seu praxis inquisitorum*, which was published posthumously.[41] He brought considerable expertise to his task as editor of the volume of the *Tractatus uniuersi iuris* in which Ugolini's manual appeared. The version of the text that appears there does not represent a simple reprint of Campeggi's edition but instead incorporates advances in inquisitorial practice since 1568. Peña made use of Diego de Simancas's revised edition of Ugolini, which included a number of criticisms of Campeggi. For example, Peña inserted a criticism of Campeggi's discussion of the application of torture during heresy proceedings into Campeggi's note 'a' to chapter 9: 'Hoc quoque displicet Simanca in adno. ad Zanchinum c. 7, et plane haec Camilli sententia tuta non est'[42] (This also displeases Simancas in his notes of Zanchino, chapter 7, and clearly this opinion of Camillo is not sound). Peña also included numerous references to his edition of the *Directorium inquisitorum* of Eymerich and other inquisitorial texts. These references appeared in parenthetical additions to Ugolini's text itself as well as Campeggi's notes. Normally, but not always, they were clearly differentiated from the text by being set in italics.[43]

Like the manuscript, this printed edition represents an effort to make Ugolini's treatise relevant to a period long after its original composition. There are also some notable differences between the two, however. Campeggi's edition revises the *Tractatus* much more systematically, and Peña's reworking of Campeggi updates it yet more. Its references are intended for persons with access to an extensive legal library, while the manuscript's more limited additions to the text do not refer to other texts, with the exception of chapter 42 on heretics added to Ugolini's text.[44] Also, Campeggi delineates authorship clearly, identifying Ugolini as the author of the treatise and clearly setting off his own contributions. By contrast, the manuscript version omits both Ugolini's name and the preface in which he identifies himself, and it also treats added materials as if they were integral, original parts of the *Tractatus.* These differing treatments of authorship may reflect some important differences between manuscript and print cultures or between the religious environments in which each was produced. Many antiheretical treatises and inquisitorial manuals in medieval Italy were anonymous and untitled.[45] Indeed, Ugolini may not have originally given his treatise a title. The title *Tractatus super materia hereticorum* appears in Vat. lat. 2648, but in the *Tractatus uniuersi iuris* it is called *Zanchini Ugolini Ariminensis iuriscons. Tractatus de haereticis.*[46] The compiler of the manuscript needed the text for purely local purposes, while Campeggi may have seen the author's name and the antiquity of the text as essential to its credibility and authority in the pan-European struggle against Protestantism.[47] Additionally, humanist philological techniques, as adopted by scholars such as Campeggi and Peña, would require careful attention to authorship.[48]

Suggestions for an Edition

As with many other medieval texts, a classic Lachmannian approach would serve Ugolini's treatise poorly. One could, of course, attempt to produce a stemma and recreate the archetypal text, but this procedure would discount the specific circumstances and historical significance of individual manuscripts and also early printed editions. Inquisitorial manuals are *textes vivants*, texts not fixed immutably by tradition, such as the Bible or a work of classical literature. As the example of Trivulziana 404 shows, users added to these manuals and changed them as they saw fit. Producing a stemma for such a text would be difficult if not impossible. An edition based on only one manuscript, while simpler to produce, would likewise be insufficient. One should give *some* attention to variants, both in the manuscripts and in at least the two earliest printed editions to see if the work circulated in more than one recension.[49] One ought to present the text in a form that makes clear how it functioned in the different contexts in which it was used, whether the early 1300s, the mid-1400s, or the later 1500s.

Ideally an edition of this text would serve not only the needs of medievalists but those of scholars of the Counter-Reformation. Presenting an edition of a text with different recensions and complex source annotations has traditionally been difficult to accomplish in print,[50] but changing technologies offer new options. The best way to create such an edition would be to present the text in an electronic medium, using a set of hyperlinked electronic files. This could be done on a CD-ROM, or perhaps more effectively on the World Wide Web. (Such an approach would also help to solve the pragmatic issues of cost and accessibility.) An electronic format would allow for keyword searching and the production of a concordance, which would be useful for philologists and linguists as well as historians. Formatted as HTML (or whatever improved hypertext system emerges as a replacement standard), the text of the manual could include not only links to an *apparatus criticus* and *apparatus fontium* but also links to Campeggi's annotations and the added comments of Simancas and Peña. Marginal glosses and materials added to a single manuscript (for example, chapter 42 and the additional letters in chapter 41 in Trivulziana 404) would also get a set of links.[51] The use of hypertext would allow each user of the edition to employ it efficiently, in a manner that suited his or her needs. A medievalist could ignore the links to sixteenth-century commentaries, while an early modernist might follow them and ignore the variant readings or glosses in the manuscripts.[52] Links might be color-coded or otherwise distinguished by category to make it easy for readers to find those elements they need. If the edition was placed on the World Wide Web, some links might themselves contain other links. For example, most of the sources in the *apparatus fontium* would be canon law references. In an ideal world, one would want connecting links to the actual texts of the references so as to see what point of law Ugolini (or Campeggi or Simancas or Peña) is employing. This last hope may be a long time coming, given the difficulties presented by editing canon law texts and the unlikelihood of an imminent replacement for the Friedberg editions of Gratian and the decretal collections, but the usefulness of links to electronic texts of canon law would be obvious to anybody working with inquisitorial manuals or other legal texts.

In any case, an edition of this text should not simply ignore the varying contexts in which it was copied and used. Any modern edition would make this text much more accessible to scholars. But an edition that in some way represented the earlier presentations of the text would be far more valuable than a simple edition of the original text. Using hypertext would be the likeliest way to produce an accessible and user-friendly edition that gives due attention to the ways in which medieval and early modern people received and employed Ugolini's manual.

NOTES

1 See for example, Emmanuel Le Roy Ladurie, *Montaillou: village occitane de 1294 à 1324* (Paris: Editions Gallimard, 1975), a study based on a close examination of the inquisitorial registers of Jacques Fournier, Bishop of Pamiers, and the critique of this work by Leonard Boyle, 'Montaillou Revisited: Mentalité and Methodology,' in *Pathways to Medieval Peasants*, ed. J. Ambrose Raftis (Toronto: Pontifical Institute of Mediaeval Studies, 1981), pp. 119–40.

2 Henry Charles Lea, *A History of the Inquisition of the Middle Ages*, 3 vols (New York: Macmillan, 1909; originally published 1887), 2:242.

3 Lea, *Inquisition of the Middle Ages,* 2:242 cites the Rome 1568 ed.; at 1:229 he cites a transcription of Paris BN lat. 12532.

4 Antoine Dondaine, 'Le manuel de l'inquisiteur (1230–1330),' *Archivum Fratrum Praedicatorum* 17 (1947): 85–194, remains the best survey of medieval inquisitorial manuals. Of the eleven manuals discussed there, only the *Practica inquisitionis haereticae pravitatis* of Bernard Gui had been adequately edited. One text mentioned by Dondaine has since been edited competently: *Il 'De officio inquisitionis': La procedura inquisitoriale a Bologna e a Ferrara nel Trecento,* ed. Lorenzo Paolini (Bologna: Editrice Universitaria Bolognina, 1976). An edition of sorts of the late fourteenth-century *Directorium inquisitorum* of Nicolas Eymerich appeared in 1973: Nicolau Eymeric and Francisco Peña, *Le manuel des inquisiteurs,* ed. and trans. (into French) Louis Sala-Molins (Paris: Mouton, 1973). On the numerous deficiencies of this edition, see Agostino Borromeo, 'A proposito del *Directorium inquisitorum* di Nicolas Eymerich e delle sue edizioni cinquecentesche,' *Critica storica* 20 (1983): 499–547 at 524–47.

5 Unless otherwise indicated, quotations from the *Tractatus super materia hereticorum* are taken from the only widely accessible printed edition, *Tractatvs vniversi iuris, duce & auspice Gregorio XIII ... in vnum congesti: additis quamplurimis antea nunquam editis, hac nota designatis: XVIII. materias, XXV. voluminibus comprehendentes. Praeter svmmaria singvlorvm tractatvvm, accessere locupletmissimi indices ...* 28 vols (Venetiis: Franciscus Zilettus, 1584–6), vol. 11, pt. 2 *Tractatus illustrium in utroque tum pontificii, tum caesarei iuris facultate iurisconsultorum de iudiciis criminalibus S. Inquisitionis* (henceforth TUI). The quotation comes from chapter 15 (TUI 248vb): 'Quia inquisitores, ut plurimum, sunt iuris ignari, et possent faciliter sic decipi ex processibus, quod absoluerent condemnandum, idcirco ut in talibus procedant semper preuia iustitia, debent circa occurrentia et processus conuocare consilia peritorum in iure.'

6 Dondaine, 'Le manuel,' 123.

7 For an overview of these collections and their significance, see James A. Brundage, *Medieval Canon Law* (London: Longman, 1995), pp. 44–69. The standard edition of these texts remains *Corpus iuris canonici,* ed. Emil Friedberg, 2 vols (Leipzig: B. Tauschnitz, 1879; reprinted Graz: Akademische Druck- und Verlagsanstalt, 1959), with Gratian's *Decretum* in vol. 1 and the decretal collections in vol. 2 (henceforth cited as Friedberg ed.).

8 Chapter 1 (TUI 234rb): 'idcirco est sciendum, quod nomen haeretici descendit, seu haereticus quosdam ab erro, quasi sit compositum ex, er, & recto, vnde haereticus, idest errans a recto, siue a rectitudine fidei catholicae.'

9 On the Cathars, see Malcolm Lambert, *The Cathars* (Oxford: Blackwell, 1998), pp. 282–9; the last arrest for Catharism occurred in Florence in 1342, but there had been few arrests anywhere in Italy since the first decade of the 1300s. Lambert notes (pp. 290–6) that some Catharist ideas survived as late as the 1370s in a syncretistic form among the Waldensians of the western Alps. For the Waldensians, see Amedeo Molnar, *Storia dei valdesi 1. Dalle origini all'adesione alla Riforma* (Turin: Claudiana, 1974), pp. 91–7.

10 On the Spirituals and Fraticelli, see Malcolm Lambert, *Medieval Heresy: Popular Movements from the Gregorian Reform to the Reformation,* 2nd ed. (Oxford: Blackwell, 1992), pp. 189–99, 206–12. On the 'Heresy of the Free Spirit' (essentially a construct of inquisitors' imaginations), see Lambert, *Medieval Heresy,* pp. 212–14, and Robert E. Lerner, *The Heresy of the Free Spirit* (Berkeley: University of California Press, 1972).

11 Bernard Gui, *Practica inquisitionis heretice pravitatis,* ed. Célestin Douais (Paris 1886) is the only complete edition of this text, which Gui compiled in 1323–4. Part V of the manual, where Gui describes the heretics of his day and how to interrogate them, has also been published in a second edition: Bernard Gui, *Manuel de l'inquisiteur,* ed. and trans. (into French) Guillaume Mollat, 2 vols (Paris 1926–7). Walter L. Wakefield and Austin P. Evans, *Heresies of the High Middle Ages* (New York: Columbia University Press, 1969), pp. 373–445, provide an English translation with valuable annotations.

12 Dondaine, 'Le manuel,' 124. Chapter 22 of the *Tractatus,* entitled 'De diuinatoribus, incantatoribus et similibus,' fols. 256ra–vb in TUI.

13 Ugolini cites a decretal of Boniface VIII, 'Inter cunctas' (TUI fol. 256rb) which limits the inquisitors to jurisdiction in cases when the magical belief clearly smacked of heresy: 'quando excessus talim saperet heresim manifeste.' This principle had already been established in 1258 by Pope Alexander IV (*Liber Sextus* 5.2.8 [Friedberg ed. 2:1071–2]). On the limits of inquisitorial authority in cases of magic, see Edward Peters, *The Magician, the Witch and the Law* (Philadelphia: University of Pennsylvania Press, 1978), pp. 98–102.

14 Dondaine, 'Le manuel,' 121 n. 14.

15 On Simancas, see Henry Kamen, *The Spanish Inquisition: A Historical Revision* (London: Weidenfeld and Nicholson, 1997), p. 247, and Henry Charles Lea, *A History of the Inquisition of Spain,* 4 vols (New York: Macmillan, 1906), 2:71, 2:476, n.

16 Dondaine, 'Le manuel,' 122, mentions these editions. For more complete bibliographical details, see Emil van der Vekené, *Bibliotheca bibliographica historiae sanctae inquisitionis,* 3 vols (Vaduz: Topos Verlag, 1982–92), 1:27, 28, 32, 34, nos 92, 97, 111, 118.

1. De Haereticis D. Zanchini Ugolino Senae Ariminen. Iur. Consul. Clariss. Tractatus Aureus. Cum locupletissimis additionibus et summariis R. P. F. Camilli Campegii Papiens. Ord. Praed. Pro communi Sacri Officii Ministrorum utilitate, Pii V Pont. Max. impensis, nunc primum in lucem editus. Accesserunt illustrium quorundam Doctorum Consilia aliquot nusquam antae impressa eiusdem F. Camilli Campegij diligentia in unum collecta, cum triplici Indice copiosissimi, opera D. Matthaei Anibaldi ex oppido Valentiae Papien., Diocesis studiosissime confecto. (Romae: Apud Haeredes Antonij Bladij Impressores Camerales, 1568).
2. Tractatus novus ... De Haereticis, in quo omnia, quae ad Officium Inquisitorum contra Haereticam pravitatem spectant ... Domini Ioannis Calderini tractantur ... Adiecta est nova forma procedendi contra Haeresi inquisitos ... (Venetiis: Ad Candentis Salamandrae Insignis, 1571). [The ascription in Vekené to Calderini is mistaken (cf. Dondaine, 'Le Manuel,' 122, Paolini, *De officio inquisitionis*, p. vii, n. 7).]
3. De Haereticis D. Zanchini Ugolino Senae Ariminen. I. C. Clar. Tractatvs Avrevs. Cum locupletissimis additionibus et summariis R. P. F. Camilli Campegii Papiens. Ord. Praed. ... Accesserunt in hac secunda editione Iacobi Simancae adnotationes in Zanchinum cum animadversionibus in Campegium: item breves ac perutiles notae in margine, e regione singularium disputationum D. Honorati Giguerolae patricij Valentini Iuris Utriusque Doctoris Denique multiplex & copiosissimus Index. (Romae: In aedibus Populi Romani, 1579).
4. *Tractatus uniuersi iuris* (TUI); see n. 5 above.

17 Vekené, 1:14–43.

18 John Tedeschi, 'Inquisitorial Sources and Their Uses,' in his *The Prosecution of Heresy: Collected Studies on the Inquisition in Early Modern Italy*, Medieval and Renaissance Texts and Studies 78 (Binghamton, NY: Center for Medieval and Early Renaissance Studies, 1991), pp. 47–88 at 56.

19 Patricia H. Jobe, 'Inquisitorial Manuscripts in the Biblioteca Apostolica Vaticana: A Preliminary Handlist,' in *The Inquisition in Early Modern Europe: Studies on Sources and Methods*, ed. Gustav Henningsen and John Tedeschi with Charles Amiel (Dekalb, IL: Northern Illinois University Press, 1986), p. 46, describing Vat. lat. 6600. This has a citation of Ugolini in its *explicit*: 'Zanchini c. 39 in se.' Jobe dates this manuscript to the early seventeenth century and describes it as a 'very rough copy which is perhaps only notes for a proposed handbook.'

20 Exemplars of the printed editions of this manual are rare; Vekené lists none in North America. *The National Union Catalog of Pre-1956 Imprints*, vol. 606,

p. 697, lists one copy of the Venice 1571 edition, which I have not seen, at the University of Pennsylvania. The TUI edition is more accessible, though copies of the TUI are not numerous. My study of the printed form of the text is based on a microfilm copy of the *Tractatus uniuersi iuris* in the University of California, Los Angeles library. I have examined two manuscripts, Biblioteca Trivulziana cod. 404 and Vat. lat. 2648, the latter only on microfilm. (My thanks to Henry Ansgar Kelly for lending me this microfilm.) Dondaine, 'Le manuel,' 154–67, provides a detailed analysis of the contents of Vat. lat. 2648.

21 There is a brief description of the manuscript in Caterina Santoro, *I codici medioevali della Biblioteca Trivulziana* (Milan, 1965), 67–8. Santoro does not identify the contents of the manuscript. On the dating of the manuscript see also Gilles Meersseman, 'Études sur les anciennes confréries dominicaines. II. Les confréries de Saint-Pierre-Martyr.' *Archivum Fratrum Praedicatorum* 21 (1951): 51–196 at 141, who dates the first part of the manuscript to 1451–8.

22 A rubric at the top of fol. 66r reads: 'In nomine Domini amen. Incipit compendium episcopale ad honorem Dei et uirginis gloriose.' A dedication follows: 'Reuerendo in Christo patri et domino, domino Iohanni diuina clementia et apostolice sedis electo Vercellensi.' The dedicatory letter fills the rest of fol. 66 and fol. 67r. The treatise is divided into three sections as follows:

A rubric at the top of fol. 67v reads: 'Ista prima pars tractat de hiis que per canones circa dispenssationes et alia episcopo sunt concessa.' This section runs to fol. 81v. Inc.: 'In primis potest dispensare cum ordinato extra tempora constituta.' Expl.: 'Iacobus frater Domini fuit primus episcopus Ierosolimitanus.' (fol. 81v).

A rubric at the top of fol. 82r reads: 'Hec sunt eis per canones interdicta, quia pro maiori parte sunt summo pontifici reseruata.' This section runs to fol. 83v. Inc.: 'in primis cum homicida non dispenssat.' Expl.: 'Vbi tollitur priuilegium.' (fol. 83v).

A rubric at the top of fol. 84r reads: 'Hec tria particula tractat [*sic*] de hiis que spectant ad officium pastorale.' Inc.: 'Iusticiam colere et iura sua cuilibet exhibere.' Expl.: 'In uisitationibus tamen et unionibus capitulum requirere consueuerunt.' (fol. 89v).

23 Lorenzo Paolini, 'Le origini della "Societas crucis,"' *Rivista di storia e letteratura religiosa* 15 (1979): 173–229, argues, against Meersseman, that the fifteenth-century group of this name originated in that century and did not represent a revival of thirteenth-century confraternities such as the *Societas*

fidelium of St Peter Martyr. He notes, 201–6, that the fifteenth-century rules do not characterize members as crusaders of a sort, in contrast to the 1254 decretal, *Malitia huius temporis,* of Pope Innocent IV.

24 Meersseman, 'Confréries,' 70–1.

25 C. 24 q. 3. c. 39 (Friedberg ed. 1:1001–1006), drawn from Isidore, *Etymologiae* 8.5.

26 Fol. 51r: 'Hec pestis multum uiguit in Marchia Anchonitana multo tempore, nec Florentia hac immunis fuit, et alicubi adhuc pululat, licet multum debilitata et quasi in occultis. Multi pertinaces in hac opinione combusti sunt anno Domini 1440 Fabriani et Florentie et unus anno sequenti.'

27 John N. Stephens, 'Heresy in Medieval and Renaissance Florence,' *Past and Present* 54 (1972): 25–60, at 47–48 discusses this episode. He quotes (48 n. 112) St. Antonino *Summa theologica* (Nuremberg, 1479) pt. IV Tit. XI, Cap. 7, sect. 5: 'Nec pestis multum viguit in marchia anchonitana et longo tempore, nec florentia fuit ab ea libera. Adhuc pullulat talis heresis etsi multi debilitata sit. Multi pertinaces in dicta opinione fuerunt conbusti Anno domini MCCCCXLIX. Fabriani et florentie et unus anno sequenti.' The author of the chapter in Trivulziana 404 may have followed Antonino (d. 1459) in this passage, or they may both have drawn on a common source. Further investigation of the relations between Antonino's *Summa theologica* and this text is needed.

28 Peter D. Diehl, 'The Papacy and the Suppression of Heresy in Italy, 1150–1254' (PhD diss. University of California, Los Angeles, 1991), pp. 534–6, contains a transcription of the narrative.

29 These are the five decretals adopted at Como. 'Po.' refers to the number assigned to papal letters by August Potthast, *Regesta pontificum Romanorum inde ab a. post Christum natum MCXCVIII ad a. MCCIV,* 2 vols (Berlin: Rudolph Decker, 1874–5). Letters not known to Potthast (many, since he produced his catalog before the opening of the Vatican Archives to scholars) lack a number.

1. Ad extirpanda, 20 May 1254 (Po. 15375). First issued by Innocent IV, 15 May 1252 (Po. 14592) and reissued by him, 25 May 1252 (Po. 14602). Substantially the same decretal was reissued by three of Innocent's successors: Alexander IV, 30 Nov. 1258 (Po. 17714); Clement IV, 3 Nov. 1265 (Po. 19433); Clement IV, again, 18 Jan. 1266 (Po. 19523); Nicholas IV, 22 April 1289 (Po. 22946).
2. Cum in constitutionibus, 20 July 1254 (Po. 15474). Reissued by Nicholas IV, 23 Dec. 1288 (Po. 22843).
3. Nouerit uniuersitas uestra, 15 June 1254. Reissued by: Alexander IV,

25 April 1260 (Po. 17840); Nicholas IV, 23 Dec. 1288 (Po. 22846); Nicholas IV, 3 March 1291 (Po. 23589).
4. Cum aduersus hereticam prauitatem, 22 May 1254 (Po. 15378). First issued by Innocent IV, 28 May 1252 (Po. 14607), and reissued by him, 31 Oct. 1252 (Po. 14762). Reissued by: Alexander IV, 27 Sept. 1258 (Po. 17383); Alexander IV, 17 Nov. 1258 (Po. 17405); Clement IV, 31 Oct. 1265 (Po. 19423); Clement IV, 1 Nov. 1265 (Po. 19428); Nicholas IV, 23 Dec. 1288 (Po. 22389).
5. Malicia huius temporis, 1 July 1254 (Po. 15429, at 19 June). First issued by Innocent IV, 30 May 1254 (Po. 15411); reissued by him, 31 May 1254 (Po. 15413); 12 July 1254 (Po. 15457); 13 July 1254 (Po. 15458).

30 On the rise of witchcraft prosecutions in northern Italy and elsewhere in the fifteenth century, see Richard Kieckhefer, *European Witch Trials: Their Foundation in Popular and Learned Culture, 1300–1500* (Berkeley: University of California Press, 1976) and Jeffrey Burton Russell, *Witchcraft in the Middle Ages* (Ithaca: Cornell University Press, 1972), pp. 244–61 and notes at pp. 339–40.

31 Kieckhefer, *Witch Trials*, p. 23. Kieckhefer, pp. 106–48, lists no trials at Vigevano in his 'Calendar of Witch Trials,' though there were a few trials nearby in Milan and Como during the later 1400s and many in slightly more distant locales such as Brescia and the Swiss Alps.

32 Kieckhefer, *Witch Trials*, pp. 19–21; see also Carlo Ginzburg, *Ecstasies: Deciphering the Witches' Sabbath* (New York: Pantheon, 1991), pp. 63–80, who describes the later 1300s and early 1400s as pivotal in the development of the stereotype of the witches' sabbath, which began to feature regularly in trial accounts.

33 The title of the edition includes the provision: 'Pro communi Sacri Officii Ministrorum utilitate, Pii V Pont. Max. impensis, nunc primum in lucem editus.' For a brief summary of the career of Pius V, see J.N.D. Kelly, *Oxford Dictionary of Popes* (Oxford; Oxford University Press, 1986), pp. 268–9.

34 On Campeggi's life, see V. Marchetti, 'Campeggi, Camillo,' *Dizionario biografico degli Italiani*, 17:439–40.

35 See n. 5 above.

36 TUI fol. 237rb.

37 One thinks of the Editio Romana of Gratian's *Decretum* (Rome, 1585) and similar texts. For a recent attempt to recreate the physical appearance of a medieval legal text surrounded by glosses, albeit in English translation, see Gratian, *The Treatise on Laws (DD. 1–20) with the Ordinary Gloss*, trans. Augustine Thompson and James Gordley (Washington, D.C.: The Catholic Uni-

versity of America Press, 1993). Typesetting Campeggi's *additiones* as marginal glosses was probably too expensive for the TUI, which is not the handsomest of sixteenth-century books.

38 TUI fols. 238rb–vb (text); 238vb–40vb (notes). Similarly, chapter 6 occupies twenty-seven lines of fol. 237rb, while the *additio* (fols. 237rb–va) takes up seventy-nine lines.

39 Tedeschi, 'Inquisitorial Sources,' p. 70 n. 31, lists them as J. Simancas, J. de Rojas, C. Campeggio, B. da Como, B. Spina, P. Ghirlandi, C. Bruni, F. Ponzinio, and Peña himself.

40 Borromeo, 'A proposito,' 508–18, sketches Peña's career. Peña also served on the commission that produced the Editio Romana of Gratian's *Decretum* and the *Decretals of Gregory IX*.

41 On the edition of Eymerich, see Borromeo, 'A proposito,' 520–4, and Edward Peters, 'Editing Inquisitors' Manuals in the Sixteenth Century: Francisco Peña and the *Directorium inquisitorum* of Nicholas Eymeric,' *The Library Chronicle* 40 (1974): 95–107.

42 TUI fol. 243ra. Campeggi was arguing for strict limits on the admissibility of evidence obtained through torture.

43 The typesetters and proofreaders of the TUI occasionally failed to set these references correctly, as, for example, in chapter 6 (fol. 237rb) where the following reference appears in regular type and without parentheses: 'Turrecerem. in sum. de eccles. lib. 4 par. 2 cap. 21. Simanc. cathol. institu. titul. 15 Pegna lib 2 adno. in Directorum [*sic*] Schol. 57.' (Pegna is the Italianized form of Peña.)

44 This chapter makes many references to canon law texts, but it garbles a number of them. It may be a somewhat incompetent adaptation of a passage in the *Summa theologica* of St Antonino of Florence (see n. 26 above).

45 Paolini, *De officio inquisitionis*, p. xvii. Paolini suggests, p. xviii, that Ugolini's treatise may have been untitled originally. The work bears no title in Trivulziana 404.

46 TUI fol. 234ra. The title *Tractatus super materia hereticorum* was assigned by Dondaine, 'Le manuel,' 121.

47 Catholic authors of the Counter-Reformation (and even later) followed the common medieval practice of identifying the dissenting movements of their day with heresies of the past, on which see Jeffrey Russell, 'Interpretations of the Origins of Medieval Heresy,' *Mediaeval Studies* 25 (1963): 26–53 at 27. Borromeo, 'A proposito,' 522, notes that Peña regarded Protestantism as largely reviving or continuing the errors of the Waldensians, rather than as truly novel.

48 Borromeo, 'A proposito,' 521; Peters, 'Editing Inquisitors' Manuals,' 100–2, discusses Peña's techniques of textual criticism and philological erudition.

49 It is not known if Campeggi used one of the extant manuscripts as his base text for the Rome 1568 edition. Based on a preliminary comparison of Vat. lat. 2648 and Trivulziana 404 to the text as presented in TUI, I can say that neither of them served as his base text. The Venice 1571 edition appears from its title information not to be a reprint of Campeggi's edition but rather a new one, based perhaps on a different manuscript or group of manuscripts.

50 To take one example from the field of medieval heresiology, *The Summa contra haereticos Ascribed to Praepositinus of Cremona*, ed. Joseph N. Garvin and James A. Corbett (Notre Dame, IN: University of Notre Dame Press, 1958) represents one valiant effort to reduce a complicated manuscript tradition to scholarly order. The editors employed complex page layouts, often with parallel columns and other devices splitting up the printed page. This presentation of the text works to a degree, though it is sometimes hard to read and must be very expensive to typeset.

51 In his edition of the *De officio inquisitionis*, Paolini was able to include an apparatus containing glosses found in one of the two extant manuscripts. Where more exemplars of a text survive, as perhaps with the *Tractatus super materia hereticorum*, the number of glosses could potentially make the typesetting of such an apparatus difficult. This would certainly be the case with many canon law collections and probably with works of theology and other heavily glossed texts produced in medieval universities.

52 Since a formal stemma is probably of limited value, the *apparatus criticus* could be limited to those variants useful for identifying different recensions of the text or significant additions appearing in individual manuscripts.

5

Editing Sung Objects: The Challenge of Digby 23

ANDREW TAYLOR

Pour engager d'autres savants à faire des recherches de ce genre, en les étendant à tous les siècles et à toutes les variétés de sujets, il convient de parler à l'esprit et aux yeux, de décrire et montrer en même temps les objets chantés et dessinés.

[To incite other scholars to conduct research of this kind, reaching out to them across the centuries and in all fields, we must appeal to the spirit and to the eyes, describing and showing at the same time these sung and drawn objects.]

In the final sentence of a note in the second volume of the *Annales archéologiques* the editor, Adolphe Napoléon Didron, one of the founders of modern iconography, evokes the challenge of doing justice to medieval manuscripts, acknowledging their acoustic and visual complexity as 'objets chantés et dessinés.'[1] In the matter of visual complexity editors and critics of medieval texts have responded vigorously to Didron's challenge for over a decade. Paleography is no longer limited, if it ever was, to identifying and dating hands or expanding abbreviations. Letter forms, punctuation, and even the spacing of letters all carry cultural significance, as M.B. Parkes, Paul Saenger, and many others have demonstrated.[2] We are attentive to minor textual differences, for what once might have been dismissed as bad grammar or bad spelling is now *variance*, and Bernard Cerquiglini has sung its praises.[3] Sylvia Huot and John Dagenais have shown how integral a program of illustrations or a pattern of recopying can be to the meaning of a collection.[4] Michael

Camille, Richard Emmerson, and Siân Echard have extended this attention to the layout and choice of type-face in printed editions, showing how they reinforce the editorial construction of works ranging from the *Vie de St. Alexis* to Gower's *Confessio Amantis*.[5] *Ordinatio*, rubrication, textual apparatus, capitalization, punctuation, letter forms, marginal illustrations, or commentary – it all matters. We are committed to the fullest possible consideration of all aspects of a text's appearance. The case for such close attention has been neatly summed up by Roger Chartier: '[i]n contrast to the representation of the ideal, abstract text – which is stable because it is detached from all materiality, a representation elaborated by literature itself – it is essential to remember that no text exists outside of the support that enables it to be read.'[6] As modern readers, we always read a specific material object, hence the importance of attending to the precise physical nature of the object, whether in manuscript or print. The textual materialism advocated by Chartier has carried the day.

In the matter of sound, however, we have largely failed to meet Didron's challenge, passively accepting conventions that conceive of a line of letters as a non-acoustic representation. We have moved into an exciting new world of multimedia medieval studies that offers us hypertext editions of Langland, Alain Chartier, and Chrétien de Troyes, elaborate ultraviolet and computer-enhanced scrutiny of the *Beowulf* codex, and electronic access to miniatures from any number of libraries, including the Vatican, the Bodleian, the British Library, and the Bibliothèque Nationale.[7] If no modern edition can ever hope to do justice to the specificities of the manuscript page, it is increasingly possible to direct readers to full electronic visual facsimiles that may. But all the web sites just mentioned are silent, as are most of the others devoted to medieval materials. Do you think *Beowulf* was intoned with ritual dignity or was rapped with frenetic energy – Kevin Kiernan's site will not tell you. As editors, we pick up at the point where a text ceases to be an acoustic score and silent reading begins.

Of course there remain technological difficulties in the presentation of sound, as anyone who has waited for audio files to download can testify, but they are not the fundamental problem. After all, such simple solutions as producing a tape to accompany a book have been available for years, and yet only a handful of medieval scholars have chosen to exploit these opportunities.[8] Rather, it is our understanding of what constitutes a text, or of what constitutes information, that is hampering us from doing better. Consider the objection to the unexamined visual paradigms of modern design offered by David Small of the MIT Media Lab: 'The display of information by computers does not often fulfill the promise of the computer as a *visual* information appliance.'[9] Small's point is well taken, and his article offers some intriguing suggestions for the visual presentation of texts. But he himself falls into the characteristic modern assumption that information is inherently visual. The same might be said of the influential design theorist Edward Tufte, one of whose beautifully illustrated books has the revealing title *Envisioning Information.*[10] Sound too is information, yet we appeal almost automatically to what we can see. Our very vocabulary indicates that we are animals who navigate chiefly by the eye: imagining, envisioning, taking a particular view, getting the picture, seeing ideas clearly, or putting them into a certain perspective. We do not even have a verb for the mental sounding of a text, what we might call its acoustic imagining – a paradoxical coinage like 'oral literature' whose awkwardness says much about our cultural norms.

The dominant assumption of most modern editions is that visual presentation is acoustically neutral; in other words, that it is possible to present an edition that in no way predetermines or presupposes the question of how the work might have sounded. We are with regard to sound where we were five or ten years ago with regard to design. Until comparatively recently, editors often felt that as long as one got the words right it did not matter much what the edition looked like. Certainly the recognition that modern typography and layout is a crucial component in the formation of medieval literary canons is a recent idea. Now, apparently, we feel that as long as we get the words right and acknowledge their original visual presentation, it does not much matter what the words sounded like in the Middle Ages, or how they might be sounded today. Of course, scholarly editions provide detailed accounts of a text's dialect, but these passages of phonological algebra are among the least read parts of the apparatus and serve more as a means of locating a text geographically than as a guide to singing it in the mind's ear. The prevailing attitude would seem to run somewhat as follows: Questions about a medieval poem's sound (Was the poem sung or recited? How fast was it delivered? Was there musical accompaniment?) may be interesting but they are supplemental and do not affect the text's basic meaning. Those who wish to pursue such questions are free to do so, but their reconstructions of medieval performance are highly speculative. For the most part, therefore, scholars should leave such matters to musicians, actors, conductors, or directors. Giving voice to a medieval poem may be art but it is not historical scholarship. After all, the more sophisticated proponents of the early music movement are often the first to admit that for all their use of period instruments, what they actually perform is modern music.[11] Since authentic reconstruction is impossible it is perhaps best not even attempted.

Now in part this attitude is entirely sensible; reconstructing the sound or the performance history of a medieval poem is a highly speculative and methodologically impure business. Two of the chief sources for such reconstruction are explicit contemporary references and ongoing performance traditions. So, for example, if we wish to know what a minstrel sounded like when he sang a *chanson de geste*, we might extrapolate from passing references made in contemporary sermons, chronicles, or other writings or, alternatively, we might imitate the tradition of free instrumental improvisation still practised by some North African musicians. The first is the approach taken by historians of minstrelsy from Thomas Warton, Joseph Ritson, and Bishop Percy, through Gervais de la Rue, writing in the wake of the French Revolution, to Edmond Faral in the early twentieth century, and this approach is still used by contemporary performance historians.[12] The second approach was pursued most aggressively by the late Thomas Binkley and the Studio der Frühen Musik (also known as the Early Music Quartet), whose extensive instrumental introductions, often beginning as tuning sessions that swirl around until they gradually discover a dominant melody, owe much to Moroccan traditional musicians.[13]

Both sources are highly suspect. Performance traditions change dramatically from place to place, and the search for an unbroken oral tradition to carry us back to the Middle Ages can easily become mere nostalgia. The written references to performance, on the other hand, are taken out of context and used as if they were direct social reporting. This is inherent in the method of extrapolation itself, and although historians may apply it with greater or lesser subtlety, they cannot escape its limitations.[14] The historian of performance seeks to reconstruct a plausible account of a lost event, or the general conditions of a series of lost events, on the working assumption that contemporary references, no matter how heavily shaped by their textual form, nonetheless refer to actual human activities. Unfortunately, since direct references to musical or dramatic performances in the Middle Ages are few and far between and are usually skimpy, a few lines at best, the historian is compelled to sift through a large pile of material to winnow out a few references. A case in point is the account of Duke William's minstrel Taillefer at the

Battle of Hastings, who, according to Wace's *Roman de Rou*, rode ahead, 'chantant de Karlemaigne e de Rollant,/ e d'Oliuer e des vassals/ qui morurent en Rencevals' (singing of Charlemagne and Roland, and Oliver and the men who died at Roncesvalles).[15] These lines from Wace, supplemented by a handful of equally brief contemporary references, have served many scholars, myself among them, as vital evidence for how minstrels actually performed: singing short passages, singing on the field of battle, singing while juggling a sword. None of us, however, has examined how the passage fits into the work as a whole and how its literary structure might affect our reading of the passage as plausible reportage.[16]

Literary critics are apt to turn up their noses at what cannot but seem a willful misappropriation of a text. This is especially true in the field of romance philology, which established a strong theoretical foundation for itself more than thirty years ago by a structuralist repudiation of naive literalism. Paul Zumthor demonstrated in his influential *Essai de poétique médiévale* that within a literary system the persona who speaks the lyric, the lyric 'I,' 'n'a pour nous d'existence que grammaticale' (has for us only a grammatical existence).[17] The principle is easily extended to literary representations of the performer or reader. Literary analysis should rise above mere human contingency. As Zumthor notes, 'Il convient donc de distinguer l'homme comme tel et l'homme dans le texte. Le second seul importe.' (We should distinguish, therefore, between the man as such and the man within the text. The second alone concerns us.)[18] Given its methodological crudity, it might well seem that speculation about performance, which concerns itself with the singer outside the text, is best kept well and truly separate from scholarship and confined to concert programs or liner notes.

As I have already suggested, a crucial assumption underlying this rejection is that a modern edition of a text is vocally neutral, neither presupposing nor predetermining the ways a text is performed. If this were true, it might indeed be possible to keep philology in one box and performance in another. I will argue, on the contrary, that modern editions both rest on and reinforce fundamental and often highly questionable assumptions about how medieval texts were originally performed. When we read a medieval poem, be it a lyric, a romance, a *chanson de geste*, or any other medieval work, we cannot do so without conceptualizing it as something that would be delivered, performed, or read in a certain way in the Middle Ages. This means that not only do we read a specific printed object – Chartier's point – but that while reading this object we imagine in what manner the text as a whole might have been vocalized. Editors do this every bit as much as general readers. Oxford, Bodleian Library MS Digby 23 provides an illustration of just how important the vocal dimension is in the modern understanding of medieval poetry, and has challenging implications for how this poetry should be edited or otherwise reproduced.

Digby 23 now contains two texts, both dating from the twelfth century. The first is a copy of Calcidius's translation of the *Timaeus*; the second, which has made the manuscript famous, is the 4002–line poem beginning 'Carles li reis,' now generally known as *La Chanson de Roland*.[19] The title *La Chanson de Roland* is found nowhere in the Oxford manuscript. It was supplied by the poem's first editor, Francisque Michel, in his edition of 1837, and has been accepted without significant dissent.[20] This poem, in other words, has always been understood as a song. I hope to show, first, that this understanding of the poem is a vital part of any modern reader's experience, and, second, that it has played a shaping role in the poem's editorial construction. Finally I wish to address the paradox that the *Roland*, although defined as a song, has so rarely been sung, asking why its performance history has been treated so casually by otherwise responsible scholars. How is it that the acoustic imagining of this work has been both fundamental – indeed the source of the poem's very existence in modern editions – and yet so feeble?

Ironically, it is Paul Zumthor, censor of naive appeals to the world outside the text, who provides one of the most telling accounts of how a certain concept of a poem's original delivery becomes a vital part of the experience of reading it today. 'I take down from my library an edition of the *Song of Roland*. I know (or assume) that in the twelfth century this poem was sung to a tune that, for all intents and purposes, I have no means of reproducing. I read it. What I have before my eyes, printed or (in other situations) handwritten, is only a scrap of the past, immobilized in a space that is reduced to the page or the book.'[21] Zumthor describes his reading as a negotiation between his own cultural perspective and that of the medieval audience: 'On the one hand, there is the discontinuity arising from the historical set of my critical concepts and their presuppositions, which project my own cultural identity onto a different object. On the other hand (for a text over which hangs some presumption of orality), there is my lack of knowledge about the auditory mode of articulation, as opposed to the visual, for a civilization with a predominantly strong oral characteristic.' An imaginary reconstruction of the lost performance is therefore an essential part of any modern reading of the poem. We are 'forced to come up with an event – a text event – and to *perform* the text-in-action, and integrate this representation with the pleasure that we experience in reading – and take this into account, if the need arises, in our study of the text.'

The discontinuity Zumthor describes is not just a discontinuity between world views or cultural identities but a discontinuity between modes of textual reception, between the assumptions governing the modern printed edition he takes down from the shelf and the assumptions governing medieval manuscripts or performances, and so touches directly on editorial questions about what aspects of a manuscript we should endeavour to reproduce. We can probably assume, for example, that Zumthor, like most of us most of the time, is reading silently. He is not reading the text aloud to an audience, nor is he half-mumbling it to himself; rather, he is practising a mode of reading that was still relatively rare in the days when the poem was copied. Silent reading, as Paul Saenger has shown, was rare even in monastic communities before about 1000, and only gradually spread outwards to clerics and then lay people, and from Latin texts to vernacular ones.[22]

The point is worth exploring more fully because it serves as a link between the visual and the vocal, and may even suggest ways in which we might move from the intense visual literalism of modern textual materialism to an equally precise insistence, line by line and word by word, on the lost sounds. Saenger has demonstrated that as the practice of silent reading became more common so did the introduction of space between words; or alternatively, that space between words provides the primary evidence of the increase in silent reading. Whichever came first, the space in the manuscript is associated with a kind of performance. The unspaced line of *scriptio continua* becomes the sign of semi-vocalization; word division the sign of a new kind of silence. Since silent reading is how we read today, it now seems normal, but it should be understood instead as a culturally specific convention that early medieval texts would not necessarily share. Bernadette Masters, for example, has gone so far as to argue that in the thirteenth-century manuscript containing the *lais* of Marie de France (London, British Library MS Harley 978) the flexible spacing and continual shifts in word division introduce an element of deliberate word play and also attempt to capture the spoken rhythms of the poem. She argues that the 'syllables are treated in this text much as notes might be in a musical score ... By these remarkable graphic means the rhythm of the poetry is built into the scripting process itself and the scripted text becomes at once a musical composition, and a fully rhythmed, so musical, performance in its own right.'[23] In keeping with recent emphasis on the significance of a text's precise visual form, she concludes that modern editors should use the resources of electronic technology to reproduce or at least draw attention to a manuscript's flexible spacing, rather than squeezing letters and breaking up words according to modern conventions.

This suggestion represents a valuable new direction in editorial practice, one more way in which we might endeavour to do justice to the specificities of the manuscript and acknowledge its difference from the modern printed edition. But Masters's notion of a musical score seems just as remote from actually making sounds as the philological analysis that heads up modern editions. The claim that a medieval handwritten vernacular text is akin to a score surely calls for modern efforts at performance. If a good reader found that he or she actually could vary the pace of delivery in response to the spacing in a particular manuscript, then Masters's hypothesis would seem far more persuasive. Yet Masters offers no help here: there is no discography, no discussion of her own reading of the poem, no suggestion of what she makes of the references to musical performances in the *lais* or of the musical section of the Harley manuscript, which unquestionably is a score.[24] Without such concrete demonstration, the variable spacing she advocates will remain a purely visual phenomenon.

The same deafness runs through the discussion offered by Zumthor. I am in complete agreement with his initial principle that an individual modern reader's experience involves some imaginative acknowledgment of the way the poem might have been delivered in the past, but Zumthor's analysis also provides a terrible warning. It is indeed a *presumption* of orality, rather than a careful examination of orality, that hangs over the poem and Zumthor's reading. Earlier in the same article Zumthor notes that he 'can distinguish without difficulty between a luxury manuscript, individualized by its dedication, and a quite ordinary minstrel manuscript.'[25] This is alarming. The notion of a 'minstrel manuscript' or 'manuscrit de jongleur' – that is, of a manuscript that can be identified by appearance alone as the property of a minstrel – does not stand up well under scrutiny. There are any number of small, plain, single-column manuscripts, rather like the second half of Digby 23, that have no connection to minstrels. In fact, the whole notion of a 'minstrel manuscript' is little more than a giant piece of circular reasoning: a minstrel manuscript is a plain, single-column manuscript that contains a text, such as a *chanson de geste* or a romance, of the kind minstrels were known to recite; we know these texts were recited by minstrels because they occur in minstrel manuscripts.[26] What is even worse is that in claiming Digby 23 as a minstrel manuscript Zumthor ignores the detailed paleographical and codicological discussion offered by Charles Samaran in his introduction to the facsimile edition.[27] Admittedly, Samaran couches his remarks with caution. However, he notes that neither the primary scribe nor the reviser was familiar with epic material, and that by the thirteenth century the manuscript was bound together with a copy of the *Timaeus* and belonged to someone who copied out lines from Juvenal on one of the flyleaves.[28] Anyone who has read his careful demonstration should realize that there are, at the very least, grave doubts about the possibility that the manuscript ever had the slightest connection to a minstrel.

Zumthor's approach seems paradoxical. On the one hand, he offers a powerful account of how assumptions about performance are part of a medieval text's modern reception and laments how little we know about medieval performance. On the other hand, he ignores such evidence as there is and, in his own work on medieval poetics, provides a theoretical justification for this methodological disdain.[29] This indifference to the manuscript, however, is by no means limited to Zumthor. The desire to find in the Digby manuscript the great original French epic has repeatedly stood in the way of a full acknowledgment of what the manuscript actually suggests about the poem's delivery. Until the manuscript was digitized and mounted on the Oxford Early Manuscripts website in 2001, the fame of one half of the manuscript rendered the other half all but invisible.[30] The Bodleian staff had microfilmed the entire manuscript but made only a limited number of plates of the first part, the *Timaeus*; the historical importance of the *Roland* prevented them from taking further photographs of the manuscript and, to this day, makes them limit access. Samaran's facsimile omits the *Timaeus* completely, and I know of only one book that contains a plate from the first section: a 1935 paperback translation into modern French, which shows the juncture of the two booklets.[31] Most readers of the poem today are not even aware of the other text that lies beside it.

The occlusion of the first half of Digby 23 is in keeping with the *Roland*'s editorial construction, going right back to its rediscovery and publication by Michel in 1837 under the title *La Chanson de Roland*. This title is far more than just a convenient addition. It claims the poem as a minstrel's song, and in doing so sums up an editorial mission that sought to find what nineteenth-century France desperately needed, an oral chivalric epic.[32] Nineteenth-century scholars and men of letters alike cried out for a poem that could stand by Homer's *Iliad*, for a poem that would capture the national spirit of reckless courage and simple faith. As François Génin declared in his popular edition of 1850, 'Désormais on ne reprochera plus à la littérature française de manquer d'une épopée: voilà le Roland de Theroulde' (Henceforth, no one will reproach France with not having an epic; here is the *Roland* de Therould).[33] This epic dignity was closely associated with the poem's oral delivery. Devoid of the sophistication of the later written romances, the *Roland* spoke directly to the simple and courageous barons, who could not read.

One might assume that this nationalist and romantic vision would have little appeal for contemporary Old French scholars, but it has only been partially dislodged. Critics such as Eugene Vance and Peter Haidu have challenged the view of the *Roland* as a simple, monovocal work that celebrates the martial values and social cohesion of its audience.[34] They have not, however, challenged the fundamental notion that the poem is a minstrel's song. This notion obviously would gain strength if Digby 23 could be associated directly with a minstrel – hence the reluctance to attend to Samaran's demonstration that it cannot. Although most editors were scornful of the Digby copyist's Anglo-Norman dialect, and in that sense regarded his version as a belated and impure witness to an earlier and truer poem, they long retained the notion that the manuscript belonged to a jongleur, and so remained almost willfully indifferent to the manuscript's fuller history. The canons of Oseney Abbey, the first identifiable owners of the complete manuscript, have barely been mentioned, and then only to be dismissed.[35] Henry Langeley, the man who owned at least the *Timaeus* section and donated it to Oseney, remains but a name, even though it is no great challenge to identify him.

I wish now to return to what is perhaps my most tendentious claim: that the way we have edited medieval texts depends on the assumptions we make of how they were performed. In the case of the *Roland,* the choice of title, the treatment of the codicological context, and the drive to make the poem available in popular paperbacks and in school texts all depend on the poem's being a minstrel's song. This possibility, in turn, depends on a specific theory of performance that claims that the poem was recited in a series of linked sessions, since nobody claims that the poem could have been recited in its entirety in a single performance. Jean Rychner first suggested that these sessions might typically have extended for 1000 to 2000 lines, from dinner to dusk, and a figure in this range has been widely accepted.[36] Ian Short, for example, claims that the *chansons de geste* were delivered in with musical accompaniment in 'séances épiques jongleresques' of 1000 to 1300 lines.[37]

The idea of the 'séance épique' or epic session actually has a precise origin, and it is a distressingly recent one. The term enters romance philology in 1895 in Léon Gautier's work *La Chevalerie*, where he offers a detailed description of an entirely fictitious performance. At a wedding feast a dignified jongleur recites at length, working through a series of great moments in French epic. Finally, for the day is passing, he offers one last song, bringing the performance to a close: 'La séance épique est achevée; la nuit tombe' (The epic session is completed. Night falls).[38] Surprisingly, although Gautier draws support from references to performance in the *chansons de geste* themselves, his 'séance épique' is actually modelled on an eighteenth-century poem, André Chénier's *L'Aveugle*, that includes an account of an extended performance by Homer, in which the blind bard sings in succession the great moments of Hellenic epic while the simple shepherds listen rapt.[39] Gautier quotes several lines from the poem, using Chénier's words to help him do justice to the inspiration of the medieval jongleur.

Now perhaps minstrels actually did engage in serial recitation, working through an epic poem of 4000 or so lines, section by section over two, three, or four days. All that can be said is that there is very little evidence to support this hypothesis. Passing references in a diverse body of material, ranging from sermons to romances to account books, have allowed a tentative reconstruction of medieval performance practice. What this evidence suggests is that while professional entertainers frequently sang about the deeds of knights, often accompanying themselves on a viol, their performances, especially at great chivalric feasts, were normally short and subject to interruption. There is little evidence of anything approaching the *séances épiques*. There were unquestionably oral *chansons de geste*, but these would appear to have been short performances bearing a complex (and largely unexplored) relation to the longer written poems on the same topics.[40]

This is not the occasion for a full investigation of this complex question, which I have addressed elsewhere. All I wish to insist on here is that there is a close relation between a hypothetical performance history and the editing and reception of a medieval poem. Even if it could be established that medieval minstrels did perform linked sessions of substantial length, the original source for the idea would still be an eighteenth-century poem and the piece of nineteenth-century historical fiction it inspired. The emotional appeal of the *Roland* for the scholars and men of letters who first edited it and made it famous would remain its association with Orphic song and Homeric epic. This romantic vision is fading, but the lines of reception laid out by the first few generations of editors remain in effect, like an ancient path directing our steps centuries later. The *Chanson de Roland* remains a foundational text in French literature, and it is the true French *Chanson de Roland*, a poem that does not actually survive, that has been the subject of virtually all the criticism, not the surviving Anglo-Norman copy. If the editorial history of the *Roland* is epitomized by the invented title, the study of the manuscript is epitomized by its incomplete photographic reproduction. In several different senses, it is because the manuscript is so important that nobody may see it.

Paradoxically, the invisibility of the manuscript as a whole is combined with a scrupulous respect for the *letters* of the text. The opening lines provide as good an example as any.[41] The page is slightly worn, but a diplomatic transcription might run as follows:

> Carles li reis nostre emper*er*e magn[es]

The last two letters are so smudged as to be unrecognizable and Michel actually gave the last word as 'magne,' but the scribe should have written 'magnes' and the smudge is about two letters wide, so 'magnes' it has become. Hasty scribes (and the Digby copyist is certainly hasty) frequently omit abbreviation marks, so the expansion to 'emperere' presents no difficulty either; the only question is whether the emendation can be made silently, or requires a note, or should be marked in the text itself by the use of italics or brackets. It is an indication of the tendency to respect the manuscript that Jean Dufournet, in a popular facing-page edition, allows emendation only within brackets. At line 28, however, the copyist makes a more serious error and editors are forced to take a stance. Blancandrin advises the Saracens to offer to Charlemagne, to that proud and haughty man, their service: 'Mandez Carlun al orguillus 7 al fier/ Fedeilz service.' If we take notice of the Tyronian abbreviation, which may be expanded to either 'et' or 'e,' the line has one beat too many. Some editors find it easier to ignore the abbreviation. Gautier is one example. He also modernizes the text slightly by modifying the spacing, adding diacritics, and changing *ui* to the modern French *oi* ('à l'orgoillus, à l'fier'). Bédier follows the scribe most closely, expanding the abbreviation and keeping the second 'al.' Cesare Segre, the most aggressively interventionist of the modern editors, keeps the 'e' but drops the second 'al,' noting six other instances in the manuscript where in a parallel series the preposition is omitted on the second occasion. Ian Short locates his own approach somewhere between the extremes of Bédier's fidelity and Segre's interventionism, but he cannot tolerate the unmetrical line, and so chooses to drop the 'e.'

One might be tempted to argue, in defence of traditional editorial practice, that the visual is actually there for us to see, while the acoustic is not actually there for us to hear. But the difference is more complicated. We see through cultural codes. Thus modern editors, who generally accept that every single deviation from the individual grapheme must be explicitly acknowledged, have been quite cavalier in their treatment of a manuscript's variable word spacing. This is the case with editions of the *lais* of Marie de France in Harley 978, as Masters shows, and it is equally true of Digby 23. Even the arch-conservative Bédier followed Gautier and offered 'a l'orguillus,' as do Segre, Brault, and Short, and one must return to Michel to find an editor who preserves the manuscript's spacing, 'al orguillus.' In other respects, however, editors have treated the unquestionably mediocre copying job of Digby 23 with respect. Gautier is the last to make any effort to silently modernize or standardize the spelling and to supply modern French diacritics. Emendation has never been extensive, and the prevailing tendency is one of high conservatism, even in editions intended for a relatively popular market, such as that of Short.

This respect, however, is tinged with an extreme unease at the manuscript's Anglo-Norman dialect, seen in Bédier's dismissive characterization of the surviving manuscript as 'une tardive transposition en français insulaire' (a late transposition in insular French).[42] This may help to explain a further paradox: that this work, whose modern existence depends upon its classification as a song, has so seldom been recorded, and that those few recordings are so casual in their discussion of phonology. One prominent Anglo-Norman specialist I consulted could not think of a single recording of the poem in its original language. I have done little better. So far I have located only three full or extensive recordings in French; two were made in the 1960s, and one of these is no longer commercially available.

Before turning to these few recordings, it is worth comparing the situation to that of English studies, where making Middle English sounds remains a crucial rite of passage. In fact, medieval English has been read so often (and so well) that it merits a full discography.[43] As early as 1949, Nevill Coghill recorded selections from *The Canterbury Tales* for the British Broadcasting Corporation. From the 1950s on there has been a spate of recordings, often by distinguished scholars, including Norman Davis, Marie Borroff, John Burrow, and Elizabeth Salter. More recently, the Chaucer Studio has undertaken to provide recordings of almost all Chaucer's works as well as a sampling of Old and Middle English poetry. These recordings pay close attention to phonological accuracy, giving voice to the kinds of full phonological analysis that in Old French studies rarely seem to make it out of the critical apparatus. Those whose appetite was whetted by Davis's discussion of Middle English vowels (especially the mysteries of the closed and open *e*), which accompanies his 1966 recording with Coghill, can turn for more extensive treatment to Helge Kökeritz's *A Guide to Chaucer's Pronunciation*, which also has a corresponding recording. *The Riverside Chaucer*, the standard modern edition, notes that the poet 'cannot be appreciated without attention to the effect of reading aloud' and the general editor, Larry Benson, provides good sound clips on his website for the 'Balade de bon conseyl.'[44] V.A. Kolve and Glending Olson, in their introduction to the Norton edition of *The Canterbury Tales*, specifically address the question of how we are to make the right sounds. They wisely note that '[t]he best way to learn ME is to hear it spoken' and recommend J.B. Bessinger's recordings on the Caedmon label.[45] While I think it is still fair to complain that even in medieval English, recording is regarded as a supplement, it is a valued supplement and an integral part of teaching.

Why the difference between the two fields? Part of the answer may lie in the difference between the two languages: one the mother tongue and peasant tongue of a specific region, the other the more dialectally generalized language of an international elite. Walter Scott's famous comment in *Ivanhoe* captures this difference: 'French was the language of honour, of chivalry, and even of justice, while the more manly and expressive Anglo-Saxon was abandoned to the use of rustics and hinds, who knew no other.'[46] The view is widespread. Seamus Heaney has explained that he agreed to translate *Beowulf* because he needed to get back to his linguistic roots. Teaching at Harvard had exposed him to 'the untethered music of some contemporary American poetry' and the *Beowulf* project would be 'a kind of aural antidote, a way of ensuring that my linguistic anchor would stay lodged on the Anglo-Saxon sea floor.'[47] His comment is in keeping with his view of Old English as the language of place, patrilineal blood-line, and bass register, the language of 'big voiced

Scullions' such as his father's relatives.[48] Admittedly, the tradition of modern performance has generalized Middle English. There has yet to be much effort to capture the range of Middle English dialects; poems such as *Sir Gawain and the Green Knight* are delivered in more familiar southern English rather than that of the west Midlands. Nonetheless, it seems at least arguable that the fascination with the sound of Middle English is related to the nostalgia for medieval England as a geographical place (the land of shires and hundreds) and medieval English as the concrete and earthy heritage of the common man. Crossing the vowel shift to make the archaic noises is an act of almost shamanistic embodiment that links the modern scholar with the old country.

In contrast, the *Roland* belongs to 'dulce France,' the vast and ever-shifting empire conquered by Roland for Charlemagne that embraces Anjou, Britanny, Poitou, Normandy, Provence, and Acquitaine, but also Lombardy, Bavaria, Flanders, Bulgaria, Poland, Saxony, England, and Ireland (lines 2322–33). 'Dulce France' is the area conquered by the French spirit, the area that shares the language of high chivalry and courtly love. The language of 'dulce France' is not that of a parish or county; it is no local patois; it is international and aristocratic. To this day, when Old French is recorded it is most often as courtly lyric.[49]

Part of the reason for the disparity in the number of recordings of medieval French and English spoken poetry surely also lies in the special status of Chaucer, many of whose *Canterbury Tales* not only revolve around the theme of tale telling but also seem admirably suited for dramatic reading, since they are presented by well-defined characters with distinct voices. As Betsy Bowden notes, 'Much twentieth-century Chaucer criticism has centered on questions first raised by Kittredge, who carefully described characters' voices in the pilgrimage drama he envisioned.'[50] Unlike the chanting of a twelfth-century jongleur, dramatic reading remains a strong tradition to this day, one now enjoying a commercial renaissance through the format of the talking book. Its standards remain those established by Dickens, who, in his sell-out performances in the 1850s and 1860s, mesmerized audiences with his powers of mimicry as he brought his vivid and idiosyncratic character sketches to life.[51] Chaucer's works are easily assimilated into this tradition and seem to call out for such skilled ventriloquism. In comparison, a poem such as the *Roland*, copied down some two and a half centuries earlier, seems to require a solemn and archaic mode of performance that has long since vanished. Characterization is less important and none of the personages are individualized by their manner of speech, although some lines do indeed invite impersonation. As Gerard Brault notes, 'the formulaic locutions signifying the acts of buckling on a sword, drawing it from its sheath, brandishing it, and striking someone – all seemingly static expressions when considered in that fashion ... leap to life if one imagines the jongleur acting out these motions.'[52] But these are impersonations of iconographically charged actions rather than of individual mannerisms and, as Brault indicates, would require a professional trained in a style of performance that we no longer know. Those few who have dared to perform the *Roland* have produced alarmingly different results and have often ended up inadvertently slipping into conventions of dramatic reading that seem completely anachronistic.

Georges Hacquard, the musical director for an undated phonograph recording in modern French (possibly released in the 1960s) calls the *Roland* 'un monument d'exaltation destiné à soulever les montagnes' (a cry of exultation destined to raise mountains), and this understanding shapes the performance.[53] He takes a strong stance on the mysterious letters 'AOI,' echoing Michel, who thought they were the very words of Taillefer: 'S'il est vrai que tout jongleur en exercice psalmodait en s'accompagnant sur le luth, il nous apparaît que le graphisme AOI ne peut représenter autre chose qu'une vocalise improvisée à la faveur de la coupure à effet, sur la voyelle même de l'assonance, dans le ton et le mouvement du récit' (If it is true that each jongleur chanted while accompanying himself on the lute, it would seem that the letters AOI can only represent an improvised cry, based on the vowel of the assonance, that deliberately breaks into the tone and development of the story).[54] The narrator, Pierre Maillard-Verger, recites the poem but delivers the AOI as a baritone chant, giving it an almost operatic quality and drawing the single syllable out for ten or fifteen seconds at a time. Apart from the AOI, however, Hacquard appears to have abandoned any attempt to reproduce the performance of a medieval jongleur. On a few occasions, the recording layers in other voices. At one point Maillard-Verger recites over background liturgical chanting, and at two other places he is joined by either a second or a second and third baritone voice.

The approach taken by Lucie de Vienne and the actors of the Proscenium Studio in Montreal in their 1961 recording is more restrained but moves even further from any possible jongleur's performance.[55] Here we are offered a dramatic reading complete with an atmospheric soundtrack that begins with the ringing of church bells followed by a peal of distinctly un-medieval trumpets, which gradually fades out after the manner of the modern studio recording. A total of eleven actors read the roles, with de Vienne herself acting as the narrator. Some effort has been made to use medieval music and to take into account medieval performance conditions, but the justification is vague. De Vienne notes that the recording drew on music from the thirteenth and fourteenth centuries, but says nothing more about it, and explains that the group used mostly brass because they doubted 'if any army would travel with instruments other than trumpets or horns,' as if the performance were actually taking place during a campaign and not just describing one. Unless it is based on the belief that a *chanson de geste* might be delivered by a score of minstrels, this big band performance is not even attempting to be historically authentic. As de Vienne put it, the performance was recorded not as 'a literary landmark of an obsolete past' but as a means of 'reviving the work with its popular and at times rural atmosphere.'

What de Vienne does claim, however, is to have reproduced the essential vocal quality of French:

> Language did evolve and undergo many changes within the course of centuries, but this does not happen as haphazardly as one may think. For instance, the French spirit is an indomitable one; French love to quarrel, to argue and – as one should admit – to fight. Whether or not this is due to the geographical situation of France is beside our present purpose but it remains that the French are quick-tempered and temperamental, that they resent any form of tyranny which they do not recognize as being just necessary [*sic*]. French think fast and speak fast, and their language has progressed accordingly.

The Proscenium recording, in other words, is rooted in the nineteenth-century romantic vision of the French people. The geographical situation she refers to is that of the French nation state, hemmed in by imperial forces; the indomitable spirit is what most appealed to nineteenth-century editors. This understanding of the poem's underlying spirit is reflected in the pace of delivery:

> Whereas literary Spanish is somewhat solemn and one could say even pontifical, whereas Italian is lightly bouncing up and down, both having retained short and long syllables, French trotts [*sic*] forward at a rapid pace. This explains why so many consonants have been dropped or reshaped, why the 'accent tonique' bears upon the last voiced vowel, why the melodic line is plane, why the resonance is forward in the face and the

> clean-cut articulation done mostly with the lips and the tip of the tongue. In other words, [the] French language is a rather extroverted one, always tending toward the end of the words or of sentences with an increasing vocal tension along the line.

De Vienne appeals to a trans-historical continuity, a bond uniting the French spirit across the ages that furnishes the modern performer with a crucial sense of which sounds are the right ones. Her understanding of the essential qualities of French and English, which is not that far removed from that of Heaney, also suggests why recording has played such a limited role in medieval French studies: 'French language is a language spoken by a people more concerned with the intellectual meaning of words than with the sensorial impact of sound, in opposition with German or English, whose language (both derived from Saxon) and especially poetry, count more for effect on the weighty stress bearing on syllables thus establishing the metric of verses according to the number of stresses rather than to the number of syllables, as is the case in French poetry.' Ponderous English needs to be voiced if it is to have this sensory impact; its recitation will seem natural and sound authentic. Intellectual French, on the other hand, gains less by its embodiment.

Given such attitudes, it is perhaps not surprising that there are so few recordings of the *Roland* in Old or modern French, or that I have been able to find almost as many recordings of the *Roland* in English.[56] The first English recording was made years ago, perhaps as early as the late 1960s, by Anthony Quayle using Dorothy L. Sayer's translation.[57] It lays no special claims to historical authenticity, noting that 'we may leave scholars to argue about origins: our business is with the poem itself – the *Song of Roland.*' Quayle reads calmly but with considerable dramatic range, as one might expect from a professional actor who had also recorded a wide range of English poetry. The version produced by Kathleen Kent Watson for Blackstone Audiobooks in 1996, on the other hand, claims on its cover that 'it makes it possible for the listener to hear the story exactly the same way that it was presented in medieval times. People gathered from the countryside to watch and listen to the "jongleur" (or troubadour) recite the poem in the village square.' In fact, the production pays no heed to medieval performance whatsoever, offering a full modern dramatization, with a narrator and eleven principal and nine secondary speakers. The actors do not chant or sing the lines but rather speak them naturalistically, trying to evoke the emotional state of each speaker. Blancandrin is sneaky, Charlemagne cautious, Roland resolute. When Marsile refers to Charlemagne's God at line 82 his voice is filled with disgust. At line 148, Blancandrin hesitates in his list of what his lord will offer Charlemagne, as if to create the effect of sincerity, and when he hears that Marsile will agree to become a Christian, Charlemagne responds with joy. There is no musical accompaniment, although passages of medieval music (portable bells and a recorder) are used to mark shifts from one episode to the next and there are a few special effects, such as whinnying mules at line 120 when the envoys dismount, and distant chant at line 160, just before Charlemagne rises to hear Matins. For all the talk of a single jongleur in a market square, Watson has employed a large and well-qualified team to ensure that the production meets the expectations of those raised on modern radio plays.

The recordings I have mentioned so far serve more easily as negative examples. Whatever the *Roland* sounded like, it probably (and in some cases, certainly) did not sound much like any of them. The Blackstone audiobook does, however, contain a short reconstruction by Joseph Duggan that does match some of the work of musicologists and is far more plausible. As the narrator explains, Duggan delivers the first six lines in Old French, chanting each line to the same melody, a method of recitation that 'was said to have produced a hypnotic effect on the medieval audience.' Duggan chants slowly, taking fifty seconds for these six lines, whereas de Vienne takes only twenty. Duggan's ritualistic chanting is dramatically different from the ululating battle-cry of Maillard-Verger. His formal and impersonal delivery excludes narratorial irony or the imitation of individual idiosyncracies heard in the Dickensian dramatic readings offered in the English translation that follows or even in the performance of the Montreal Proscenium Studio.

The basic principle underlying Duggan's performance is that a *chanson de geste*, monophonic song of high seriousness, would draw heavily on contemporary liturgical chant. While there is no indication of how we know this in the audiobook (whose written commentary is confined to a short blurb on its plastic case), Duggan's premise is indeed supported by current scholarship. Admittedly, only a handful of manuscripts that provide music for *chansons de geste* survive and they are limited to a single line. The best known is the burlesque version of a line from *Girard de Rousillon* sung by the peasant Gautier in Adam de la Halle's *Le Jeu de Robin et Marion*: 'Audigier dist Raimberge bous vous di' (Audigier, said Raimberge, I say shit to you). A modern recording, such as that of Guy Robert's Ensemble Perceval, has a ponderous mock solemnity that is not that far from Duggan's chanting.[58] However, there is no way of telling how often this single line might be repeated. For evidence of repetition, we can turn to a thirteenth-century manuscript of the romance *Aucassin,* which uses three basic melodic phrases, or to saints' lives, which metrically and stylistically are not that far removed from the *chansons de geste.* When these lives were incorporated into the liturgy, musical notation was commonly added. This is the case in two troped epistles of St Stephen, celebrating his feast on the 26th of December. One, from Chartres, makes use of two melodic phrases; the other, from Provence, makes use of three.[59] The musicological account of these matters is highly technical and has accordingly had a limited impact. Duggan's reconstruction is a valuable initial demonstration of what this scholarship actually implies about the lost sounds. If the Oxford canons heard the poem delivered in the refectory it may have been delivered in something like this fashion.[60]

Duggan's recording is important not just because it is the only one that pays any heed to what scholars have been able to find out about how the *chansons de geste* were actually sung, but also because it raises the question of how they might have been transmitted, and under what circumstances an audience might have been gathered. The notion of the *séance épique* and the repeated serial performance by a valued jongleur in a great hall provides one possible explanation of how this might have occurred. If we are forced to discard it as a piece of nineteenth-century romanticism, we will need something to put in its place. Duggan's reconstruction links the minstrel's performance to a well-established set of performance conventions and techniques, those of liturgical chant. His performance suggests a number of hypotheses about what the poem's moral status and social function might have been and how the material might have been passed on. Those who wish to keep the word 'song' in the poem's title will need to have such a specific vocalization in mind or the word will mean little at all.

A certain conception of the poem's acoustic materiality is an integral part of our understanding of what the poem was in the Middle Ages. Whether we conceive of a poem sung by a minstrel to the accompaniment of a viol or read from a pulpit by an Austin canon or read in the privacy of a canon's cell, or chanted to a liturgical melody makes a great deal of difference to how we respond to it. What we must reject is attenuated acoustic imagining. As long as we merely write (for the eye) about sounds, our imaginings will remain vapid and imprecise. They will, consequently, be difficult to challenge. Generations of Old French scholars have, like Zumthor, known that the *Chanson de Roland* was sung and known that they could identify an ordinary minstrel's manuscript, because they never paid the matter serious attention. Once we begin to discuss how we imagine the poems sounded, or actually have the courage to sing them, we open ourselves to criticism. In some cases, such as the notion of the *séance épique* or the big-band approach to medieval minstrelsy, it may be possible to find evidence to discredit the assumptions; this is one of the best reasons for trying to make assumptions about performance explicit. In most cases, however, we will remain in a state of frustrating uncertainty. Better this than false assurance. The alternative to overt speculation is not neutrality but rather covert speculation and unconscious assumption, which makes no effort to seek out what evidence might be found and gives free rein to romantic stereotypes. We cannot successfully bracket the questions of how a medieval poem was delivered – if we ignore these questions we end up classifying the poem by default. We must confront these issues directly, recognizing that the way these objects were sung is as important as the way they were designed. Our editions must help us hear what a medieval poem might have sounded like. Phonological commentary must escape from the obscurity of the philological apparatus and join the text, so that there are at least passages where we can hear what the experts are telling us. Discography must join the other forms of commentary. Using the new medium of digital information (which reduces sound, space, and grapheme to a common denominator) we must link the rich visual variety of the medieval text to the various ways it might have been sounded. If we insist on calling medieval poems songs we should be prepared to sing them.

NOTES

1 Adolphe Napoléon Didron, 'Note du directeur,' *Annales archéologiques* 2 (1845): 271. I owe this reference to Michael Camille.

2 M.B. Parkes, *Pause and Effect: An Introduction to the History of Punctuation in the West* (Berkeley: University of California Press, 1993); Paul Saenger, *Space between Words: The Origins of Silent Reading* (Stanford, CA: Stanford University Press, 1997).

3 Bernard Cerquiglini, *Éloge de la variante: Histoire critique de la philologie* (Paris: Editions du Seuil, 1989).

4 Sylvia Huot, *The Romance of the Rose and Its Medieval Readers: Interpretation,*

Reception, Manuscript Transmission (Cambridge: Cambridge University Press, 1993); John Dagenais, *The Ethics of Reading in Manuscript Culture: Glossing the Libro del buen amor* (Princeton, N.J.: Princeton University Press, 1994). For further examples of this emphasis, see *Reading from the Margins: Textual Studies, Chaucer, and Medieval Literature*, ed. Seth Lerer (San Marino, Cal.: Huntington Library, 1996).

5 Michael Camille, 'Philological Iconoclasm: Edition and Image in the *Vie de Saint Alexis*,' in *Medievalism and the Modernist Temper*, ed. R. Howard Bloch and Stephen G. Nichols (Baltimore: Johns Hopkins University Press, 1996); Richard K. Emmerson, 'Reading Gower in Manuscript Culture: Latin and English in Illustrated Manuscripts of the *Confessio Amantis*,' *Studies in the Age of Chaucer* 21 (1999): 143–86; and Siân Echard, 'Typography and the (Mis)Representation of Middle English Texts,' paper delivered at Cultural Studies, Medieval Studies, and Disciplinary Debate, The University of Saskatchewan, March 13–14, 1998.

6 Roger Chartier, 'Texts, Printings, Readings,' in *The New Cultural History*, ed. Lynn Hunt (Berkeley and Los Angeles: University of California Press, 1989), p. 161.

7 See, for example, the following sites:
Hoyt Duggan, *The Piers Plowman Electronic Archive*, http://jefferson.village.virginia.edu/piers/archive.goals.html (this site has now been supplemented by two CDs, edited by Robert Adams, Hoyt N. Duggan, Eric Eliason, Ralph Hanna III, John Price-Wilkin, and Thorlac Turville-Petre, *The 'Piers Plowman' Electronic Archive, Vol. 1: Corpus Christi College, Oxford, MS 201 (F)* and *The 'Piers Plowman' Electronic Archive, Vol. 2: Cambridge, Trinity College, MS B.15.17 (W)* [Ann Arbor: University of Michigan Press, 2000]); Joan Grenier-Winther, *Alain Chartier's 'La Belle dame qui eut merci,'* http://www.innoved.org/BelleDame/; Karl D. Uitti, et al., *The Charette Project* (on Chrétien de Troyes) http://www.princeton.edu/~lancelot/; Kevin Kiernan, *Electronic Beowulf*, http://www.uky.edu/~kiernan/eBeowulf/guide.htm (This site has now been largely supplanted by the CD-ROM of the same title published by the University of Michigan Press in 2000.); The British Library: *Collections, Treasures*, http://www.bl.uk/collections/treasures.html; *Digital Scriptorium*, http://sunsite.berkeley.edu/scriptorium/; *Early Manuscripts at Oxford University*, http://image.ox.ac.uk or the Bodleian's *Image Catalogue*, http://www.bodley.ox.ac.uk/dept/scwmss/wmss/medieval/browse.htm; The Library of Congress *Vatican Library* exhibit, http://metalab.unc.edu/expo/vatican.exhibit/exhibit/Main_Hall.html; Bibliothèque Nationale, *Virtual Exhibitions*, http://expositions.bnf.fr/usindex.htm

8 While there have been numerous records, audiotapes, videotapes, and CDs containing medieval material, I am aware of only three books that also come with a tape. They are Betsy Bowden, *Chaucer Aloud: The Varieties of Textual Interpretation* (Philadelphia: University of Pennsylvania Press, 1987); Rebecca A. Baltzer, Thomas Cable, and James I. Wimsatt, eds, *The Union of Words and Music in Medieval Poetry,* with music by Sequentia (Austin: University of Texas Press, 1991); and Howell Chickering and Margaret Switten, *The Medieval Lyric* (privately published; copies may be ordered from Margaret Switten, Mount Holyoke College). William D. Paden's *An Introduction to Old Occitan* (New York: Modern Language Association of America, 1998) is one of the first books in the field of medieval studies to come with a CD. Ward Parks makes a plea for such editions in 'Song, Text, and Cassette: Why We Need Authoritative Audio Editions of Medieval Literary Works,' *Oral Tradition* 7 (1992): 102–15. It is worth considering why so little has changed despite technological improvements.

9 David Small, MIT Media Lab, 'Navigating Large Bodies of Text,' *IBM Systems Journal,* 35.3 and 4 (1996): 14–25, my italics, available at http://www.research.ibm.com/journal/sj/mit/sectiond/small.html

10 Edward R. Tufte, *Envisioning Information* (Cheshire, Connecticut: Graphics Press, 1990). See also his *Visual Explanations: Images and Quantities, Evidence and Narrative* (Cheshire, Conn.: Graphics Press, 1997) and *The Visual Display of Qualitative Information* (Cheshire, Conn.: Graphics Press, 1983).

11 See, for example, Roger Norrington's remark that there is no such thing as 'authentic' early music, in Bernard D. Sherman's collection *Inside Early Music: Conversations with Performers* (Oxford: Oxford University Press, 1997), p. 357.

12 Gervais de la Rue, *Essais historiques sur les bardes, les jongleurs et les trouvères normands et anglo-normands,* 3 vols (Caen, 1834); Edmond Faral, *Les jongleurs en france au moyen âge* (Paris: Champion, 1910); Christopher Page, *The Owl and the Nightingale: Musical Life and Ideas in France, 1100–1300* (London: Dent, 1989); John W. Baldwin, 'The Image of the Jongleur in Northern France around 1200,' *Speculum* 72 (1997): 635–63.

13 See, for example, the two-volume recording 'Andalusische Musik aus Marokko,' of the Moroccan Ensemble of Fez under the direction of Hāǧǧ Abdelkarim Rais (Harmonia Mundi, 1984), for which Binkley wrote the liner notes. This performance might be compared to the long introduction to 'Kalenda maya' in Binkley's 'Troubadours, Trouvères, Minstrels,' a reissuing on CD (Teldec Classics, 1995) of recordings from 1970 and 1974. A large collection of recordings is kept at the Thomas Binkley Archive of Early Music Recordings, Indiana University (http://www.music.indiana.edu/

som/emi/tba.html). The University is also compiling a digital library of its musical holdings, *Variations*; it is currently only available for use on campus but there are plans to make it available on the Web.

14 See, for example, Paul Zumthor, 'Jongleurs et diseurs: interprétation et création poétique au moyen âge,' *Medioevo Romanzo* 11 (1986): 3–26. Baldwin provides a balanced defense of the method at the end of 'Image of the Jongleur.'

15 *Le roman de Rou de Wace*, ed. A. J. Holden, Société des anciens textes français, 3 vols (Paris, 1971), 2:183, lines 8013–18.

16 See, for example, Andrew Taylor, 'Fragmentation, Corruption, and Minstrel Narration: The Question of the Middle English Romances,' *Yearbook of English Studies* 22 (1992): 38–62; and John Southworth, *The English Medieval Minstrel* (Woodbridge, Suffolk and Wolfeboro, New Hampshire: Boydell, 1989), pp. 31–5.

17 Paul Zumthor, *Essai de poétique médiévale* (Paris: Editions du Seuil, 1972), p. 192.

18 Ibid., p. 69.

19 The poem, in an ever-shifting form, survives in eight other manuscripts, some of them mere fragments. The Oxford version, however, has for all practical purposes become the *Roland*. While the Oxford *Roland* has been edited and translated again and again, the other later versions, many of them significantly expanded, are mostly available only in a single scholarly edition, Raoul Mortier, ed. *Les textes de la Chanson de Roland*, 9 vols (Paris: Éditions de la Geste Francor, 1940–3).

20 Francisque Michel, *La Chanson de Roland ou de Roncevaux du XIIe siècle publiée pour la première fois d'après le manuscrit de la bibliothèque bodléienne à Oxford* (Paris: Silvestre, 1837; reprint, Geneva: Slatkine Reprints, 1974), pp. xi–xiii.

21 Paul Zumthor, 'The Text and the Voice,' *New Literary History* 16 (1984): 67–92 (at 71).

22 Paul Saenger, 'Silent Reading: Its Impact on Late Medieval Script and Society,' *Viator* 13 (1982): 366–414; and *Space between Words*.

23 Bernadette A. Masters, 'Computer Editing of Medieval Texts: A Caveat,' *Literary and Linguistic Computing* 8 (1993): 131–42 (at 137). She clarifies that the manuscript should really be considered 'a counterfeit, on vellum, of the circumstances of a *viva voce* performance, not a prescriptive "score."'

24 In the case of Harley 978, a major difficulty for Masters's thesis is that the lyrics for the musical works in the opening leaves (which include the well-known lyric 'Sumer is icumin in') make no effort to follow the rhythms indicated by the musical notation. Admittedly, the hand that copies this

section is not the hand responsible for the *lais* and fables of Marie, but it is roughly contemporary. I discuss this manuscript further in *Textual Situations: Three Medieval Manuscripts and Their Readers* (Philadelphia: University of Pensylvania Press, 2001).

25 Zumthor, 'Text and Voice,' p. 69.

26 Andrew Taylor, 'The Myth of the Minstrel Manuscript,' *Speculum* 66 (1991): 43–73.

27 Charles Samaran, 'Étude historique et paléographique,' in *La Chanson de Roland: Reproduction du manuscrit Digby 23 de la Bodleian Library d'Oxford*, ed. Comte de Laborde (Paris: Société des anciens textes français, 1933).

28 Ibid., pp. 28–33. For a contrasting position, see Ian Short, 'L'avènement du texte vernaculaire: la mise en recueil,' in *Théories et pratiques de l'écriture au moyen âge*, Actes du colloque, Palais du Luxembourg-Sénat, 5–6 mars 1987, ed. Emmanuèle Baumgartner and Christiane Marchello-Nizia (Nanterre: Centre de recherches du département de français de Paris X-Nanterre, 1988), pp. 11–24.

29 Zumthor's attitude to medieval performance is perplexing. His powerful evocations of oral poetics, such as *L'Essai de poétique médiévale* and *La Poésie orale*, never allude to his own considerable dramatic experience as one of the Théophiliens, the troupe who performed the *Jeu de Robin et Marion* under the direction of Gustave Cohen in 1935, attempting to relive the medieval experience by imitating the gestures seen in medieval manuscripts. See Helen Solterer, 'Revivals: Paris 1935,' *Alphabet City*, 'Fascism and Its Ghosts,' issues 4 and 5 (1995): 76–83, for a critical assessment of this 'incarnational' approach and its drive for direct contact with the Middle Ages.

30 http://image.ox.ac.uk. One of the few to consider the two sections of the manuscript together (although concluding they have little significant connection) is Ian Short, 'L'avènement du texte vernaculaire.'

31 Fernand Flutre, ed., *La Chanson de Roland: Extraits, traduits d'après le manuscrit d'Oxford* (Paris: Hachette, 1935), p. 5.

32 I discuss this editorial construction further in 'Was There a Song of Roland?' *Speculum* 76 (2001): 28–65.

33 F[rancois] Génin, *La Chanson de Roland: Poëme de Theroulde* (Paris: Imprimerie Nationale, 1850), p. vi.

34 Eugene Vance, 'Roland and the Poetics of Memory,' in *Textual Strategies: Perspectives in Post-Structuralist Criticism*, ed. Josué V. Harari (Ithaca, N.Y.: Cornell University Press, 1979), pp. 374–403; Peter Haidu, *The Subject of Violence: The Song of Roland and the Birth of the State* (Bloomington: Indiana University Press, 1993).

35 Dominica M. Legge, 'Archaism and Conquest,' *Modern Language Review* 51 (1956): 227–9 at 229.

36 Jean Rychner, *La Chanson de geste: Essai sur l'art épique des jongleurs* (Geneva: Droz, 1955), pp. 48–9, 54.

37 Ian Short, ed. and trans., *La Chanson de Roland* (Paris: Livre de Poche, 1990), p. 12.

38 Léon Gautier, *La Chevalerie*, 3rd ed. (Paris, 1895), pp. 668–9.

39 Ibid, p. 658. André Chénier, *Oeuvres complètes*, ed. Gérard Walter (Paris: Gallimard, 1950), p. 46. On this tradition, see Brian Juden, *Traditions orphiques et tendances mystiques dans le romantisme français (1800–1855)* (Paris: Klincksieck, 1974; reprint 1984).

40 This is the argument I advance in 'Fragmentation and Corruption,' drawing in part on the evidence in Page's *The Owl and the Nightingale*.

41 The editions cited here are those of Michel (see n. 20); Léon Gautier, *La Chanson de Roland: texte critique accompagné d'une traduction nouvelle et précedé d'une introduction historique* (Tours, 1872); Joseph Bédier, *La Chanson de Roland* (Paris: Piazza, 1922); Cesare Segre, *La Chanson de Roland* (Milan: Ricciardi, 1971); Short (see n. 37); and Jean Dufournet, *La Chanson de Roland* (Paris: Flammarion, 1993).

42 Bédier, *Chanson de Roland*, p. ii.

43 Betsy Bowden, *Listeners' Guide to Medieval English: A Discography* (New York: Garland, 1988). See also Alan T. Gaylord, 'Imagining Voices: Chaucer on Cassette,' *Studies in the Age of Chaucer* 12 (1990): 215–38.

44 Larry Benson, ed. *The Riverside Chaucer* (Boston: Houghton Mifflin, 1987), p. xxx. http://www.courses.fas.harvard.edu/~chaucer/

45 Geoffrey Chaucer, *The Canterbury Tales: Nine Tales and the General Prologue*, ed. V.A. Kolve and Glending Olson (New York: Norton, 1989), p. xiii.

46 Walter Scott, *Ivanhoe, A Romance*, 3 vols (Edinburgh, 1820), 1:5.

47 Seamus Heaney, trans. *Beowulf, A New Verse Translation* (New York: Norton, 2000), p. xxii.

48 Ibid., p. xxvii. Some notion of the sounds Heaney wishes to invoke can be gained from his BBC recordings of his translation, passages of which are available on the CD attached to M.H. Abrams and Stephen Greenblatt, eds., *The Norton Anthology of English Literature*, 7th ed. (New York: Norton, 2000).

49 One encouraging exception is the workshop organized by Daniel E. O'Sullivan and Samuel Rosenberg on 'Reading Old French Aloud' at the 37th International Congress on Medieval Studies, 3 May 2002 at Kalamazoo, Michigan.

50 Bowden, *Listener's Guide*, pp. xiv–xv. Bowden explores these issues further in

Chaucer Aloud: The Varieties of Textual Interpretation (Philadelphia: University of Pennsylvania Press, 1987).

51 Helen Small, 'Dickens and a Pathology of the Mid-Victorian Reading Public,' esp. pp. 285–90, in *The Practice and Representation of Reading in England*, ed. James Raven, Helen Small, and Naomi Tadmor (Cambridge: Cambridge University Press, 1996).

52 Gerard J. Brault, *The Song of Roland: An Analytical Edition*, 2 vols (University Park, Pa.: Pennsylvania State University Press, 1978), 1:112–13, drawing on the work of Jeanne Wathelet-Willelm.

53 *La Chanson de Roland*, disque 270E047, in the series L'Encyclopedie Sonore (Paris: Hachette, nd).

54 Ibid., liner notes, pp. 2–3.

55 *La Chanson de Roland* (Folkways: FL 9587, 1961), released as 2 CDs by Smithsonian Folkways Recordings. All quotations are from page two of the liner notes.

56 David Lass has kindly brought to my attention a third recording of passages from the *Roland*, which I have not yet been able to hear, 'Roncevaux: Echos d'une bataille' (Mandres les Roses, France: Mandala, MAN 4953, 1999, distributed by Harmonia Mundi, France, HMCD 78).

57 *The Song of Roland* (New York: Caedmon, nd), two LPs, released as two cassettes.

58 *Adam de la Halle, Le Jeu de Robin et Marion.* Ensemble Perceval, directed by Guy Robert, record (Paris: Arion, 1980).

59 The influential early studies by Jacques Chailley, 'Études musicales sur la chanson de geste et ses origines,' *Revue de Musicologie* 27 (1948):1–27; and J. Van der Veen, 'Les aspects musicaux des chansons de geste,' *Neophilologus* 41 (1957): 82–100 have now been expanded by John Stevens, *Words and Music in the Middle Ages: Song, Narrative, Dance and Drama, 1050–1350* (Cambridge: Cambridge University Press, 1986), pp. 222–7, 239–49.

60 Ibid., p. 247.

6

The Boy and the Blind Man: A Medieval Play Script and Its Editors

CAROL SYMES

Le garçon et l'aveugle, a dialogue for 'The Boy and the Blind Man,' is one of the oldest surviving plays in any European vernacular.[1] It may, in fact, be the oldest medieval play not directly associated with the institutional Church – that is, with a religious community, with the liturgy, or even with the dramatization of an episode drawn from the Bible or the lives of the saints. Datable on internal evidence to some time after 1266,[2] it is preserved in a single manuscript codex (Paris, Bibliothèque nationale de France, fonds français 24366) and occupies portions of three leaves left over at the end of a copy of the *Roman d'Alexandre* completed, according to its colophon, in May 1228.[3] The play was brought to the attention of modern readers by Paul Meyer, who printed a transcription in 1865. A critical edition, published by Mario Roques in 1911 and reliant in part on Meyer's work, has since provided the basis for Jean Dufournet's edition and translation of 1989.[4] But as my analysis will demonstrate, any attempt to present a definitive version of this script is bound to mask some of its most intriguing characteristics, since the distribution of lines and other important features were altered by a number of different hands working over a period of at least two hundred years. These alterations suggest that ways of reading, interpreting, and performing the play also changed drastically over the same period of time. Moreover, as I shall argue here, the successive metamorphoses of *The Boy and the Blind Man* have been obscured in modern versions of this text, as have the implications of these changes. As a result, some widely held assumptions about the nature of medieval play scripts, and even about the nature of medieval drama, have long gone unchallenged.

Described in a series of explicits as *du garcon et la veule*,[5] the dialogue between a self-professed blind beggar and a roguish boy showcases the quintessentially urban practices of deception and the making of a fast buck, as the pair team up in order to play – and fleece – the crowd. Like the tavern-folk of related plays from thirteenth-century Arras, the *Jeu de saint Nicolas* of Jehan Bodel, the *Courtois d'Arras*, and the *Jeu de la feuillée* of Adam de la Halle, these characters live a hand-to-mouth existence, preying on passers-by and appealing to their baser instincts, funny-bones, and sympathies.[6] Hence, *The Boy and the Blind Man* is made up of a series of verbal and physical gags whose arrangement and execution would have depended on the professional performers' intimate knowledge of the material and more intimate knowledge of each other's skills and their audiences' expectations.

The very appearance of the manuscript reinforces this impression: the piece is only a step or two removed from improvisational comedy, a rough-and-ready pretext that was adapted to suit changing tastes, circumstances, and the needs (financial or dramaturgical) of the entertainers. It may be little more than the outline for a more extended series of comic riffs, or possibly a tour-de-force for a single jongleur and his bauble, the fool's scepter.[7] It is also an important indication that entertainers were not without the resources for translating their work from stage to page, and it complicates the received notion of the relationship between performers and texts. While most jongleurs would have learned routines like this one through contact with other performers, there clearly came a time when theirs ceased to be 'a craft which was not learned in books.'[8] The rich theatrical legacy of this particular sketch, or of the oral traditions on which it draws, is discernible in a variety of later French farces and even in English plays of the medieval and early modern periods, from the codependency of Cain and Garcio in the Towneley *Mactatio Abel* to the bittersweet relationship of Lancelot Gobbo and his blind father in Shakespeare's *The Merchant of Venice* or the harrowing alliance of Edgar (disguised as Poor Tom) and his blinded father, Gloucester, in *King Lear*.[9]

The Boy and the Blind Man thus provides a highly instructive example of the way a stock medieval routine might have been recorded, handed down, and re-used over an extended period. It is a work 'in process.' Yet editors have tended to ignore the telling ambiguities of its manuscript, preferring to regard the play as a theatrical monument providing a fixed point in the development of a new, worldly æsthetic. It has been hailed by French scholars as a farce *avant la lettre* and the precursor of modern comedy,[10] and by their English-speaking counterparts as evidence for the survival of mimic entertainment in the antique tradition.[11] Michel Rousse has pronounced it the herald of 'a theatre secular, popular, without ambitions either literary or didactic.'[12] Dufournet calls it a 'true stage play,' although his judgment is more acute and less anachronistic when he imagines that it began with the kind of impromptu foolery appropriate to the marketplace of a busy town or fairground.[13]

None of the studies devoted to the play has remarked on the fact that, when it was committed to writing in the last third of the thirteenth century, only minimal stage directions were provided by the original scribe; nor have they noted that most of the character designations added to the right and left of the text on each of the four two-column pages were changed long after the lines were first copied (see Figures 6.1–6.4). The significance of these accretions is briefly stated: this early specimen of vernacular drama is not only untrammeled by notions of a fixed text, authorial intention, or definitive production, it also hovers on the verge of obscurity. For without these marginalia, it would look a great deal like any fabliau or verse story, and would not necessarily be readily identifiable as a play.

Le garçon et l'aveugle is therefore a veritable advertisement for the benefits conferred by a coherent script, benefits that were evident to those already familiar with the finished product, the performers themselves. Yet it appears that the dialogue's original scribe thought that he could dispense with rubrics altogether, at least until he was a quarter of the way down on the second page of his text; only at this late stage did he realize that a few markings might be helpful to himself, to his reader, or to posterity.[14] This absence, or tardy appearance, of character designations has hitherto been a matter of little consequence to the modern editors of *The Boy and the Blind Man.* Alluding briefly to the manuscript, Richard Axton and John Stevens noted that 'only half the speeches are headed by an indication of the speaker's identity, and most of these headings were added by a scribe in the fifteenth century.' Dufournet, too, identified only two hands at work: the thirteenth-century scribe who provided the character designations 'placed sometimes following the first verse of a piece of dialogue, and sometimes after the last verse of the preceding speech,' and a fifteenth-century annotator, who, Dufournet assumed, was correcting the latter character designations by placing them after the first verse of each speech. In other words, Dufournet posits a whimsical, careless, or illogical approach to the initial transcription, and a unified program of 'necessary' emendations made by a more systematic reader at a later date.[15]

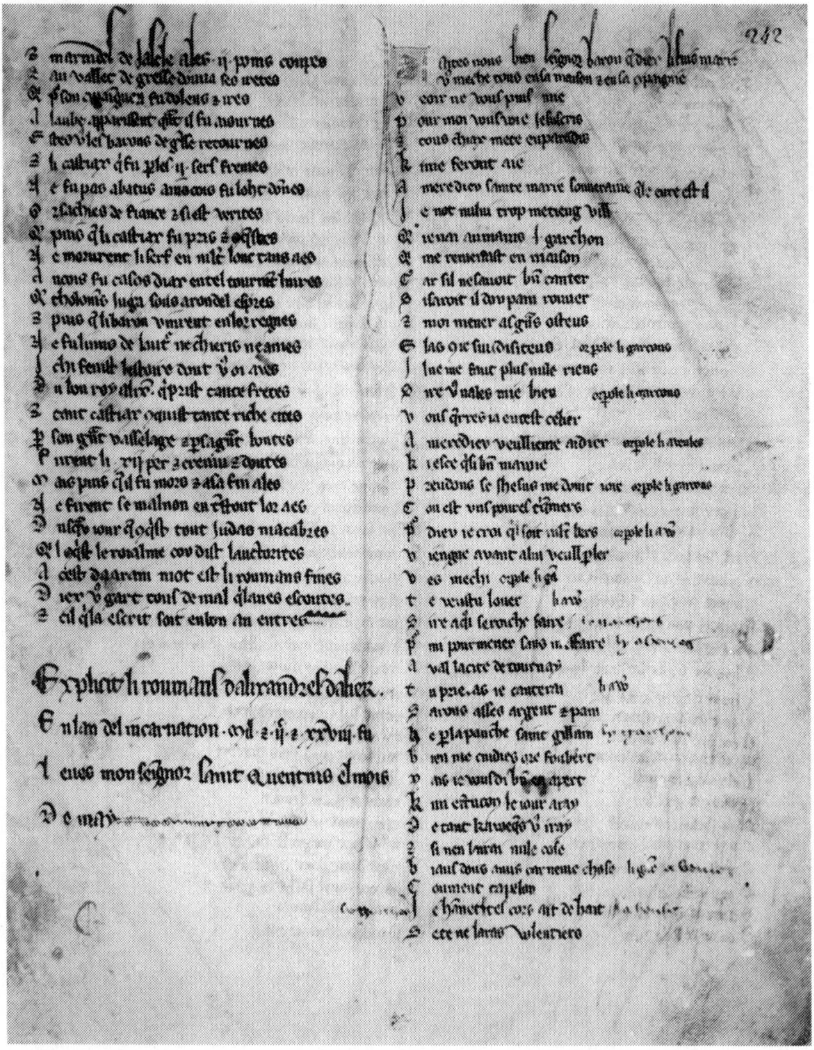

Figure 6.1 Paris, Bibliothèque nationale de France, fonds français 24366, page 242.

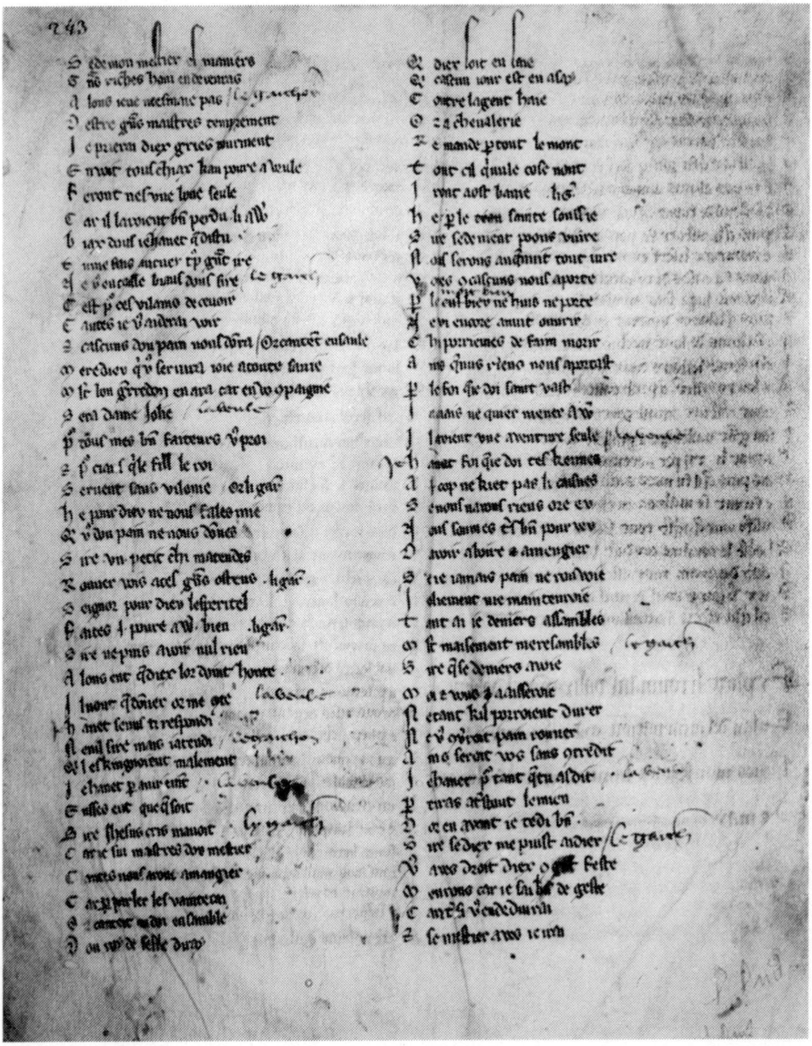

Figure 6.2 Paris, Bibliothèque nationale de France, fonds français 24366, page 243.

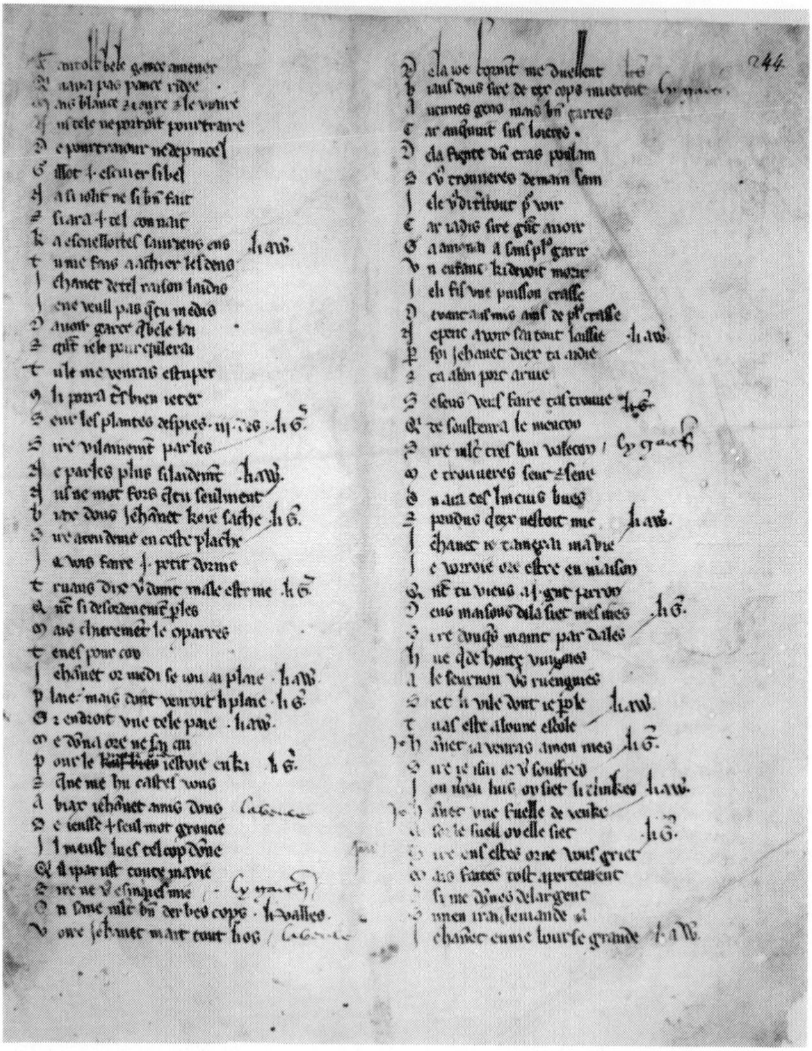

Figure 6.3 Paris, Bibliothèque nationale de France, fonds français 24366, page 244.

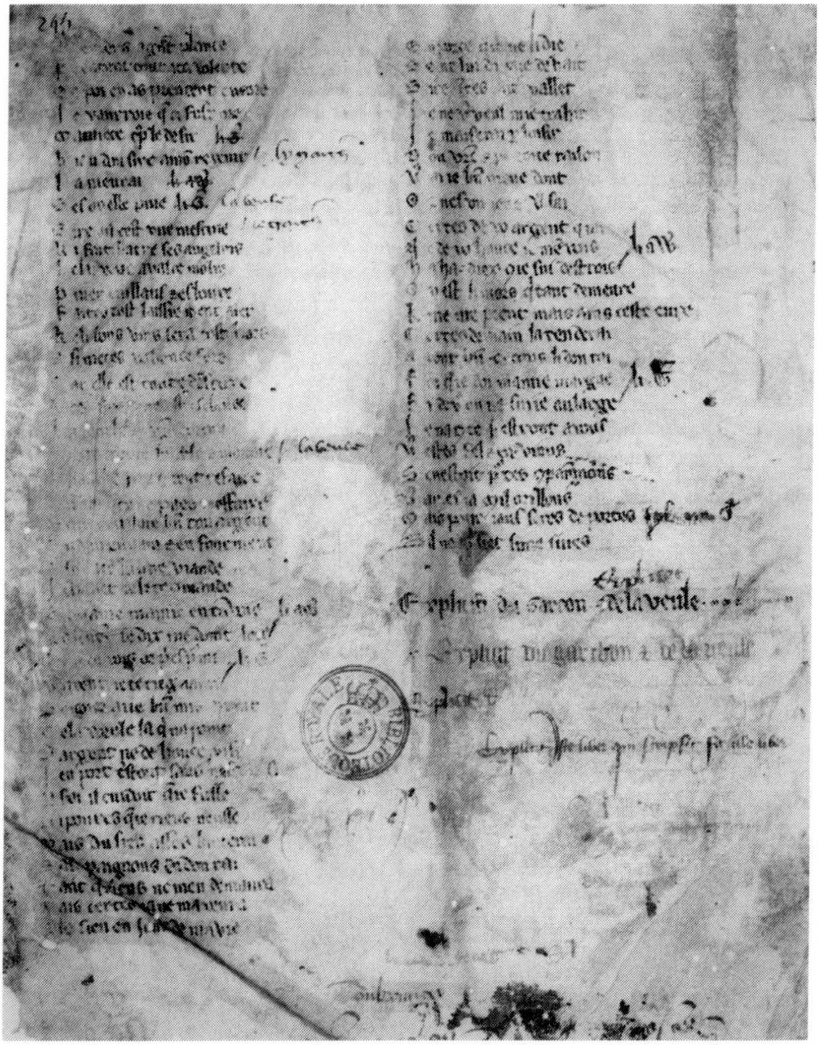

Figure 6.4 Paris, Bibliothèque nationale de France, fonds français 24366, page 245.

In fact, all but four of the stage directions included in the script of *Le garçon et l'aveugle* represent additions made according to two or more incompatible systems, provided on at least four separate occasions. Furthermore, it is clear that later performers of the dialogue either did not understand the methods of character designation used by their forebears in the thirteenth century, or that they chose to re-assign parts by using arrows, slashes, or (less frequently) erasures to alter prior annotations. These changes (or, as Dufournet would have it, 'corrections') have largely been adopted by modern editors, although with a new degree of inconsistency. Going a step further, Dufournet has even supplied some of his own stage directions, cast in Old French on the right-hand side of the page and 'translated' into modern French on the left, giving the misleading impression that they are authentic. However, he scruples to translate some of the actual words, as when the Old French phrase 'je le pourquenlerai' is demurely rendered 'je l'enc ...' on the facing page.[16] A viable edition of *The Boy and the Blind Man* is certainly necessary; but which one? And is it necessary to do violence to the medieval record in order to achieve that desirable goal?

Although it is impossible to distinguish and date all of the successive changes made to the play's manuscript text, five main phases in transmission can be identified: the original transcription campaign, carried out sometime around 1270 (Scribe);[17] an initial attempt at clarification, either by the same scribe working at a later time (with a better pen) or by a close contemporary (Hand A);[18] a further attempt at clarification, effected sometime between the end of the thirteenth and middle of the fourteenth centuries (Hand B);[19] and two periods of radical revision and censorship in the mid to late fifteenth century, the heyday of the farce (Hands X and Y).[20] Indeed, the later hands are not dissimilar to that of the copyist responsible for the oldest manuscript of *Maistre Pierre Pathelin*, dated 1484–5.[21] In addition, the five separate explicits that grace the ending of the play suggest that other reader-performers sought to leave their marks, but given the abbreviated nature of the changes made to the body of the text, it is hard to match these hands with those of the annotators. One explicit may have been supplied by Hand B, one is from the mid-fourteenth-century,[22] two are roughly contemporary with Hands X and Y,[23] and the last may also date from the fifteenth century.[24]

Based on these assessments, I maintain that the only instructions for performance supplied by the scribe at the time of transcription are the three narrative stage directions and one of the abbreviated character designations, all appearing on page 243 of the manuscript (Figure 6.2).

They are: / 'Or cantent ensanle' (Now they sing together) before the first song on line 14 of column A; / 'Or li gar' (Now the Boy) at the end of that song, line 20; 'Or cantent en doi ensamble' (Now they both sing together), which occupies line 39 of column A, before the second song; and' / 'li G.' after the second song, line 7 of column B. In other words, the scribe was concerned only with the indication of changes in the register of performance (speaking versus singing) and with clarifying who was to speak first after the songs had been sung (the Boy). The belated insertion of the first 'Or cantent,' for which he did not leave adequate space, further attests that he had not planned even that much editorial intervention when he began to copy out the play; the two indications for the Boy's speeches are also the result of afterthought. All of this strongly suggests that the scribe regarded most of the requirements for performance as self-evident, either because he himself had authored or performed the piece, or because it was acceptable or usual to leave performance choices – even at the level of line distribution – open to the individual performer.

Indeed, most of the (very few) contemporary plays available for comparison with *Le garçon et l'aveugle* were not subjected to the later rubrication and re-editing to which that script bears witness. For instance, both *Courtois d'Arras* and Rutebeuf's *Miracle de Théophile* have come down to us in forms so vague that they have perpetuated a division of opinion as to their genres (secular play? monologue? fabliau? liturgical drama? 'semi-liturgical' drama?). But similar indications of performance practice are a distinguishing feature of the contemporary *Aucassin et Nicholette*, whose *genus* 'chantefable' is derived from the rubrics in the sole manuscript, which call for three different modes of performance: 'Or cantent' (now they sing), 'Or fablent' (now they recount the story), and 'Or dient' (now they speak).[25] The combined testimony of such indeterminate texts is that medieval scribes usually took it for granted that performers would extract most of the information they needed from the content of the piece, and required only minimal direction at certain key points, in the form of half-lines (broken to show the exchange of rapid-fire dialogue) or other aids.

However, judging from the manuscript appearance of two other texts widely regarded as *bona fide* plays, there were more elaborate methods of layout and glossing available to scribes working in the vernacular: one derived from the liturgy, and one adapted from the apparatus used in scholarly circles. The scribe of the Anglo-Norman *Ordo representacionis Ade* (or *The Play of Adam*), copied at the end of the twelfth or beginning of the thirteenth century,[26] developed a technique adapted from the standard treatment of the dialogic elements in liturgical prosæ, combined with that employed in manuscripts of vernacular romance: he placed initials in the right-hand margin of the page, just above the first line to be spoken by the character so designated.[27] An entirely different system, and one that depends on superior copying skills, is employed in the contemporary manuscript of another Anglo-Norman verse play, the *Seinte Resureccion* ('The Holy Resurrection').[28] In this case, characters' names appear directly opposite the speeches to which they refer, in the left- or right-hand margin of the two-column page, with a rubricated *paragraphus* marking the beginning of a speech and corresponding to another rubricated *paragraphus* placed to the left of the speaker's name.[29] But the dangers inherent in relying on such a sophisticated layout are advertised in the second surviving manuscript of the same Resurrection play, which has lost all of the rubrics that help to identify it as a dramatic text.[30]

Could some plays, then, be disguised in manuscript form as unrubricated texts? And conversely, could a likely text be turned into a play by an enterprising scribe or editor? Over a decade ago, Paul Zumthor remarked on the adaptation, in vernacular contexts, of the glossing techniques of the schools, and on the performance tradition of *ars legendi*, exemplified by the close kinship of sermons, plays, letters, dialogues, and treatises. He also paid attention to the importance of layout in the manuscripts of many medieval texts intended for public reading or recitation, pointing to the systems of notation in copies of Wolfram von Eschenbach's *Parzival* and the *Iwein* of Hartmann von Aue.[31] Often, such indications of performance practice are subtle: in manuscripts of liturgical chant, romance literature, and sermons alike, alternating red and blue initials can stand for changes of voice or emphasis.

Yet evidence that reliance on these conventions, which were prevalent in the eleventh through fourteenth centuries, was not sufficient for readers or performers of a later era is provided by *The Boy and the Blind Man*, as well as by the testimony of what would seem to be a very different kind of witness: the rubrics added to an early fourteenth-century codex made for Dominican preachers.[32] Here, narrative tales are paired with dialogues that reinforce the spiritual messages of the exempla by reenacting them, much as liturgical drama expanded or commented on the liturgy per se. For example, a story concerning 'Du frere quie dit que Nostre Dame estoit une sote, pource quele est trop debonnair' (The brother who said that Our Lady was an idiot, because she was too good-natured) is followed by 'Item un dyalogue du sage et do fol' (A dialogue of a wise man and a fool, fols $119v^{a}$–$121r^{b}$) which hearkens back to *Le garçon et l'aveugle* and *Aucassin* while anticipating later moralities such as *Mankind.* But the original scribe did not identify the speeches of Wise Man and Fool; instead, he provided red and blue initials to distinguish their lines. It is a fifteenth-century hand that has added the names of the characters in the right-hand margin, opposite the first line of the speech, according to the practice used in the Paris copy of the *Seinte Resureccion* (not on the line before, as in the *Ordo representacionis Ade*).

> **S**eignors ie di pour voir. .Li sages.
> Oians tous en apert
> Que cil est fol prouvez
> Que sa ioenesse pert
> Et qui de paradis
> La ioie ne dessert
> La ou toutes bontez
> Et toutes clartes pert
> **D**aler en paradis .Li foulz.
> Ne men parole mis
> Il mua forz que vieles
> Et que vilains bossus
> Et mesiaus. et contrais
> Et gent de tel refus
> Iames un bon conpains
> Ni seroit receus.

(*The Wise Man:* Seigneurs, I speak to show: / Listen to what you hear, /To what this Fool should know, / Whose youth has cost him dear, / Who's barred from Heaven's bliss. / Those joys will not appear / To him, no blessings flow: / All good will disappear. *The Fool:* To go to Heaven's bliss / Is no part of my wish! /You'd best stay out, my friend, /With crooked low-lived scum /And bad-lots and yes-men, /Folks shunned by everyone. / The fun forever ends /If you get into that slum.)

The later marginal annotations could be taken to mean that this piece was only adapted as a play during the fifteenth century.

But it is also likely, given the evident function of this dialogue as a dramatization of familiar themes, that the fifteenth-century editor was following a practice similar to that observed in the manuscript of *Le garçon et l'aveugle*, thereby making the performative possibilities of the extant script more clear. This hypothesis is reinforced by another text in the same fourteenth-century manuscript, 'Item un dyalogue en la passion du viel homme. et de la ioene fame' (A dialogue on the Passion, by an old man and a young woman, fols. 203r[a]–203v[a]) which elaborates on its companion story, 'De la pierre sus la quele Nostre Dame ploura en la passion de son fil' (Concerning the stone upon which Our Lady wept during the Passion of her Son). It could have reminded a right-thinking audience of Jesus' conversations with Mary Magdalene, or suggested a loose adaptation of the story of his encounter with the Samaritan woman by the well at Sychar (John 4). In this case, there is enough narrative material to guide the reader, so no later annotations supplement the initials indicating different registers of discourse and changes of voice or character (the prologue and the Old Man's first speech are directed to the audience, his second speech to the Young Woman). A further example is provided by a dialogue that boasts fifteenth-century narrative directions, this time added in Latin ('vir loquitur / mulier respondet'). It extends the moral offered by a miracle story 'Du dyable qui enforme domme temp[te] une fame. qui senfui a linvocation N[ostre] Dame' (Concerning a devil who, in the form of a man, tempted a woman, and who ran away at the invocation to Our Lady). Once again, the dialogue translates a universal, divine message into specific, human terms by showing how the teaching of the Church should be applied to real-life situations. In a fourth example, 'Item un dyalogue comment un hons prioit une fame. Et comment e[le] li respondit' (A dialogue showing how a man wooed a woman, and how she answered him, fols. 229v[a]–230v[a]), the techniques of seduction popularized by courtly literature and fabliaux (as well as by encounters such as that between Satan and Eve in *The Play of Adam*) are brought to their logical conclusion – with the young woman looking ahead to an unwelcome pregnancy and a life of shame.

This brief overview of contemporary scribal methods used either to clarify or create dramatic texts delineates a set of adaptive techniques that must have been very common in the Middle Ages. But certain modern editorial practices, many of which have already been abandoned by scholars working with non-dramatic texts, still pose a fundamental threat to our understanding of how plays were variously transmitted and reconceived during this period. Indeed, the study of medieval theatre has been particularly, perhaps uniquely, affected by the way editorial criteria have been applied not only to the texts of plays but also to the very identification of certain texts *as* plays. As I have argued elsewhere, there seems to have been little contemporary interest in promoting a generic definition of a 'play' as an entity distinct from other performance pieces. A bold assertion that '[t]he uniqueness of medieval drama' as a literary phenomenon 'is even reflected in the manuscripts' is based on the more self-conscious play scripts of the late fourteenth and fifteenth centuries,[33] while an observation that 'the speaker's name was carefully indicated from the very beginning' of the transmission of plays in writing is certainly not borne out by the evidence presented here.[34] On the contrary, the manuscript of *The Boy and the Blind Man* teaches us to place renewed emphasis on the concepts of *mouvance* and *variance*, now increasingly influential among scholars interested in orality, textuality, and performance.[35]

At the very least, the infinite internal variety of *The Boy and the Blind Man* challenges forced distinctions such as those articulated by Edmond Faral, whereby the essential boundaries between 'plays' (for two or more actors), 'dialogues' (for a single reader), and 'mimes' (dialogues for a single performer playing all roles) are scrupulously maintained.[36] It even challenges more pervasive attempts to subdivide surviving vernacular plays into categories labeled 'religious' and 'secular,' a practice dating back to the nineteenth century and taking no account of manuscript provenance, chronology, audience, or occasion.[37] Even within the last scholarly generation, when the journal *Research Opportunities in Renaissance Drama* asked two leading experts to write review articles on the study of medieval French theatre, dividing the field into 'Religious Drama' and 'Comic Drama,' neither reviewer questioned the validity of those classifications.[38] While at first glance it seems hard to believe that *The Boy and the Blind Man* may have been composed for a didactic purpose, Lester K. Little has argued that urban audiences were demanding of 'a spirituality that would express itself in speech,'[39] and the play could easily have been pressed into service by friars as well as jongleurs in order to illustrate any number of doctrinal messages. Take, for example, the favourite Biblical text of the well-known preacher Michel Menot, Matthew 15:14: 'Leave them: for they are blind and leaders of the blind; for if a blind man offers to lead a blind man, they will fall into the pit together.'[40] It is instructive that the play opens with the Boy saving the Blind Man from just such a tumble and, if framed appropriately, this incident would amuse an audience even as it showed whither such misdirection led. (Who knows? Some performances of *Le garçon et l'aveugle* could have ended with a fall into the pit, or a journey to Hell Mouth.) The Dominican dialogues surveyed above employ a similar kind of reverse psychology, teaching good behavior by staging the inevitable outcome of bad, through a suggestive juxtaposition of pious exempla with bawdy situation-comedies.

Plays have been neglected in the many re-evaluations of editorial praxis published in recent years, perhaps because the collation of variants, coupled with questions of authorial intention, are the issues around which current theory tends to revolve – issues that have little bearing upon most medieval scripts.[41] But here we have ample evidence that variant readings were performed over a two-hundred-year period in the history of a single play's reception, and at this stage it may be useful to ask how medieval and modern readings of *The Boy and the Blind Man* might differ. To take one fairly straightforward example, we see that on the first page of the manuscript text (242^{b}, Figure 6.1), all parties involved in its transmission appear to have agreed that the first fourteen lines are spoken by the begging Blind Man. No character designations have been added, and there is not even an incipit to mark the beginning of the text.[42] Starting at line 14, however, Hand A has added a number of narrative directions. Bearing in mind the available models discussed above, we must ask whether we should read the script as though, like *The Play of Adam,* the character designations in the right-hand margin carry over to the line below; or whether, according to the conventions of the *Seinte Resureccion,* they refer to the line directly opposite.

Modern editions chart a course similar to the latter, giving the line to the left of the first stage direction to the Boy, rather than connecting that line to the preceding speech of the Blind Man and taking the following line as the beginning of the Boy's speech. Here is a translation of a sample passage as it was left by the original scribe:

Elas con ie sui disiteus	Alas for want of drink I'm dry
Il ne me faut nule riens	Just now there's nothing more to say
Sire vous nales mie bien	Mister you've really lost your way
Vous querres ia en cest celier	Look out you'll fall into that hole
A meredieu veullie me aidier	O Mary help me some good soul
Ki esce qui isi bien mavoie	Who's that who helps me now to see
Preudons se Jhesus me doint ioie	Fellow Christ grant you joy for me
Cou est uns poures triquemers	Well here's a pathetic trickster
Pour dieu ie croi quil soit mult bers	By God I bet he's a master

A contemporary reader, following the indications of Hand A, might apportion the lines in the following way.

[blind man>>] Alas, for want of drink I'm dry! **now the boy speaks [aside >>]**
[>>] Just now there's nothing more to say –
Mister, you've really lost your way. **now the boy speaks [to him >>]**
[>>] Look out! you'll fall into that hole!
O Mary! Help me, some good soul! **now the blind man speaks [>>]**
[>>] Who's that? Who helps me now to see?
Fellow, Christ grant you joy for me! **now the boy speaks [>>]**
[>>] Well, here's a pathetic trickster –
By God, I bet he's a master! **now the blind man speaks [>>]**

Dufournet construes the passage this way, as perhaps a later reader might have done.[43]

now the boy speaks [aside>][44]	Alas, for want of drink I'm dry!
[seeing the blind man>][45]	Just now there's nothing more to say:
now the boy speaks [to him>][46]	Mister, you've really lost your way.
	Look out! you'll fall into that hole.
now the blind man speaks[>	O Mary! Help me, some good soul!
	Who's that? Who helps me now to see?
now the boy speaks[>]	Fellow, Christ grant you joy for me!
	Well, here's a pathetic trickster.
now the blind man speaks[>]	By God, I bet he's a master!

Either scenario makes sense, and either could be made to work in performance. Perhaps both were used at one time or another; perhaps lines were mixed and matched, or unwanted designations discarded. The confusion created by the editions, emendations, and erasures on page 243, for example, could have tripped up readers of any century.[47] But for all that, the play was not recopied. Perhaps contemporary performers valued the tangible record of past performances more than we do.

The Boy and the Blind Man confirms the premise that expectations regarding the inscription of plays could vary over time – even systems of line attribution, roughly contemporary with one another, were not entirely compatible. Looking ahead to the fifteenth century, printed farces still show traces of the techniques employed by the thirteenth-century scribe responsible for *The Play of Adam*, with designations appearing on the line above a character's speech, oriented slightly to the right. When they occupy a blank space between segments of dialogue, the effect is clear; but when space must be conserved, they are pushed farther to the right and are juxtaposed with the preceding line. (In all probability, they were literally pushed as the compositor added extra type to the tray.) The first page of Nicolas Chrestien's impression of *Le Couturier et Esopet* (Paris, ca 1550), for example, features both extremes, and would baffle a reader trained in scholastic techniques of rubrication (such as the scribe of the *Seinte Resureccion*) or accustomed to construing scripts the way some annotators of *Le garçon et l'aveugle* evidently did.[48] Such instances of miscommunication in transmission were by no means uncommon. Malcolm Parkes has illustrated the ways in which texts could suffer at the hands of copyists unfamiliar with the conventions of another place and time, pointing out the differences between the twelfth-century exemplar of a treatise by St Augustine and its fourteenth-century copy, whose scribe mistook the *punctus flexus* for an abbreviation and, as a result, unwittingly emended the text to read *et* in two places on the same page.[49] A harmless change – although wars have been waged over the proliferation or absence of conjunctions in the articulation of dogma.

The consequences of misinterpretation in *Le garçon et l'aveugle* are far less weighty, but they do have interesting implications, since the personalities of the characters alter considerably depending on one's reading of the parts. Is the Blind Man an unwitting accomplice, an innocent front for the 'cruel deceptions practised by the Boy'?[50] Or is he a charlatan, a corrupter of youth, the mastermind behind the pair's shady dealings? The many possibilities suggest that this ambivalence was one of the play's selling points, at least in the first hundred years or so after it was written down. However, the vehemence of the changes made in the late fifteenth century is suggestive of the growing intolerance for multiple meanings to which the fixity of print – and the changing religious climate – must surely have contributed. It was then that the two oaths originally sworn by 'God's ass' (*cul bieu*) were converted to 'God's death' (*mort bieu*), and a reference to 'the hole' (*le trau*) of Sainte-Sophie was crossed out.[51] Over time, scholarly editions would place further restraints on the unruly manuscript remnants of medieval theatre.

NOTES

This paper was originally based on portions of *A Medieval Stage: Theatre and the Culture of Performance in Thirteenth-Century Arras* (unpublished PhD dissertation,

Harvard University, 1999). It has benefited from the comments of the editors of this volume and those of Elton Cormier. I discuss the larger context of the evidence presented here in my article "The Appearance of Early Vernacular Plays: Forms, Functions, and the Future of Medieval Theatre,' *Speculum* 77 (2002): 778–831.

1 See the bibliographical essays in *The Theatre of Medieval Europe: New Research in Early Drama*, ed. Eckehard Simon (Cambridge: Cambridge University Press, 1991), especially pp. 119–28 (English), pp. 155–8 (French), pp. 170–1 (Italian), pp. 189–90 (Spanish and Catalan), p. 208 (German), p. 227 (Dutch).

2 The song 'Dou roy de Sesile' included in the play (vv. 83–90; see Figure 6.2, p. 243[a], l. 40 – p. 243[b], l. 6) refers to the campaigns of Charles of Anjou, created king of Sicily on Epiphany in 1266.

3 The manuscript measures 265 × 220 mm and is written in two columns. The romance occupies pp. 1–242r[a] of the codex, the pages of which are numbered in Arabic numerals that were probably added in the fourteenth or fifteenth century. The colophon (see Figure 6.1) reads: 'Explicit li roumans dalixandres dalierz / En lan del incarnation.mil.&. cij. &. xxviii. fu / leues mon sei*n*gnor saint Quentins el mois / De may.' The reference to 'my lord Saint Quentin' suggests that the parent text may have been copied in the town bearing his name, at the abbey of Mont-Saint-Quentin near Arras, or perhaps even in the town of Aisnes where the saint was the dedicand of a prominent church.

4 Paul Meyer, '*Du garçon et de l'aveugle,* saynète du XIIIe siècle,' *Jahrbuch für romanische und englische Literatur* 6 (1865): 163–72; *Le garçon et l'aveugle: Jeu du XIIIe siècle*, ed. Mario Roques (Paris: Champion, 1911) and tr. Jean Dufournet (Paris: Champion, 1989), hereafter abbreviated as *G&A*. See my transcription and analysis in the Appendix. This is not a diplomatic edition *in strictu sensu* because I have expanded abbreviations and *tituli*, although I indicate (in italics) where I have done so. Where applicable, I have also noted variant readings adopted by Dufournet, who supplemented Roques's edition of the text, as he explains, with a few corrections drawn from his own perusal of the manuscript and from the marginal notes made by Gaston Paris in Paris's own copy of Meyer's 1865 edition, now at the Sorbonne. See *G&A*, 89. The only English translation of the play currently available is that of Richard Axton and John Stevens, published in *Medieval French Plays* (Oxford: Basil Blackwell, 1971), pp. 193–206.

5 See Figure 6.4, p. 245[b], ll. 25–31. On the importance and relative frequency of explicits over incipits see Paul Zumthor, *La lettre et la voix de la 'litterature' médiévale* (Paris: Seuil, 1987), p. 123.

6 I have included *The Boy and the Blind Man* among contemporary plays associated with the town and city of Arras for two special reasons. In the first place, the song lampooning the exploits of the new 'roy de Sesile' refers to Charles of Anjou, uncle of Count Robert II of Artois; Robert was one of King Charles's most loyal supporters, and it was at the king's Neapolitan court that Adam de la Halle's *Jeu de Robin et de Marion* had its probable première. In the second place, it is significant that the Boy declares himself to be from Arras when he swears 'By the faith that I owe Saint-Vaast,' the patron saint of the town (*Par la foi que ie doi saint Vast,* v. 99; see Figure 6.2, p. 243b, l. 16). While the version of the play preserved in the sole manuscript was apparently intended for performance in Tournai, since that city and its environs are mentioned in the text (vv. 28–31; see Figure 6.1, p. 242b, ll. 26–9), the basic scenario could have played itself out anywhere in the region. Moreover, it is perfectly possible that the name of the town could have been changed to match the venue of performance. Although the word 'Tournai' sets up a rhyme to be completed in the following line, 'Tu prieras, je canterai,' a new couplet could easily be invented if the next day's destination was Aire, Amiens, or Saint-Omer. (Cambrai, of course, would pose no difficulties.)

7 On the uses of the fool's bauble see William Willeford, *The Fool and His Scepter: A Study in Clowns and Jesters and Their Audience* (Evanston, Ill.: Northwestern University Press, 1969), pp. 32–7 and passim.

8 About the jongleurs who would have developed pieces such as *Le garçon et l'aveugle* Michel Rousse says: 'Quant à eux, ils étaient gens de métier, d'un métier qui ne s'apprend pas dans les livres.' See 'Le *Jeu de Saint Nicolas.* Tradition et innovation,' in *Arras au moyen âge: Histoire et littérature,* ed. Marie-Madeleine Castellani and Jean-Pierre Martin (Arras: Artois Presses Université, 1994), pp. 153–62 at 154.

9 On the blind man and his boy in the French tradition see Gustave Cohen, 'La scène de l'aveugle et de son valet dans le théâtre français du moyen âge,' *Romania* 61 (1912): 346–72, and Dufournet's commentary on his edition of the play. I am not aware of any studies that comment on the resemblance between this scenario and those in English drama.

10 Edmond Faral, *Les Jongleurs en France au Moyen Age* (Paris: Champion, 1910), p. 228. For a brief summary of critical opinion see Dufournet's introduction, *G&A,* 11–26. See also Michel Rousse, 'Propositions sur le théâtre profane avant la farce,' *Tréteaux* 1 (1978): 4–18.

11 Axton and Stevens, p. 195. See also Richard Axton, *European Drama of the Early Middle Ages* (London: Hutchinson, 1974), p. 19; and William Tyde-

man, *The Theatre in the Middle Ages: Western European Stage Conditions, c.800–1576* (Cambridge: Cambridge University Press, 1978), p. 29.

12 Michel Rousse, 'Le théâtre et les jongleurs,' in *Naissances du théâtre français (XIIe–XIIIe siècles),* ed. Jean Dufournet in *Revue des langues romanes* 95 (1991): 1–14 at 4: 'un théâtre profane, populaire, sans ambition littéraire ou édifiante.'

13 Dufournet in *G&A,* 11: 'une véritable pièce' or 'sans doute à l'origine une parade de foire, mimant une scène de rue, une scène de la vie quotidienne.' See also Tydeman, 126, who mentions that this setting would even be appropriate for Rutebeuf's quack doctor of the *Dit de l'herberie.*

14 For parallel instances in medieval music transcription see Leo Treitler, 'Oral, Written, and Literate Process in the Transmission of Medieval Music,' *Speculum* 56 (1981): 471–91.

15 Axton and Stevens, p. 195; *G&A,* 113: 'Les indications du copiste du XIIIe siècle sont placées tantôt à la suite du premier vers de la réplique, tantôt à la suite du dernier vers de la réplique précédente; dans ce dernier cas le lecteur du XVe siècle les a grattées ou rayées ou a noté d'un trait le déplacement nécessaire.'

16 *G&A,* 100–101, v. 137; compare Figure 6.3, p. 244^a, l. 14. For examples of Dufournet's supplementary stage directions see *G&A,* 92–3, 102–103, 104–105.

17 The basic characteristics of handwriting and layout resemble those of Chantilly, Musée Condé MS 476, fol. 55 (copy of *L'image du monde* of Gossuin de Metz), dated 1270. See *Catalogue des manuscrits en écriture latine portant des indications de date, de lieu ou de copiste,* vol. 1 (Paris: Centre national de la recherche scientifique, 1959), p. 35 and pl. 15.

18 Hand A makes only minor clarifications or corrections with a different pen, and is responsible only for the *or parole* phrases and some abbreviations on pp. 242 and 243.

19 Hand B adds further abbreviated designations throughout, as well as the erroneous *li valles* at the bottom of p. 244^a, which may have been crossed out immediately.

20 I have made this distinction based on slight differences in *ductus* and consistently different spelling habits: Hand X writes *la veule* and *le garchon,* while Hand Y writes *ly aveules* and *le garchons.*

21 Paris, Bibliothèque nationale, fonds français 25467, fols 48 ff. See *Recueil de farces,* ed. André Tissier, 12 vols (Geneva: Droz, 1986–98), VII: 13 (facs.) and 32.

22 Compare the hand at work on Paris, Bibliothèque de l'Arsenal, MS 5218,

fol. 91v (copy of *Le quête du saint Graal*), dated 1351; *Catalogue des manuscrits*, 191 and pl. 47.

23 Compare Paris, Bibliothèque de l'Arsenal, MS 3357, fol. 339v (copy of *Le roman de Tristan*), dated 1488; *Catalogue des manuscrits*, 161 and pl. 145.

24 Compare Paris, Bibliothèque de l'Arsenal, MS 2886, fol. 305v (copy of *Les propriétés des choses* of Barthélemy l'Anglais), dated 1472; *Catalogue des manuscrits*, 151 and pl. 131b.

25 Paris, Bibliothèque nationale, fonds français 2168, fols. $70r^{b}$–$80r^{d}$. On the dramatic qualities of this and other 'non-dramatic' texts, see Jean-Claude Aubailly, 'Aux sources du théâtre: Le «poème» de *Piramus et Tisbé* (vers 1170),' in *Naissances du théâtre français*, pp. 15–30; and André de Mandach, 'Le rôle du théâtre dans une nouvelle conception de l'évolution des genres,' *Stylistique, rhétorique et poétique dans les langues romanes* 8 (1986): 27–46 at 36–7.

26 Tours, Bibliothèque municipale, MS 927, fols. 20v–40r. See Paul Aebischer's edition, *Le Mystère d'Adam* (Geneva: Droz, 1964), p. 11; and Wolfgang von Emden's preface to his edition, *Le Jeu d'Adam*, British Rencesvals Publications, 1 (Edinburgh: Société Rencesvals British Branch, 1996), pp. v–ix. Photographs of each manuscript page are published by Leif Sletsjöe in *Le mystère d'Adam: Édition diplomatique* (Paris: Klincksieck, 1968).

27 Pierre-Marie Gy, 'La mise en page du Canon de la messe,' and Geneviève Hasenohr, 'Les romans en verse,' in *Mise en page et mise en texte du livre manuscrit*, ed. Henri-Jean Martin and Jean Vezin (Paris: Promodis, 1990), pp. 112–20 at 113 and pp. 244–63 at 249–52, respectively.

28 Paris, Bibliothèque nationale, fonds français 902, fols. 97r–98v.

29 On the origins and uses of such systems, see Richard H. Rouse and Mary A. Rouse, '*Statim invenire*: Schools, Preachers, and New Attitudes to the Page,' in *Renaissance and Renewal in the Twelfth Century*, ed. Robert L. Benson and Giles Constable (Cambridge, Mass.: Harvard University Press, 1978), pp. 201–25 at 209; also Rouse and Rouse, 'Concordances et index,' in *Mise en page*, pp. 218–28.

30 London, British Library, MS Additional 45103 (copied at St Augustine's, Canterbury, around 1275). The texts of both manuscripts were combined in the edition of T.A. Jenkins (Oxford: Blackwell, 1943), who appears to have considered the lack of rubrication in the Canterbury manuscript to be a minor problem, mentioning it only in passing, p. xxii.

31 Zumthor, *La lettre et la voix*, pp. 86, 119–23, 263, and *passim*. See also Geneviève Hasenohr, 'La prose,' in *Mise en page*, pp. 264–71, especially p. 266, pl. 212. For an excellent description of the chief features of vernacular *mise en page*, with many facsimile examples, see Carleton W. Carroll, 'Medi-

eval Romance Paleography: A Brief Introduction,' in *Medieval Manuscripts and Textual Criticism*, ed. Christopher Kleinhenz (Chapel Hill: University of North Carolina Press, 1975), pp. 39–83.

32 Paris, Bibiothèque nationale, fonds français 12483.

33 Graham Runnalls, 'Towns and Plays,' in *Études sur les mystères: Un recueil de 22 études sur les mystères français, suivi d'un répertoire du théâtre religieux français du Moyen Age et d'une bibliographie* (Paris: Champion, 1998), pp. 61–82 at 62; in the same volume see 'The Theatre in Paris in the Late Middle Ages,' pp. 83–100 at 85.

34 Geneviève Hasenohr, 'Les manuscrits théâtraux,' in *Mise en page*, pp. 334–40 at 336: 'Dès les origines, le nom des locuteurs est soigneusement indiqué.'

35 Paul Zumthor, *Essai de poétique médiévale* (Paris: Editions du Seuil, 1972), and *La lettre et la voix;* and Bernard Cerquiglini, *Eloge de la variante: Histoire critique de philologie* (Paris, 1989). On the impact of these concepts see, for example, Gregory Nagy, *Poetry as Performance: Homer and Beyond* (Cambridge: Cambridge University Press, 1996).

36 Edmond Faral and Julia Bastin, eds., *Œuvres complètes de Rutebeuf*, 2 vols (Paris: A. et J. Picard, 1959 and 1960), 2:168–9; see also Faral's *Mimes français du XIII*e *siècle* (Paris: Champion, 1910), p. xiv.

37 This has long been a trend in French scholarship. See Gustave Cohen, *Histoire de la mise en scène dans le théâtre religieux français du moyen âge*, 2nd ed. (Paris: Champion, 1926); and *Théâtre en France au Moyen-Age. II. Le théâtre profane* (Paris: Rieder, 1948), especially pp. 13–48. Of course, Cohen was merely following the lead of Edmond Faral, who in turn followed Joseph Bédier and Gaston Paris. The traditional segregation is preserved by Grace Frank, *The Medieval French Drama* (Oxford: Clarendon Press, 1954); Jean Frappier, *Le théâtre profane en France au moyen-âge (XIII*e*–XIV*e *siècle)* (Paris: Centre de documentation universitaire, 1965); and Giuseppe Macrì, *Teatro comico francese del Medio Evo: Appunti per una storia del teatro* (Galatina, [1973]), among many others.

38 Graham A. Runnalls, 'Medieval French Drama: A Review of Recent Scholarship. Part I: Religious Drama,' *RORD* 21 (1978): 83–90 and 22 (1979): 111–36; and Alan Hindley, 'Medieval French Drama: A Review of Recent Scholarship. Part II: Comic Drama,' *RORD* 23 (1980): 93–126.

39 Lester K. Little, *Religious Poverty and the Profit Economy in Medieval Europe* (Ithaca: Cornell University Press, 1978), pp. 198–9; see also pp. 31–4.

40 Etienne Gilson, 'Michel Menot et la technique du sermon médiéval,' in *Les idées et les lettres* (Paris: J. Vrin, 1932), pp. 93–154 at 117.

41 But see the introduction of William D. Paden, *The Future of the Middle Ages:*

Medieval Literature in the 1990s (Gainesville and Tallahassee: University Press of Florida, 1994), pp. vii–xiii; and the critiques of Rupert T. Pickens, 'The Future of Old French Studies in America: The "Old" Philology and the Crisis of the "New,"' pp. 53–86; and Peter F. Dembowski, 'Is There a New Textual Philology in Old French? Perennial Problems, Provisional Solutions,' pp. 87–112. For a helpful introduction to the history of Old French textual criticism and conventions, see Alfred Foulet and Mary Blakely Speer, *On Editing Old French Texts* (Lawrence, Kans.: Regents Press of Kansas, 1979), pp. 1–39. A thoughtful summary of the myriad issues affecting textual criticism across the board is offered by Peter L. Shillingsburg, *Scholarly Editing in the Computer Age: Theory and Practice,* 3rd ed. (Ann Arbor: University of Michigan Press, 1996). A major exception to the trend noted above is the attention given to editing in English theatre studies, but here the focus of endeavor is on the fifteenth, sixteenth, even seventeenth centuries. See David Bevington, 'Drama Editing and Its Relation to Recent Trends in Literary Criticism,' and Peter Meredith, 'Stage Directions and the Editing of Early English Drama,' in *Editing Early English Drama: Special Problems and New Directions,* ed. Alexandra F. Johnston (New York: AMS Press, 1987), pp. 17–32 at 29–31 and 65–94 at 88–91, respectively.

42 Dufournet supplies, without comment, a designation before line 1. The absence of an incipit contrasts with the plethora of explicits, as I noted above, and may suggest that this play, very literally, needed no introduction. Potential performers knew what it was at sight, where to find it, and opened automatically to it. But these same performers, who were also the editors and annotators, left their marks at the end of the play in a series of scribal curtain calls.

43 This makes for creative editing: *G&A*, 93–5, ll. 17–26.

44 Dufournet adds the direction *à part* before v. 17 of his edition.

45 Dufournet adds the direction *il aperçoit l'aveugle* before v. 18.

46 Dufournet supplies the direction *à l'aveugle.*

47 For example, T. Bercham, 'Quelques remarques critiques sur une scène du *Garçon et l'aveugle,*' in *Mélanges de philologie romane dédiées à la mémoire de Jean Boutière,* ed. Irénée Cluzel and François Pirot (Liège: Editions Soledi, 1971), I:139–52; especially pp. 140, 144–5. This study tries to make sense of several obscure passages but without attempting to reapportion the lines as given in Roques's edition. Despite the fact that Bercham makes specific reference to the manuscript (p. 145, n. 4 and p. 151, n. 18), he deals only with trifling difficulties posed by the indeterminacy of individual words or letters, not with the problem of line attribution at its most basic level.

48 *Recueil de farces,* VII: 7 (facs.).

49 Malcolm B. Parkes, *Pause and Effect: An Introduction to the History of Punctuation in the West* (Aldershot: Scolar Press, 1992), pp. 250–3 and pl. 51–2.

50 Axton and Stevens, p. 195.

51 Figure 6.2, p. 243[b], ll. 8 and 12, and Figure 6.3, p. 244[a], l. 32.

APPENDIX

A transcription and analysis of *Le garçon et l'aveugle*

(Paris, Bibliothèque nationale, fonds français 24366, pp. 242^{b}–245^{b})

p. 242^{b} – Figure 6.1^{B}

Faites nous bien sei*n*gnor baron q*ue* diex li fuis[1] Marie
V*ous* meche tous en sa maison *et* en sa *con*paignie
Veoir ne vous puis mie
Pour moi vous voie Jesuscris
Et tous chiax mete en paradis
Ki me feront aie
A mere dieu sainte Marie souveraine q*ue* le eure est il
Je not nului trop metieng vill
Q*ue* ie nai aumains .j. garchon
Que me remenast en maison
Car sil ne savaoit b*ie*n canter
Si saroit il dov pain rouuer
Et moi mener as g*ra*ns osteus
Elas *con* ie sui disiteus — **or p*ar*ole li garcons** [Hand A]
Il ne me faut plus nule riens
Sire v*ous* nales mie bien — **or p*ar*ole li garcons** [Hand A]
Vous q*ue*rres ia en cest celier
A meredieu veullie me aidier — **or p*ar*ole li aveules** [Hand A]
Ki esce q*ui* si b*ie*n mavoie
Preudons se Jhesus me doint ioie — **or p*ar*ole li garcons** [Hand A]

p. 242[b] – Figure 6.1[B] (*concluded*)

	Cou est vns poures t*ri*q*ue*mers		
	P*our*[2] dieu ie croi q*ui*l soit mult bers	**or p*ar*ole li aw'**	[Hands A, B][3]
	Viengne avant a lui veull p*ar*ler		
	Ves me chi	**or p*ar*ole li ga'**	[Hand A]
	Te veus tu louer	**li aw'**	[Hand B]
	Sire a q*uo*i seroi che faire	**/ le garchons**	[Hand X]
	P*our* mi pour mener sans mesfaire	**ly aveules**	[Hand Y]
	A val la cite de Tournay		
	Tu prieras ie canterai	**li aw'**	[Hand B]
	Sarons asses argent *et* pain		
	He p*ar* la panche saint Gillain	**ly garchons**	[Hand Y]
	Bien me cuidies ore foubert		
	Mais ie vous di b*ie*n en apert		
	Kun e*s*cucon le iour aray		
	Detant kavoeq*ues* v*ous* iray		
	Et si nen lairai nule cose		
	Biaus dous amis car neme chose	**li garc' aveules.**[4]	[Hands A, Y]
	Coument tapelon		
le garchons	Jeha*n*net[5] / tes cors ait de hait	**/ la veules**	[Hand X]
	Se te ne laras volentiers		

p. 243[a] – Figure 6.2[A]

Se de mon mestier es maniers		
G*ra*ns riches hom en devenras		
Alons ie ne mesmaie pas	**/ le garchon'**	[Hand X]
Destre g*ra*ns maistres temprement		
Je prierai diex gries tourment		
En voit tous chiax kan poure a veule		
Feront nes vne bone seule		
Car il laroient b*ie*n perdu.	**li aw'**	[Hand B]
Biax dous iehanet q*ue* distu	**<gar'>**	[<erasure> Hand B?]
Tu me fais au cuer t*rop* g*ra*nt ire		
Ne v*ous* en caille biaus dous sire	**le garch'**	[Hand X]
Cest p*our* ces vilains deceuoir		
Cantes ie v*ous* aiderai voir		
Et cascuns dou pain nous do*n*ra	**/ Or cante*n*t ensanle**	[Scribe]
Merediev q*ui* v*ous* seruira ioie atoute sauie		
M*ul*t bon g*ue*rredon en ara car en vo c*on*paignie		
Sera dame jolie	**/ laveule**[6]	[Hand X]
P*our* tous mes b*ie*n faiteurs v*ous* proi		
Et p*our* ciaus q*ui* le fill le roi		
Seruant sans vilonie	**/ Or li gar'**	[Scribe]
He pour diev ne nous fales mie		
Q*ue* v*ous* dou pain ne nous do*n*nes		
Sire.vn. petit chi matendes		
Rouuer vois aces g*ra*ns osteus	**.li gar.'**	[Hand A]

p. 243[a] – Figure 6.2[A] (*concluded*)

	Seignor pour dieu lesperitel		
	Faites .j. poure aw'. bien	**.li gar.'**	[Hand A]
	Sire ne puis avoir nul rien		
	Alons ent q*ue* diex lor doint honte.	**<li aw'>**	[<erasure> Hand B?]
	Il nont q*ue* do*n*ner or me *con*te	**laveule**	[Hand X]
Je	Ha*n*net[7] se nus respondi	**<li gar'>**	[<erasure> Hand A?]
	Nenil sire mais iatendi	**/ legarchon**	[Hand X]
	Q*ui*l es kingnoient malement	**<li aw'>**	[<erasure> Hand B?]
	Jehanet p*ar* anuiem*en*t	**/. aveule**	[Hand X]
	Eusses eut que q*ue* soit	**</ ligar'>**	[<erasure> Hand B?]
	Sire Jhesus cris mauoit	**/. ly garch**	[Hand Y]
	Car ie sui maistres dov mestier	**<?>**	[<erasure>]
	Cantes nous arons amangier	**<?>**	[<erasure>]
	Car p*ar* parler les vainterai		
	Or cante*n*t en doi ensamble		[Scribe]
	Dou roy de Sesile diray		

p. 243^{b} – Figure 6.2^{b}

	Que diex soit en saie		
	Q*ui* cascun iour est en asay		
	Contre lagent haie		
	Or a chevalerie		
	Remande[8] p*ar*tout le mont		
	Tout cil q*ui* nule cose nont		
	Iront aost banie	**.liG.'**	[Scribe]
	He p*ar* le ~~trau~~ sainte Sousfie[9]		[<crossed out>]
	Sire se de nient poons vuire		
	Nous serons anq*ue* nuit tout iure		
	Voes *con*cascuns nous aporte		
	P*ar* le ~~cul biev~~[10] ne huis ne porte		['mort bieu': Hand X]
	Ne vi encore anuit ouurir		
	Chi porriemes de faim morir		
	Ains que nus riens nous aportast		
	P*ar* le foi q*ue* ie doi saint Vast	**<?>**	[<erasure>]
	Jamais ne quier mener aw*eule*		
	Il avient une aventure seule	**/ laveule**	[Hand X]
Je	Ha*n*net[11] foi q*ue* ie doi tes kennes		[Hand X]
	A .j. cop ne kiet pas li caisnes		
	Se nous narons riens ore eu		
	Nous soumes t*res* b*ie*n pour veu		
	Davoir aluire *et* amengier		
	Se ie iamais pain ne ronvoie		

p. 243^b – Figure 6.2^b (*concluded*)

Joliement me maintenroie		
Tant ai ie deniers assambles	**<?>**	[<erasure>]
M*u*lt[12] maisement me resambles	**/ le garch'**	[Hand X]
Sire q*ue* se deniers avoie		
Moi *et* vous ~~*et*~~ a aisseroie		[<crossed out>]
Netant kil porroient durer		
Ne v*ous con*v*er*roit pain rouuer		
Ains seroit vos sans *con*tredit	**<?>**	[<erasure>]
Jehanet[13] p*our* tant q*ue* tu as dit	**. la veule**	[Hand X]
Par tiras atrestout le mien		
Dor en avant ie te di b*ie*n	**<?>**	[<erasure>]
Sire se diex me puist aidier	**/ le garch'**	[Hand X]
V*ous* aves droit diex *con* gr*a*nt feste		
Menrons car ie fai b*ie*n de geste		
Cant*er* si v*ous* en deduirai		
Et se mestier aves ie irai		

p. 244[a] – Figure 6.3[A]

Tantost bele garce amener[14]		
Q*ui* nara pas pance ridee ·		[· supplied in original]
Mais blance *et* tenre *et* le viaire		
Ans tele ne portoit pourtraire		
De pour traiour ne depincel		
Gillot .j. escuier sibel		
Na si iolit ne si b*ie*n fait		
Et si ara .j. tel con nait		
Ka escuellortes[15] sauriens ens	**.li aw.'**	[Hand B]
Tu me fais a achier les dens	[line in MS indicates later change in attribution][16]	
Jehanet[17] detel rasion laidis		
Je ne veull pas q*ue* tu medis		
Dauoir garce q*ue* bele lai ·		[· supplied in original]
Et q*uan*t iele pourqu*en*lerai[18]		
Tu le me venras estuper		
Con li porra t*re*s bien ieter		
Seur les plantes despies. iij. des.	**.li G'.**	[Hand B]
Sire vilainem*en*t parles	[line in MS denotes later change in attribution]	
Ne parles plus si laidem*en*t	**.li aw'.**	[Hand B]
Nus ne mot fors q*ue* tu seulment	[line in MS denotes later change in attribution]	
Biax dous Jeha*n*net ke ie sache	**.li G'.**	[Hand B]
Sire atende me en ceste plache	[line in MS denotes later change in attribution]	
Je vois faire .j. petit dorine		
Truans dix v*ous* doint male estrine	**.li G'.**	[Hand B]

p. 244^{a} – Figure 6.3^{A} (*concluded*)

Q*ua*nt si desordeneme*nt* p*ar*les		
Mais chiereme*nt* le *con*parres		
Tenes pour cou		
Jeha*n*net[19] or me di se iou ai plaie	**.li aw'.**	[Hand B]
Plaie; mais dont venroit li plaie	**.li G'.**	[Hand B]
Or endroit vne tele paie	**.li aw'.**	[Hand B]
Me do*n*na ore ne sai cui		
Pour le ~~kul biev~~ iestoie en ki	**.li G'.**	['mort bieu': Hand X]
Et q*ue* ne me hu castes vous		
A biax Jeha*n*net amis dous	**laveule**	[Hand X]
Se ieusse .j. seul mot groucie		
Il meust lues tel cop do*n*ne[20]		
Q*ue* il iparust toute mavie		
Sire ne v*ous* esmaies mie	**/- ly garch/**	[Hand Y]
On sane mult bien der bes cops	**~~.li valles.~~**	[Hand B <crossed out>]
Voire Jehanet mait tout li os	**/ laveule**	[Hand X]

p. 244[b] – Figure 6.3[B]

De la ioe torme*n*t me duellent	**~~li G'~~**[21]	[Hand B <crossed out>]
Biaus dous sire de tex cops muerent	**ly garch'**	[Hand Y]
Aucunes gens mais b*ien* garres		
Car anq*ue* nuit sus loieres ·		[· supplied in original]
Dela fiente du*n* cras poulain		
Si v*ous* trouueres demain sain		
Je le v*ous* di t*re*stout p*our* voir		
car iadis sire g*ra*nt auoir		
Ga aingnai a sans pl*us* garir		
Vn enfant ki devoit morir		
Je li fis vue puisson crasse		
Devant aus mis ains de pl*us* crasse		
Nepeuc avoir sai tout laissie	**.li aw'.**	[Hand B]
Par foi Jehanet diex ta aidie	[line in MS denotes later change in attribution]	
Et ta a bon port arive		
Sesens veus faire tas trouue	**~~li G'~~**	[Hand B <crossed out>]
Q*ui* te soustenra le menton		
Sire m*u*lt tres bon valeton	/ **ly garch'**	[Hand Y]
Me trouueres seur *et* sene		
On aia tes lincuis bues[22]		
Et pendus q*ui* tex nestoit mie	**li aw'.**	[Hand B]
Jehanet ie tamerai ma vie	[line in MS denotes later change in attribution]	
Je vorroie ore estre en maison		
Q*ua*nt tu viens a .j. g*ra*nt perron		

p. 244ᵇ – Figure 6.3ᴮ (*concluded*)

	Deus maisons de la siet mes mes	**.li G'.**	[Hand B]
	Sire donq*ue*s maint par dales	[line in MS denotes later change in attribution]	
	Hue q*ui* de honte vuignies		
	A le seurnon v*ous* ruengnies		
	Siet li vile dont ie p*ar*ole	**.li aw'.**	[Hand B]
	Tu as este aboune escole	[line in MS denotes later change in attribution]	
Je[23]	Hannet ia venras amon mes	**.li G'.**	[Hand X, Hand B]
	Sire ie isui or v*ous* sousfres[24]	[line in MS denotes later change in attribution]	
	Iou v*er*rai luis ou siet li clinkes	**.li aw'.**	[Hand B]
Je	Ha*n*net une fuell de venke	[Hand X, later change in line attribution]	
	A sor le fuell ovelle siet	**.li G'.**	[Hand B]
	Sire ens estes orne vous griet	[line in MS denotes later change in attribution]	
	Mais faites tost apertement		
	Et si me do*n*nes de largent		
	Simen irai ,le viande **,a**		[correction original?]
	Jeha*n*net en me bourse grande	**li aw'.**	[Hand B]

p. 245[a] – Figure 6.4[A]

A il deniers en g*ra*nt plante		
Prent ent tout a ta volente		
Se poi en as prentent encore		
Je vaurroie q*ue* a fust ore		
Mamiete t*ro*p le desir	**~~li G'.~~**	[Hand B <crossed out>]
Biau dou sire amo*n* revenir	**ly garch'**	[Hand Y]
Lamenrai	**~~li aw'.~~**	[Hand B <crossed out>]
Ses ovelle pine	**~~li G'.~~aveule**	[~~Hand B~~, Hand X]
Sire oil cest une mescine	**le garch**	[Hand Y]
Ki fait batre ses angelins		
Je lai veue aval ce molins		
Pinet caillaus *et* esboure		
Faites tost laissie ment aler		
Keli bons vins sera tost hors		
E si metes vo houce fors		
Car elle est toute desciree		
Ves sire comme est esclouee[25]		
La boucle de vostre coroie		
Prent coroie boucle et monoie	/ **laveule**	[Hand X]
Et houche porte tout refaire		
Bien sia que tu ne pues mesfaire		
*Mais em*ploie bien ton argent		
En vain en pain et en fourment		
Et saca te boune viande		

p. 245ª – Figure 6.4ᴬ (*concluded*)

Jehanet ie le te *con*mande		
Samaine mamie en ta voie	**li aw.'**	[Hand B]
Volontiers se dix me doint joie	[line in MS denotes later change in attribution]	
Je men vois or p*ri*es pour me	**.li G'.**	[Hand B]
Vatent ie te tiegn a ami	[line in MS denotes later change in attribution]	
Seignor ai ie b*ie*n mis apoint		
Ce la weule la q*ui* na point		
Dargent ne de houce *ausi*		
Jen port t*re*stout sans nes *unsi*		
Par foi il cui doit q*ue* ie fusse		
Si povres q*ue* ie riens neusse		
Mais du sien asses *humerai*		
Et as conpaignons endonrai		
Tant q*ue* riens ne men demoura[26]		
Mais certes ia ne mavenra		
Que le sien en jour de ma vie		

p. 245^{b} – Figure 6.4^{B}

En porte que ne li die
Se ne lui di iaie de hait
Sire q*ue*res autre vallet
Je ne v*ous* veul mie trahir
Je maiserai p*ar* loisir
Dou v*ostr*e et p*ar* droite raison
V*ous* ai ie b*ie*n mene dont[27]
Or nes un ie es v*ous* sai[28]
Certes de vo argent q*ue* iai
Ne de vo houce ie me*n* vois — **li aw'.** [HAND B]
Haha: diex *con* ie sui destrois — [line in MS denotes later change in attribution]
Ou est limors q*ui* tant demeure
Ki ne me prent mais ains ceste eure
Certes demain la tenderai
Adont b*ie*n .c. cops li donrai
Foi q*ue* ie doi mamie margue — **.li G'.** [HAND B]
Fi de v*ous* en ne sui ie enlarge — [line in MS denotes later change in attribution]
Je na *con*te .j. estront avous
V*ous* estes fel et envious
Senestoit p*our* des *con*pai*n*gnons

p. 245^{b} – Figure 6.4^{B} (*concluded*)

V*ous* aries ia mil millons
Mais pour iaus seres de portes **lyveule D** [Hand Y]
Sil ne vous siet si me sives

Explicet[29]
Explicit du Garcon *et* de la veule ....[30]
Explicit du garchon *et* de la veule[31]

Explicit[32]

Explicit iste liber qui scripsit fit ale liber[33]

NOTES TO APPENDIX

1 Dufournet reads 'fius.' *G&A*, 95, v. 1.

2 Dufournet reads 'Par.' *G&A*, 95, v. 24.

3 The designation *li aw'*, in contrast to the direction *or parole*, appears to be written in the slightly later hand.

4 Dufournet follows the later, fifteenth-century line reading. *G&A*, 95, vv. 38–9.

5 Dufournet has the Blind Man repeat the word 'Jehannet.' *G&A*, 95, v. 41.

6 Dufournet does not note this emendation. *G&A*, 97, v. 61.

7 Dufournet does not note the fifteenth-century emendation in the left margin. *G&A*, 97, v. 74 and 105, v. 194.

8 Dufournet reads 'remandee.' *G&A*, 99, v. 88.

9 Dufournet reads 'Souffie.' *G&A*, 99, v. 91.

10 This change occurs here and on p. 244[a], below. Dufournet adopts the original.

11 Dufournet does not note the fifteenth-century emendation and reads 'Hanot.' *G&A*, 99, v. 102.

12 Dufournet reads 'mout' here and on p. 244[b], l. 18. *G&A*, 99, v. 107 and 105, v. 181.

13 Dufournet does not note the original, substituting 'Hanet' here and elsewhere (see below). *G&A*, 101, v. 113.

14 Dufournet reads 'amenee.' *G&A*, 101, v. 124.

15 Dufournet reads 'escuelloites.' *G&A*, 101, v. 132.

16 Dufournet follows later attempts to 'correct' the placement of the designations supplied by Hand B.

17 Dufournet emends to 'Hanet.' *G&A*, 101, v. 134.

18 Dufournet reads 'pourqulerai,' but does not translate the term on the facing page. *G&A*, 100-101, v. 137.

19 Dufournet emends to 'Hannet.' *G&A*, 103, v. 151.

20 Dufournet emends to 'lancié.' *G&A*, 103, v. 159.

21 Dufournet follows the later reading here and below, at l. 16. *G&A*, 103, v. 164–5 and 105, vv. 179–80.

22 Dufournet reads 'linçuel bué.' *G&A*, 105, v. 183.

23 Dufournet does not note this emendation or the one following. *G&A*, 105, v. 194 and 106, v. 197.

24 Dufournet reads 'souffrés.' *G&A*, 105, v. 195.

25 This section of the manuscript is barely legible, even under ultraviolet light. I have followed Roques's readings in difficult places.

26 Dufournet reads 'demourra.' *G&A*, 109, v. 240.

27 Dufournet amends this verse to read: 'ne vous ai je bien mené dont?' *G&A*, 109, v. 249.

28 Dufournet amends this verse to read: 'Or nes un gré je ne vous sai.' *G&A*, 109, v. 250.

29 Added in the fifteenth century.

30 Explicit added by Hand B?

31 Explicit of a fourteenth-century editor?

32 Added in the fifteenth century.

33 Explicit added in the sixteenth century?

7

Toward a Disjunctive Philology

WILLIAM ROBINS

Disjunctive Philology

Philologists may be, in general, a verbally scrupulous lot. Nevertheless even discussions about the direction of philology occasionally suffer from conflicting, unstated, or imprecise definitions. Prudence thus suggests that, in order to indicate clearly its own point of departure, this essay begin with an explicit definition, as provisional as it is cumbersome: *philology is a respect for the contingent determinacies of textual phenomena.* A definition of this sort cannot be adequately disentangled in the course of a single essay, and I will not here embark upon a consideration of the term 'respect,' a retention of the gist of the Greek word *philo* meant to admit the inevasability of an ethical dimension when encountering the words of other persons and when engaged in a pursuit with strong pedagogical implications. Nor will I point out that philology is not this state of respect so much as it is the activity corresponding to such motivation. Nor will I be concerned to explore what shall and what shall not count as textual phenomena. I want to dwell instead on the aspects of these textual objects toward which philological respect is addressed, their *contingent determinacies.*

Only by being caught up in an array of semiotic, discursive, and material codes can any phenomenon participate in spheres of human interaction, and it is the rules and conditions of these codes that determine the textualized nature of an object. Nevertheless, the kinds of codes at work are manifold; they are perhaps infinite, to the extent that questions that can be directed to the object are infinite. Moreover, the codes are often incommensurable. It can never be finally settled which determinacies are the most influential in giving an artifact readable shape and which are negligible – a hierarchy of codes is always suspect, since it too will depend upon a certain set of codes for its legitimacy. It is in this respect that, even as all artifacts of communication are constituted by their *determinacies*, those determinacies are *contingent* and stand in an indeterminate relation to each other.

In Anglo-American traditions, the word 'philology' has usually been associated with the description of textual objects according to their position within recognized linguistic and material practices. Respect is directed toward whatever makes a set of artifacts readable, and philological methods have been elaborated to produce reliable publications such as dictionaries, catalogues, dialect atlases, and codicological surveys. Certain continental traditions allied to developments in hermeneutics have spoken of 'philology' in more radical terms, as a respect for an object's resistance to our categories of interpretation. It was as a philologist that Nietzsche grasped that categorical thinking is always an imposition of the will of the interpreter upon recalcitrant materials, and it is in this sense that Paul de Man championed deconstruction as nothing more than 'the return to philology.'[1] At moments when the field of literary studies became polarized between these two tendencies, apologists for both sides confidently affirmed their deep respect for the particulars of texts and for the parameters of interpretation, even as they fundamentally disagreed about what might constitute a particular (a detail that can be read according to established codes, or a detail that resists those codes?) and what might constitute interpretation (making sense of a text, or diagnosing the contradictions involved in making sense of it?).

Philology as *philo-logos*, love of reason, entails a respect for the categories of human communication, and finds its activity in the careful elaboration of method to raise phenomena to the status of facts. Philology as *philo-logoi*, love of words, entails respect for the facticity of utterances that resists generalizing exegesis, and finds its activity in the disclosure of any method as partial and only provisional. The field is the site of an oscillation between, to use Ricoeur's formulation, a hermeneutics of faith and a hermeneutics of suspicion. A capitulation of one approach to the importunities of the other would impoverish the discipline, and any attempt at a synthesis would threaten to squelch the dynamic tension that keeps the field alive. Philology, according to this definition, is constituted by opposing impulses and thus is inherently *disjunctive*, at least as a discipline made up of several camps. A more openly disjunctive philology would encourage the play of these impulses even within an individual study, as in, for example, a critical edition that at one moment adheres to the rigors of a particular method yet at the next moment puts this method under the sign of a question mark.

Critical editing is that branch of philology engaged in producing models of textual artifacts. Any claim that an edition *represents* a text is grievously overstated, for editions are very selective about what features of texts they attend to, and they do not in fact 're-present' any textual object in its fullness. Rather, an edition *models* some of the determinations of a text. Like any model, it raises one set of features to visibility by excluding others in order to serve a heuristic purpose. Facsimiles privilege visual artifactuality; reconstructive editions privilege a message capable of being transmitted from one material enactment to another; and so on. To ask which of these models *best* accounts for textual phenomena would be like asking a physicist whether light behaves as a wave or a particle or a quantum; the answer is, it depends upon what you want to know.

Disjunctive text-editing would not only present a first-order model of a text in the form of an edition, but would also provide a second-order model of some of the presuppositions entailed in its own editorial activity: by homing in on a crucial decision that takes place in the course of editing, by following through rigorously with not one but a plurality of ways of resolving that decision, and by putting these results into direct juxtaposition with each other. This approach is less of a method than a strategy for negotiating between various editorial methods or between the various implicit criteria often yoked to a particular method. The aim is to make an editorial problem visible, in order to draw out relevant practical, methodological, and theoretical implications. Practically, disjunctive editing asks what actual differences obtain between an edition that pursues resolution *x* and one that pursues resolution *y*? Methodologically, it focuses attention on the disciplinary presuppositions that would permit one of these resolutions to be preferred to the other. Theoretically, it queries the limits of the method itself, by advertising how even the most rigorous solutions are in fact provisional hypotheses.

Modeling different editorial solutions at one and the same time has something in common with the urge, associated now with the great promise of computer-driven multi-media projects, to present a text from as many angles as possible. A disjunctive approach, however, does not aim at exhaustivity. Such restraint derives not only from its scepticism – and an especial scepticism for any dreams of totalized representation –

but also from its aim to enact and to query methods by means of highly pointed and economical strategies. Disjunctive text-editing (which no doubt has much to gain from new information technologies, and which might suggest ways of harnessing those technologies to maximal effect) brings contrasting editorial methods into juxtaposition in order to generate usable models, and also to interrogate those models for the partialities and falsifications they effect.

A disjunctive approach to critical editing is nothing new. The critical apparatus, to take only one example, developed in order to acknowledge that the readings of an edition might in fact have been rendered differently; its subsequent function as a sign of scholarly authority teaches us that successful disjunctive strategies will almost inevitably become calcified into standard methodological steps, no longer thought of as declarations of provisionality, yet still perhaps ensuring a place for sceptical engagement. Parallel-text editions have developed yet another format for placing more than one editorial solution within the range of a single gaze, thereby attending to the 'hermeneutic gap' that opens between two or more versions of a text. Parallel-text editions are not only visibly effective and, at least compared to an exhaustive presentation of all manuscript versions of a text, cost-effective as well; they also possess a disjunctive potential that still remains largely untapped. Most parallel-text editions display different stages of a text (different manuscript versions, different authorial versions, etc.) presented according to a standard set of criteria; dwelling on aporias of method is not usually part of their stated purpose, even if problematic issues seem to be raised implicitly by considering a text through the lens of such a format. I aim to make use of this more radical potential of parallel-text editions in offering three examples of disjunctive text-editing: in the first example, to explore problems of method faced by single-text editions; in the second, problems of stemmatic editing; and in the third, problems of adjudicating between these two dominant editorial approaches.

Single-Text Editing

The paramount decision faced by single-text editing is the selection of one manuscript version of a text over others, privileging that version for the purposes of the edition. In choosing a so-called best-text, what aspects of the literary system is an editor proposing to examine? Will a focus on these aspects aid us, or hinder us, in posing the literary-historical questions we ought to be asking? Why should we try to model a 'best' text, anyway? Single-text editions traditionally have made use of various criteria of selection, not always compatible, such as the age of the manuscript, the dialect, the 'superiority' of aesthetic structure, or the 'superiority' of readings. Each of these criteria is underwritten by specific disciplinary interests. In a case where two manuscripts equally answer the editor's needs, a parallel-text edition of two candidates for a 'best-text' might be appropriate. Our assumptions about literary or historical value might be made more visible if we queried the process of selection even more radically; why not, for example, produce a 'worst-text' edition? A single-text edition of one manuscript version, chosen by the editor on the basis of such criteria as are generally accepted by the field (a 'best-text') might disjunctively face a single-text edition of the same poem, from a manuscript version that most resists those very historical or aesthetic criteria (a 'worst-text'). By these means, a reader might gain some sense of the range of discrepancies that inhere within the textual tradition, as well as some scepticism about invoking standard criteria of value.

As an example of 'worst-text' editing, the *Lai de l'ombre*, which thanks to Bédier's edition of 1913 occupies a prominent place in the history of single-text methodological reflection, might serve our purposes well. All editors of medieval texts know Bédier's negative arguments concerning stemmatic editing, but what are his positive arguments for choosing one particular text over another?

> Si nous avons choisi le manuscrit *A*, le précieux manuscrit 837 de la Bibliothèque nationale, c'est de façon tout empirique, et simplement parce que, offrant d'ailleurs un texte à l'ordinaire très sensé et très cohérent, et des formes grammaticales très françaises (à part quelques 'picardismes'), et une orthographe très simple et très régulière, il est, entre nos sept manuscrits, celui qui présente le moins souvent des leçons individuelles, celui par conséquent qu'on est le moins souvent tenté de corriger.[2]

Aesthetic criteria that were unexceptionable for his generation combine with Bédier's decision to give a text that is central, not peripheral, with respect to the relations among extant manuscripts. By 1928, although his stated criteria had not changed, Bédier came to feel that manuscript *E* (Paris, Bibliothèque nationale, nouv. acq. fr. 1104) was equal or even superior to manuscript *A* (Paris, Bibliothèque nationale, fonds français 837), and so published an edition of it as well. The four editions since have all adopted a single-text method, two preferring *A* as the best text and two preferring *E*. But what about the other manuscripts? What about 'les nombreuse fautes, souvent très grossières, de *D*, les faintaisies individuelles de *F*, les faiblesses évidentes du groupe *CG*'?[3] If centrality with respect to the rest of the tradition is the prime criterion of selection, then manuscript *F* (Paris, Bibliothèque nationale, fonds français 14971) is, as the most idiosyncratic, the 'worst' version. In the passage below, I present parallel single-text editions of a passage of the *Lai de l'ombre* as it appears in *A* and in *F*. The scene is a crucial moment in the human drama of the poem, when the knight takes back his ring from the lady yet sets in motion his plan to toss the ring to her reflection in the well in order to win her love:

***A* = Paris, BN, f. fr. 837**	***F* = Paris, BN, f. fr. 14971**
N'*ert* enviesis ne esfaciez	N'*estoit* enviezis n'esfaciés
Li *sens* del *gentil* chevalier.	L'*aniaux* du *courtois* chevalier.
Toz esprendanz de cuer entier,	*Moult joians* et de cuer entier
Le prist tout porpensseement;	Le prist tout porpenseement;
Si le *regarde* doucement;	*Moult* le *regarda* doucement
Au reprendre dist: 'Granz merciz!	Au reprendre, *et* dist: 'Grant mercis,
Por ce n'est pas li ors noirciz,'	Pour ce n'est pas li ors noircis,'
Fet il, 's'il vient de cel biau doit.'	Fet-il, 's'il vient de ce bel doit.'
Cele *s'en* sozrist, qui cuidoit	Celi sousrit, qui *bien* quidoit
Qu'il le deüst remetre el suen.	Qu'il le deüst remetre el sen.
Mès il *fist ainz* un *mout grant* sen,	Mais il *a fait* un *autre* sen,
Qu'a grant joie li *torna* puis.	*Dont moult* grant joie li *vint* puis.
The *shrewdness* of the *noble* knight	The *ring* of the *courtly* knight
was not worn-out nor faded.	was not worn-out nor faded.
All aflame with his whole heart	*Much gladdened and* with his whole heart
he took it very deliberately;	he took it very deliberately;
he *looks* at it *so* sweetly;	he *looked* at it *very* sweetly
upon receiving it he said, 'Many thanks,	upon receiving it, *and* said: 'Great thanks,
for the gold has not tarnished,'	for the gold has not tarnished,'
he says, 'coming from that beautiful finger.'	he says, 'coming from that beautiful finger.'
She smiled *at that*, believing	She smiled, *well* believing
that he would replace it on his own.	that he would replace it on his own.
But *instead* he did a *very great* ploy	But he did a *different* ploy
which soon *returned him to* great joy.	*from which* great joy soon *came to him.*[4]

Comparison of the two texts reveals numerous differences in stylistic texture, as well as several discrepancies that affect the overall significance of the poem. While in *A* it is the knight's wit that remains uncorrupted, in *F* it is the ring; this difference is recorded even in the titles given to the poem: 'Le lai de l'ombre' in *A*, where the emphasis lies on the knight's clever use of the lady's reflection (*ombre*) in the pool; and 'Du chevalier qui donna l'anel a la dame' in *F*, where emphasis lies on the ring (*anel*) as the emblem of a courtly tryst. Assessments of the knight's new stratagem lie at the heart of critical discussion of this tale, and the *A* and *F* versions differ greatly in their characterization of this ploy, both in their verbal echoes of the word *sen* and in the way that the knight's sudden decision fits into his dialogue with the lady. Although I do not here propose to trace out the implications of these differences, I do want to insist upon the fact that the implications are substantial.

One justification for single-text editing is the recognition that each copyist of a medieval vernacular poem could participate to some degree in the performance of a new version of that work, but we are rarely shown the scope and degree of elaboration to be found within a single tradition. By juxtaposing a version central to the tradition with one peripheral to it, that range of variation can be modeled not exhaustively but tactically. Moreover, the peripheral status of *F* has no necessary bearing on its stemmatic position in the transmission of the poem, and it is in fact quite possible that this manuscript, rather than *A* or *E*, more closely retains the tenor of Jean Renart's original. Although single-text editions proceed on the assumption that notions of authorship are of secondary importance in medieval literary culture, nevertheless the text of the poem that editors choose will be discussed with the name of Jean Renart and with the label 'the *Lai de l'ombre*' attached to it; a disjunctive edition might at least let us know what is at stake in permitting that slippage towards authorship and titling to occur with one manuscript version rather than another. Attention to the 'worst-text' version has the further benefit of transmuting assumptions about literary and historical value into provisional hypotheses: in the case of the *Lai de l'ombre*, for instance, criticism has deployed a tidy contrast between romance conventions and ironic realism, a tension of representational means that plays itself out rather differently in *F* than in *A*. Where might Jean Renart fit in our historical script if the privileging of *A* and *E* is foregone? Single-text editing is inevitably complicit with values that guide the process of manuscript selection, values that will predetermine the questions that will be posed to the text. A disjunctive presentation not only suggests alternative answers to traditional questions; it also asks for a reconsideration of the ground from which literary questions will be posed.

Stemmatic Editing

In stemmatic editing, crucial dilemmas are posed by attempts to resolve the relations among witnesses into a family-tree. The concepts to which editors turn when establishing a stemma (error, *lectio difficilior*, conflation, etc.) are themselves hypotheses about how textual circulation occurred in the Middle Ages, and the applicability of such hypotheses to particular cases is always open to question. The editions generated by stemmata are accordingly provisional, asking what model would be generated if we privilege certain aspects of our text and if we accept certain assumptions about textual dissemination. Instead of holding fast to a single set of assumptions, a disjunctive strategy could produce two editions alongside each other, each generated by a different stemmatic resolution.

The example below shows a disjunctive presentation of a passage from the B-Text of *Piers Plowman*, the text which ever since Kane and Donaldson's edition of 1975 has served as a reference point for much of the discussion about stemmatic methods in medieval textual criticism. A fundamental difficulty for any stemmatic edition of the poem involves the place of manuscripts *R* (London, British Library, MS Lansdowne 398 and Oxford, Bodleian Library, MS Rawlinson Poetry 38) and *F* (Oxford, Corpus Christi College, MS 201), together making up group α. Group α has many lines lacking in β, the other family of witnesses to the B-text, and vice versa. Kane and Donaldson, followed by Schmidt, treat α and β as the two branches of a bifid tradition of the B-text, thereby placing *R* and *F* in positions of great importance for determining readings of the poem. Yet recently Skeat's suggestion that α is not a branch of the B-text, but is itself a separate authorial version of the poem, has regained currency.[5] If α is a distinct version, can it still be used as a valuable witness to the B-text in the sections where they do overlap? What would be the difference between an archetype of the B-text of *Piers Plowman* that includes α and one that does not? The test-passage is XI.4–9.

B-Text with α and β	**B-Text with β alone**
Tho wepte I for wo and wraþe of hir speche	Tho wepte I for wo and wraþe of hir speche
And in a wynkynge wraþe *til I was* aslepe.	And in a wynkynge wraþe *weex I* aslepe.

A merueillous metels *me tydde to dreme,*	A merueillous metels *mette me þanne*
For I was rauysshed riȝt þere – *for* Fortune me fette	*That* I was rauysshed riȝt þere *and* Fortune me fette
And into þe lond of longynge *and loue* she me brouȝte,	And into þe lond of longynge *allone* she me brouȝte,
And in a mirour þat hiȝte Middelerþe she made me to biholde.	And in a mirour þat hiȝte Middelerþe she made me to biholde.[6]

These verses mark the point where the B-text extends beyond the A-text, inaugurating a new design for the whole poem; it presents Will falling into a dream within a dream (thus providing an occasion for meta-narrative reflection about the status of this visionary poem), and it perhaps includes a pun on the name of Langland in the phrase 'land of longing.' Anne Middleton's judgement about the interpretive pressure borne by this passage for structural, allegorical, narrative, and autobiographical dimensions of the poem might be taken as representative: 'The place where Fortune rules is called by his "kynde" name: the Lond of Longyng. This "avanture" into Fortune's realm, occurring at about the midpoint of the poem in its two long versions, proclaims a new beginning, a re-vision of the nature of his project, enabled by yet another act of retrospection.'[7] It matters, for our understanding of the predicament of the first-person narrator and of his poetic project, whether Will finds himself in the 'land of longing and love' or in the 'land of longing alone.' Considerable structural and narrative implications follow from the resolution of the conjunctions of v. 7: in one rendition Will's being 'ravished' may be synonymous with his ecstatic dreaming, whereas in the other Will's ravishment to a different land might instead denote a violent action that Fortune does to him within the world of the dream.

Do these differences exhibit the kind of intervention accorded to copyists of *Piers Plowman*, or do they point to another stage of authorial revision and retrospection? Stemmatic editing of *Piers Plowman* is at pains to distinguish between authorial 'versions' and scribal copies, relying upon a categorical distinction that is not always feasible to maintain in critical practice. Where does first-person self-revising yield to an intersubjective dynamic of creative misreading? Skeat's and Schmidt's parallel-text editions of the poem's several versions make visible their hypotheses about authorial self-revision. Nevertheless, they still adhere to a set of assumptions about what constitutes a separate version of the poem.[8] A disjunctive edition can take the parallel-text format even further in order to render some of those assumptions, and their practical implications, visible as well.

Between Methods

The great methodological rift in medieval textual editing comes along the fault-line that separates single-text and stemmatic editions. The act of deciding whether to follow one or the other method must appeal to various critical principles, and will entail a wide array of concrete implications for the presentation of a text. The format of a parallel-text could easily be adopted for an examination of these principles and these implications, by juxtaposing editions arrived at through opposing methods. Perhaps publications such as Rychner's edition of the *Lai de Lanval*, which juxtaposes a stemmatic edition at the top of the page against four single-text diplomatic editions below, can stand as precedents for such a disjunctive strategy.[9] The rarity of similar examples is no doubt a symptom of the entrenchment that tends to accompany any methodological *prise de position*, so that textual editors often proceed as if proving the usefulness of one method requires insisting upon the inapplicability of another. To work with two methods side by side demands that an editor suspend methodological insistence for the sake of a countervailing sense of provisionality.

One area where stemmatic and single-text approaches have clashed is in Italian philology, where a strongly Lachmannian tradition has at times given way to equally strong assertions about situations where a single-text method would be more appropriate. One genre of anonymous narrative poems, the medieval popular *cantare*, has provided the text-book example of the place for single-text editing ever since De Robertis spoke of his encounter with such texts as the 'experiences of a Lachmannian in non-Lachmannian territory.'

> It is the case of someone who came to textual criticism through a familiarity with Barbi's work of research and reconstruction ... and, through recent contacts, confirmed in his habit of absolute systematicity and rationality of examination and deduction, of rigorous adherence to the norms of 'stemmatics'; yet who at a certain moment found himself grappling with a different sort of tradition, that of the anonymous poems in *ottava rima*: a tradition not so much of a text as of a genre, or of an attitude, built around specific narrative models, and shaped by a process of active collaboration over its entire period.[10]

De Robertis's single-text approach to anonymous *cantari* has become orthodox, but it gives rise to difficulties when considering the *cantari* by the fourteenth-century poet Antonio Pucci, not only because these poems, not being anonymous, invite speculations about authorial originals, but also because Pucci himself was an entertainer in the recitative tradition who aspired to the fixity that might come from textual production and circulation. A single-text edition might model the performative *mouvance* of the *cantari* tradition, while a stemmatic edition might model the author's claim to enfranchisement within a system of textual controls. Both approaches can be responsibly justified. Each one on its own, however, yields a very partial view of the place of these poems in literary history.

A disjunctive approach seems especially called for in this case. In the following example, a stanza from Pucci's *La Reina d'Oriente*, III.16.1–8, is given first in a single-text edition from manuscript *K* (Florence, Biblioteca Nazionale Centrale, MS N.A. 333, a codex accorded exceptional authority for Pucci's poetry because of its antiquity and its status as a compilation of his oeuvre), alongside a stemmatic reconstruction of the archetype based on the eight extant witnesses. These verses describe a moment just after the 'King' of the Orient, who has been obliged to marry the daughter of the emperor of Rome, has told the princess that in fact she too is a young woman who has spent her life cross-dressed as a male.

K = Florence, BNC, N.A. 333	**Stemmatic Edition**
E 'nsieme si prromisser d'osservare	Insieme si promisson d'osservare
verginità mostrandosi contente,	verginità mostrandosi contente,
e *chottal cosa* non manifestare	e *questo fatto* non manifestare
in tuta la lor vita ad uon vivente.	in tutta la lor vita a uomo vivente.
Poi s'abraciaro. *E 'n* poco dimorare	Po' s'abbracciaro *un* poco dimorare.
a quela ciambra ritorno la giente	*Ed* alla zambra ritornò la gente
la qual *danzando era gitta dintorno*	la qual *era ita tutta notte attorno*
siche levarsi ch'era preso *'l* giorno.	sì che levarsi ch'era presso *al* giorno.
And together they promised to maintain	Together they promised to maintain
virginity while appearing satisfied,	virginity while appearing satisfied,
and not to reveal *such a thing*	and not to reveal *this fact*
to any living man for their entire life.	to any living man for their entire life.

Then they embraced. *And in a little while*
the people who had been going around
dancing returned to *that* chamber
to wake them, for it was nearly day.

Then they embraced *lingering a little.*
And the people who had been going around
all night returned to *the* chamber
to wake them, for it was nearly day.[11]

With the representation of the same-sex marriage that begins with this episode, *La Reina d'Oriente* presents a higher degree of explicit female homoeroticism than any other medieval work that I know. But just how explicit is it? The word *dimorare* in verse 5 means 'to dwell' or 'to stay,' sometimes carrying sexual connotations of 'dalliance,' but just as often simply indicating a passage of time ('in a little while'). *K* excludes the connotations of sexual dalliance as much as possible, attaching the act of lingering not to the same-sex couple but to the return of the celebrating wedding guests (by contrast, manuscript *F* makes those connotations unmistakable: 'then they embraced with a little loving,' *un poco d'amore*). The seven witnesses disagree on how to link the word *dimorare* to the preceding clause, perhaps because of some ambiguity (purposeful or accidental) in the archetype.

In this example, each edition brings with it its own mechanisms for delimiting, and so limiting, the meanings generated by the poem. The single-text edition of *K* respects the degree of intervention accorded to copyists in the *cantari* tradition, but that respect entails following the readings of the chosen manuscript even when they seem to close down interesting play with verbal and gender categories. The stemmatic edition puts the editor in the position of choosing among a variety of readings (or perhaps of suggesting an emendation) to construct a text that fits the editor's own aims – in my case here, the preservation of ambiguity both as a possible source of variant readings and as a possible poetic maneuver. Not only are the two results incompatible, but also the way of arriving at those results, and the criteria to which the editor appeals in justification of a reading, are of completely different kinds. One of the virtues of parallel-text editing, especially in its more radicalized potential, is its capacity to disclose the practical effects of a methodological choice while also charting the extent of collaborative scribal intervention to be met with in a complex tradition. Insofar as it draws attention to the different criteria that lie behind the preference for one edition over another – the privileging of an individual witness or the premise of textual recoverability – and insofar as it holds these two methodological resolutions next to each other in suspension, the provisional and partial nature of both becomes visible.

The Rhetoric of Disjunction

To my mind, a disjunctive approach to textual editing encourages at least three stages of reading that standard editions tend to avoid. First, it allows us to measure the practical differences that result from editorial choices. Second, it places the reader at the point where a decision between methods might be made, thus condoning a full scrutiny of the criteria that such a choice must bring in to play. Third, it calls to our attention the provisional status of our editions – that is, their function as hypothetical and heuristic models. Philology's dynamic movement between first following through with a method and then questioning the validity of that method will, in most cases, be effectively visible when the disjunction is between two rival answers to a single methodological problem. As those problems are manifold, so too are the forms a disjunctive approach might take. Complex combinations of juxtapositions would be especially useful as pedagogical tools. The effect of a disjunctive philology, however, has less to do with the range of its data-field and the multiplicity of its dimensions than with its means of rhetorical presentation, which include its *mise-en-page.*

Critical editions have traditionally deployed the rhetorical and visual means at their disposal (page layout, apparatus, introductions, etc.) in order to grant the reader a role in thinking about the process of editing. A disjunctive edition is one way to further this dialogic potential, where the reader is actually engaged in the constitution of the textual model, indeed engaged in evaluating the very parameters upon which an edition is to be based. When two different editorial *products* are contrasted, the editorial *process* stands more revealed – the edition is in fact still in process, insofar as it is still suspended at a moment of choice. The three short examples given above are not unlike the kind of heuristic exercises encountered in programs of philological instruction and training. One objective of a disjunctive philology would be the exportation of that heuristic and process-oriented attitude out of the seminar room and into the delivery of published editions. Publishing resources and expectations are often so circumscribed, however, that in many cases a disjunctive parallel-text edition of an entire work will remain impracticable; disjunctive editors may have to hit upon other strategies for revealing how editions would appear differently if opposing criteria were put into play. Nevertheless, compared to a strategy of exhaustivity, disjunctive editing has the advantages of conceptual focus, feasability of format, and economy of cost.

In thinking about the potential of a disjunctive philology, we can find compelling analogies in the theory of reading conceptualized by Charles Bernstein in support of a 'disjunctive poetics':

> The text formally involves the process of response / interpretation and in so doing makes the reader aware of herself or himself as producer as well as consumer of meaning. It calls the reader to action, questioning, self-examination: to a reconsideration and a remaking of the habits, automatisms, conventions, beliefs through which, and only through which, we see the world. It insists that there is, in any case, no seeing without interpretation and chooses to incorporate this interpretive process actively by bringing it into view rather than to exploit it passively by deleting its tracks.[12]

Disjunctive philology involves not only a respect for the contingent determinacies of textual phenomena; it also entails respect for the contingent determinacies of its own methods and models. An edition partakes in a complex array of discursive practices – scholarly, pedagogical, publicistic, institutional – so that its own significance is not entirely known even by the editor producing it. It is in no way antithetical to the rigors of academic research to welcome the participation of readers, whether colleagues, undergraduates, or a general public, in their role not simply as *consumers* but also as *producers* of meaning, as the real 'witnesses' that constitute an edition. The only catch is continually to renew the strategies of delivery so that the inherently disjunctive and dialogic nature of philology enables hypothetical models to emerge while keeping their coercive authority at bay.

NOTES

1 Paul de Man, 'The Return to Philology,' in *The Resistance to Theory* (Minneapolis: University of Minnesota Press, 1986), pp. 21–6.

2 Jean Renart, *Le lai d l'ombre*, ed. Joseph Bédier (Paris: Firmin-Didot, 1913), p. xlii.

3 Jean Renart, *Le lai de l'ombre*, ed. Félix Lecoy (Paris: Champion, 1979), p. 31.

4 The text of *A* is taken from vv. 867–77 of Bédier's 1913 edition, pp. 43–4;

that of *F* from Achille Jubinal, *Lettres a M. le comte de Salvany sur quelques-uns des manuscrits de la Bibliothèque de la Haye* (Paris: Didrion, 1846), p. 174; I have altered the punctuation of both. The translations are my own.

5 See Ralph Hanna III, 'On the Versions of *Piers Plowman*,' in *Pursuing History: Middle English Manuscripts and Their Texts* (Stanford: Stanford University Press, 1996), pp. 203–43; Sean Taylor, 'The Lost Revision of *Piers Plowman B*,' *Yearbook of Langland Studies* 11 (1997): 97–134.

6 Both passages follow the editions of Kane and Donaldson and of Schmidt, in taking manuscript *W* as a base for orthographic features. The rendition that includes α and β is substantively identical to Schmidt's, except for v. 6, where I prefer α's 'me tydde to dreme' to β's 'mette me þanne.' Cf. William Langland, *The Vision of Piers Plowman: A Critical Edition of the B-Text Based on Trinity College Cambridge MS B.15.17*, ed. A.V.C. Schmidt, 2nd ed. (London: Dent, 1995), pp. 166 and 384; and *Piers Plowman: The B-Version*, ed. George Kane and E. Talbot Donaldson (London: Athlone Press, 1975), p. 437.

7 Anne Middleton, 'William Langland's "Kynde Name": Authorial Signature and Social Identity in Late Fourteenth-Century England,' in *Literary Practice and Social Change in Britain, 1380–1530*, ed. Lee Patterson (Berkeley: University of California Press, 1990), p. 47.

8 In fact, the presence of the Z-text in Schmidt's parallel edition brings with it questions about how we distinguish between a manuscript copy and an authorial version; William Langland, *Piers Plowman: A Parallel-Text Edition of the A, B, C and Z Versions*, ed. A.V.C. Schmidt (London: Longman, 1995). The truly radical implication of the Z-text, to my mind, is that any manuscript of *Piers Plowman* could, on good grounds, be promoted to the status of a separate 'version' of the poem.

9 Marie de France, *Le lai de Lanval: Texte critique et édition diplomatique des quatre manuscrits français*, ed. Jean Rychner (Geneva: Droz, 1958).

10 Domenico De Robertis, 'Problemi di metodo nell'edizione dei cantari,' in *Studi e problemi di critica testuale: Atti del Convegno di Studi di Filologia Italiana nel centenario della Commissione per i Testi di Lingua (7–9 aprile 1960)* (Bologna: Commissione per i Testi di Lingua, 1961), pp. 119–20.

11 Antonio Pucci, *La Reina d'Oriente* III.16.1–8. The transcription from *K* and the stemmatic construction are my own; I am preparing a disjunctive edition of the entire poem. The uncritical eclectic text in Ezio Levi, ed., *Fiore di leggende: Cantari antichi* (Bari: Laterza, 1914), pp. 229–84, is unreliable.

12 Charles Bernstein, 'Writing and Method,' in *In the American Tree*, ed. Ron Silliman (Orono, Maine: National Poetry Foundation, 1986), p. 595.

8

Digitizing (Nearly) Unreadable Fragments of Cyprian's *Epistolary*

WILLIAM SCHIPPER

Unreadable or difficult-to-decipher manuscripts can be both challenging and fascinating. Sometimes they are dismissed out of hand. For example, the very beginning of Cambridge, Corpus Christi College, MS 178 (containing homilies by Ælfric and a bilingual copy of the *Rule* of St Benedict) has had several supply leaves added for a table of contents. On the back of one of these is the remains of what appears to be a word list in the hand of the Worcester Tremulous Glossator that had long been ignored as unreadable because nearly all the words on the page had been crossed out. Closer examination, using enlargements as well some ingenuity and determination, revealed that the list was the remains of a worksheet that had been used by the Tremulous Glossator to compile a bilingual glossary.[1] Often it is the very appearance of unreadability, or being declared so in print, that poses a challenge. Manuscripts can end up in this condition through any number of circumstances: fire, as in the case of some of the Cotton manuscripts in the British Library; neglect; deliberate mutilation; officially sanctioned mutilation with reagents to recover readings that had been obscured by dirt, time, or neglect; and palimpsests, in which older manuscripts, deemed more useful for their parchment than their contents, were scraped clean of their text and reused. These last often contain the oldest extant copies of classical and early Christian texts. In all cases the manuscripts are notoriously difficult to read, despite efforts of generations of students to decipher their contents.

Sometimes the survival of a problematic manuscript is the result of felicitous serendipity. Such is the case of London, British Library MS

Additional 40165A, five partial folios now bound in with two leaves containing a small part of the Old English Martyrology (Add 40165B).[2] This manuscript is a late fourth-century fragment, from a single gathering, of the epistolary of St Cyprian of Carthage, of which only portions of letters 55, 69, and 74 now remain.[3] It was written in an elegant uncial script in a north African centre, perhaps even Carthage itself, in a square format of four columns with thirty-three lines per page.[4] By the eighth century the manuscript was in England: on folio 2v (in column 3, line 8) an inelegant early hand has added an insular 'vr' over top of an uncial 'UR' at the end of INPONITUR (see Figure 8.1). Also, on folio 2v (column 1, line 1) there is an insular N above the second T in BAPTIZET (see Figure 3.1) added in the same hand, judging from the colour of ink. This addition seems to be an attempt to ensure that users of the manuscript would correctly read the word as the plural (baptizent) rather than the singular (baptizet).[5] This fragment may well be from one of the many books brought to England by Theodore of Tarsus and Hadrian when Theodore became Archbishop of Canterbury in 669, since Hadrian, with whom Theodore founded a school at Canterbury (as the Venerable Bede reports) had originally come from North Africa and had spent a number of years in a monastery in Naples. Hadrian may even have brought the book with him from Africa to Naples, and thence to Canterbury, although this cannot now be substantiated.[6] We do know that within fifty years Bede was quoting from Cyprian's letters, from which we may conclude that the collection was known in Northumbria by the early eighth century.

In the late eleventh century this particular gathering was removed from the manuscript itself, perhaps for doctrinal reasons, as Maurice Bévenot argued convincingly some years ago.[7] If Bévenot is right, that dismemberment became the means of survival for the fragment, since the rest of the book has disappeared without a trace. For the next 800 years or so it remained part of the binding of a theological miscellany. Folio 3 recto of the fragment contains a twelfth-century table of contents written over a space created when the original text was scraped away. The original manuscript must have been spectacular in appearance. The folio where the new table of contents is now located still displays one of the Biblical citations, all of which were originally in red (see Figure 8.2, column 3). The manuscript originally had four columns of text per page, with an additional eight or nine lines of text, which have now disappeared, at the foot of each column. It also had large margins at top, bottom, and sides (see Figure 8.1; the bottom margins are no longer present). When the book was lying open eight columns of text would thus be displayed at one time. The original volume, with the Biblical quotations highlighted in red, must have been an impressive sight.[8] Clearly this was a carefully made, deluxe copy of Cyprian's letters.

Nine centuries spent as part of a binding have left an indelible mark on this fragment. The upper portions of most of the surviving columns are generally readable, albeit faded. Frequently the ink has flaked away, leaving only the outlines of letters, thus making the text difficult to read even where no other damage has been done. The bottom halves of the columns on folios 1 and 2 (see Figure 8.1 and the enlargement in Figure 8.3) show how daunting the task can be: chemical reactions with the glues used for the medieval binding have eaten away not only the ink, but even the parchment itself, leaving only vague indications of letters that must have been there once upon a time. The deplorable condition of these parts of the fragment led Diercks, the editor of the recent Corpus Christianorum edition of Cyprian's letters, to declare the last ten lines of folio 2v, column 2, for example, to be 'illisible.'[9] Figure 8.3, of folio 2, shows how impossible it seems at first to read what remains on this page; the photograph for that plate, moreover, taken with a highly sophisticated and expensive digital camera, shows far more than can be seen looking at the manuscript itself under optimal lighting conditions.[10] Yet the fact that this fragment is both the oldest surviving Latin manuscript fragment in the British Library and the earliest extant copy of Cyprian's letters makes it particularly desirable to recover the full extent of the text that has survived the ravages of time and chemical damage.

Recent advances in digital photography and in photo imaging and editing software have made it both affordable and relatively easy to attempt to recover readings in such manuscripts, even when at first glance it seems simply impossible.[11] The basis for the attempt discussed here was a series of thirty digital photographs taken at the British Library at the end of March, 2000 with a Kontron camera:[12] ten overviews, ten closeups of the rectos and versos of the surviving pages, and ten closeups under ultraviolet light. For the ultraviolet photography the manuscript was exposed to ultraviolet light for only fifteen seconds. With off-the-shelf software it is possible to use these images to make all but the most recalcitrant readings visible. The best software – and the present industry standard – is Adobe Photoshop (now in version 7).[13]

This kind of software allows one to modify original digital images in a number of ways. Some of these modifications, if done with standard photography, would involve retaking photographs with a variety of lenses and exposures under various forms of lighting, and possibly trying various tricks in the dark room. But such manipulation has limitations, not the least of which is cost. Photo manipulation with software, on the other hand, requires only one image. The simplest tool is the 'fill tool'; once an area that is bounded by very similar colours has been outlined, this tool floods most of the selected area with a chosen colour. Figure 8.4 shows a series of results using part of a word from folio 2, column 2, line 1. The outline of 'RE' in HERE (the beginning of HERETICOS) was selected on the basis of similarity of colour, using a 'magic wand' that joins pixels of similar colours. Figure 8.4 shows an enlarged version of the original, which clearly reveals the outline of the letters where the original ink has flaked away. First the R and E are filled. Because software normally does not fill a selected area uniformly, the end result can look remarkably like ink on parchment. Some care is required. When letters are close enough to touch, for example, successive small areas must be selected to prevent what looks like blotting. The airbrush tool can be used to separate the letters by adding more of the general background colour between H and E, and between E and R, after which small areas can be filled one at a time, with pleasing results. Although the process is time-consuming, it is possible to subject images of an entire manuscript to this kind of manipulation, so as to produce a reconstruction of what the manuscript might have looked like fresh from the scribe's pen (see Figure 8.10). One significant advantage of using photo imaging software, however, is to clarify what appears to be invisible, which is a step beyond the simple digital restoration of what can still be read with some slight effort.

It is, of course, well known that ultraviolet light can reveal details in a manuscript that ordinary light can not. It is equally well known that long exposure to ultraviolet light is not healthy for a manuscript, and that this is especially true for very early fragile pieces such as the Cyprian fragment. With the help of image editing software, however, a manuscript need not be exposed to ultraviolet light for more than a few seconds. Figure 8.3, which shows the lower half of folio 2, as already noted, demonstrates how little can be seen under normal light, even in an enlarged portion: only a few letters – ESSET, for example, or the occasional N – can be read with confidence. Even when seen in the reading room, the lower portion of the manuscript is unreadable (or 'illisible,' as Diercks says). Conventional black and white photography can sometimes help a reader to see more in a manuscript; digital photographs take this

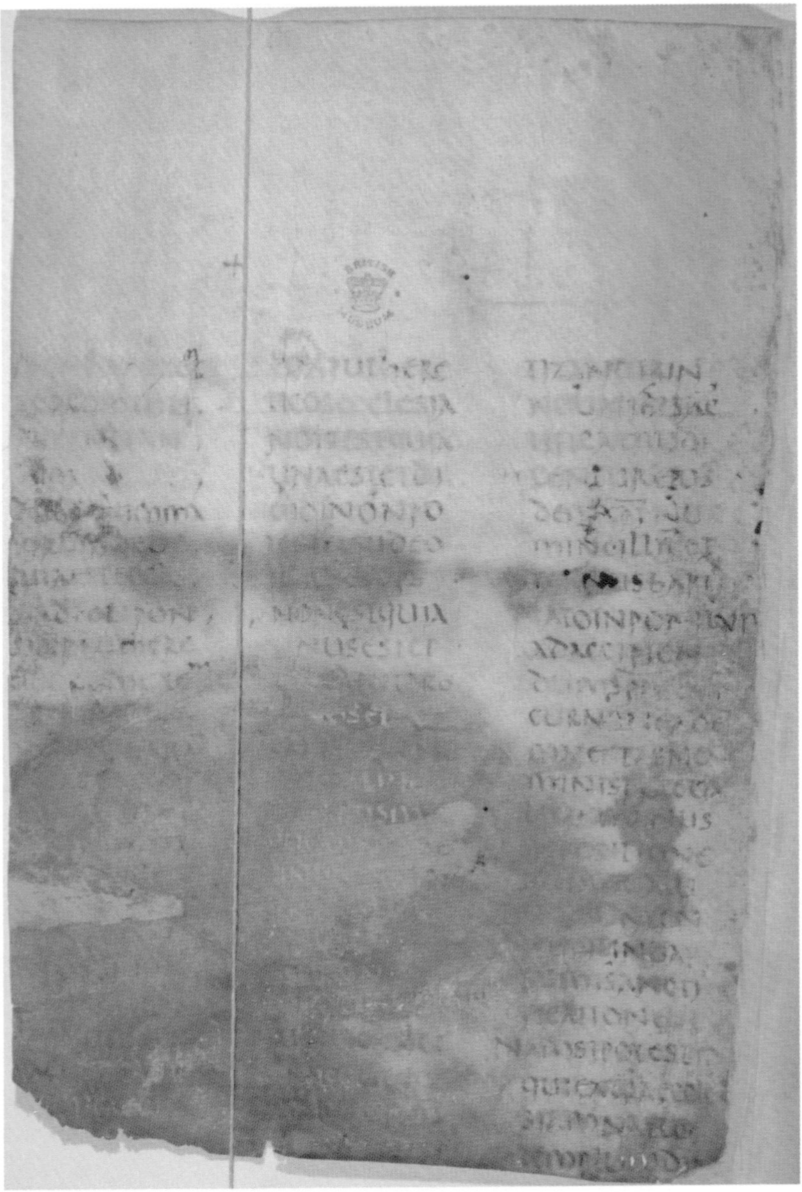

Figure 8.1 British Library, MS Additional 40165A, folio 2v (with permission of the British Library Board).

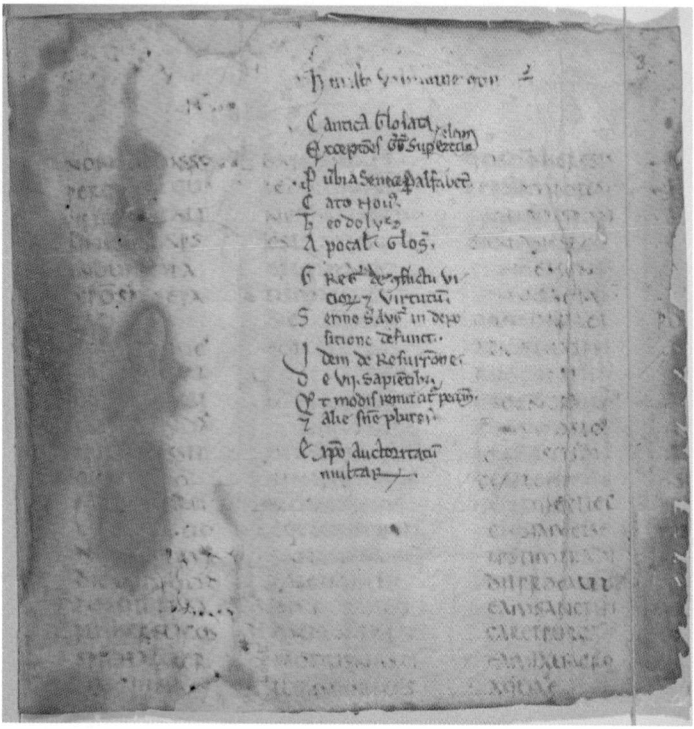

Figure 8.2 British Library, MS Additional 40165A, folio 3r (with permission of the British Library Board).

Figure 8.4 'HERE' (from 'HERETICOS') in various stages of being filled, British Library, MS Additional 40165A, folio 2v, column 2, line 1 (Ep.74.4 = Diercks, p. 569, line 81) (with permission of the British Library Board).

Figure 8.3 British Library, MS Additional 40165A, folio 2v, column 2, lower half, enlarged (with permission of the British Library Board).

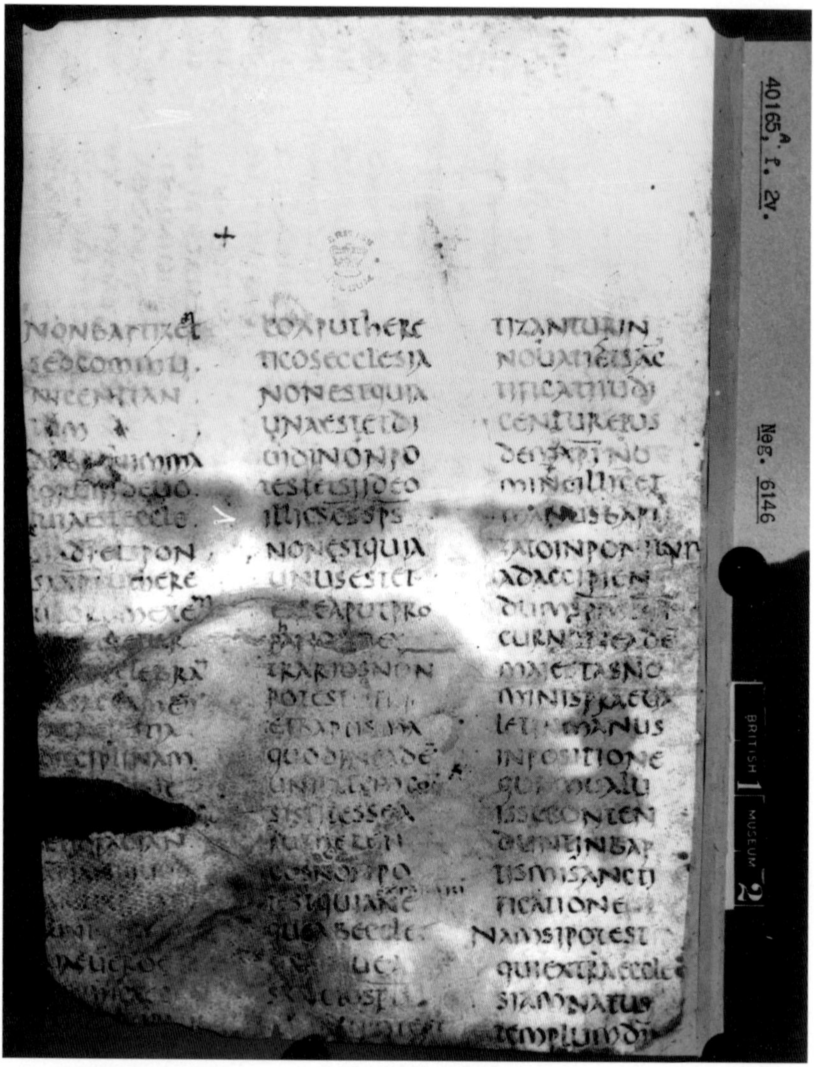

Figure 8.5 British Library, MS Additional 40165A, folio 2v, black and white photography (with permission of the British Library Board).

Figure 8.6 British Library, MS Additional 40165A, folio 2v, column 2, lower half, ultraviolet (with permission of the British Library Board).

Figure 8.7 British Library, MS Additional 40165A, folio 2v, column 2, lower half, ultraviolet image in greyscale (with permission of the British Library Board).

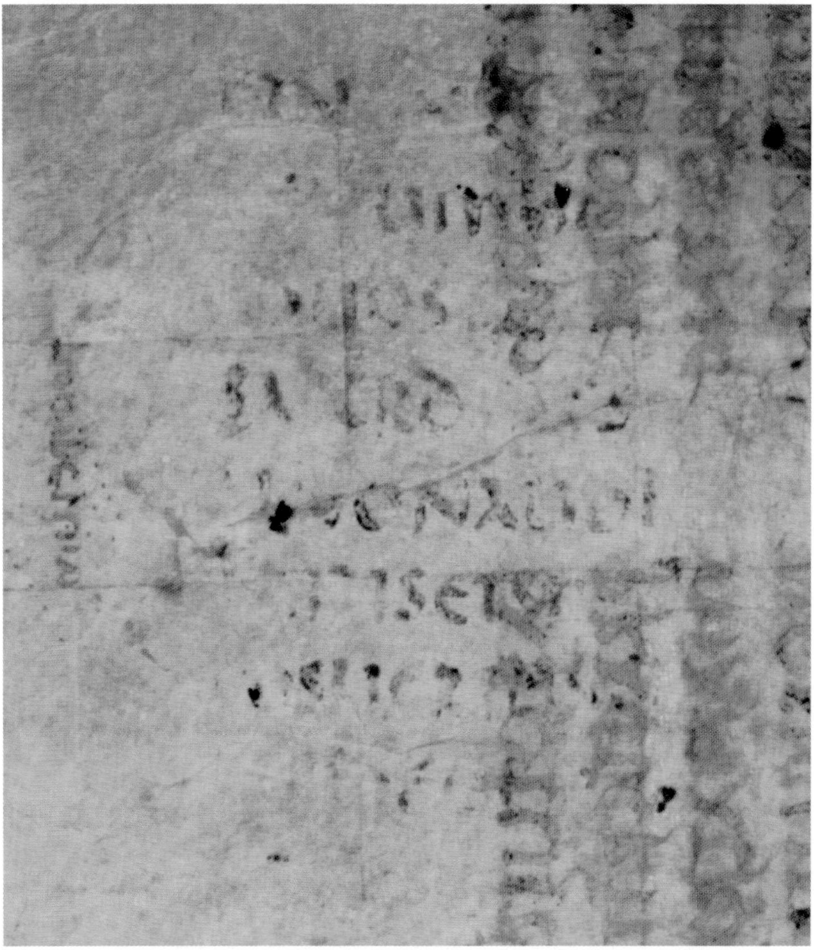

Figure 8.8 British Library, MS Additional 40165A, folio 2r, top (mirror image), showing offset from folio 3v (Diercks, p. 573, lines 146–9) (with permission of the British Library Board).

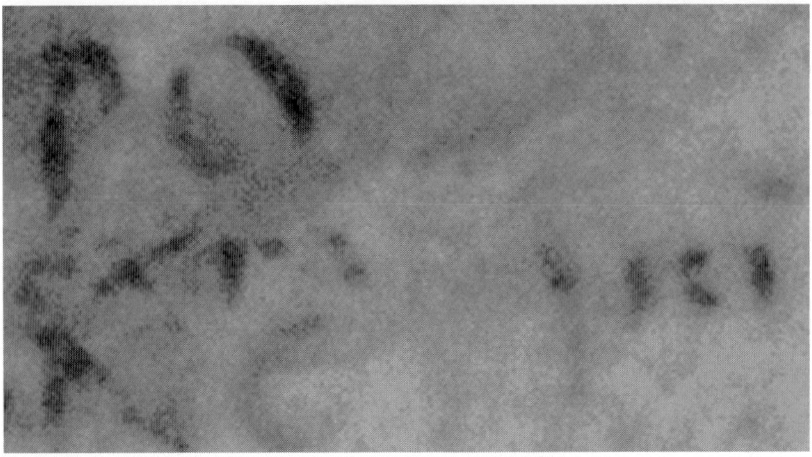

Figure 8.9 British Library, MS Additional 40165A, folio 2v, column 2, detail showing scribal insertion (with permission of the British Library Board).

Figure 8.10 British Library, MS Additional 40165A, folio 2v, column 2, enhanced, background lightened, letters touched up (Ep.74.4 = Diercks, p. 569, lines 81–2) (with permission of the British Library Board).

process of enhancement several steps further. During the process of making digital photographs, it is possible to enhance contrast; while the black and white image is not completely 'illisible,' a digital image taken under ultraviolet light is definitely more readable than one taken under normal lighting conditions – and the digital photographs can be enhanced in ways that are not readily available with older methods of photography. It is, of course, possible to use enhancements with older photography. Figure 8.5, for example, an older black and white image of folio 2v, taken under special lighting conditions, does indeed provide a readable copy of the text on the lower half of the page, including a clear interlinear scribal correction (on which more below). It is, however, likely that this photograph was taken for purposes other than textual studies, and has not received wide circulation; as others have also noted, the page is not 'lisible' under normal lighting conditions in the British Library Manuscript Reading Room.

The difference becomes especially striking when the two images are placed side by side and in close up.[14] Sharpening the contrasts in the ultraviolet version of this image makes the ghostly words quite clear. Contrasts in digital images can be further modified in a number of ways. Since all colours are produced from the three primary colours – red, blue and yellow – one of these colours can be enhanced. For example, using a higher saturation level of red produces an image that may be difficult to look at for long, but does make the text clearer in some instances. We can also lighten the background by systematically changing each shade of the background colour to a lighter one, by changing individual shades of the letters to a darker shade, or by a combination of the two methods. Images can, moreover, be reversed with ease. The top of folio 2r shows what appears to be writing in red ink, running at right angles to the main text on the page (see Figure 8.8). Rotating this image and reversing it to show a mirror image makes the mysterious writing readable. The text (from Malachi 2.1–2) turns out to be identical with the citation from Malachi on folio 3v of the same manuscript,[15] and demonstrates graphically that folio 3v must have been placed against folio 2r at right angles. Constant contact for 800 years, coupled with the chemical effects of the glue used to hold the two sheets together, caused the red ink (and some of the black) to leave an offset in mirror image at the top of folio 2r.

The most striking effects of using image enhancing software, however, come from a closer examination of scribal corrections. Between lines 10 and 11 in Figures 8.6 and 8.7 there is clearly something visible, though at first it is somewhat elusive. The editors of the New Palaeographical Society Publications in 1928 saw the word 'separari,' guided by knowing what was supposed to be there: in the majority of manuscripts 'separari' occurs after 'quia.'[16] The 'p,' the first 'a,' and the final 'ri' are reasonably clear. But the first two letters are clearly not 'se.' A closer look at the grey scale version of the ultraviolet image suggests that these first two letters are 'e' and 'x.' Certainly the third letter is a 'p,' the back of the fourth letter ('a') is clearly visible, and there is even a ghostly 'r' in fifth letter position (see Figure 8.9). It is possible to manipulate the digital image further to make the text even clearer: a copy of the second 'r' can be moved into the position of the first one, and the letters touched up to seem clearer. The result confirms that what the scribe inserted here was not 'separari' but 'exparari'; this is further confirmed by comparing the reading with what can be seen in the black and white photograph mentioned above (Figure 8.5). 'Exparari,' however, is not recorded anywhere in the surviving corpus of Latin writings: neither Lewis and Short, nor Souter, nor Ducange lists such a word.[17] Nor does a search of CETEDOC or the Patrologia Latina on CD-ROM yield an example of 'exparari.'[18] Instead, the word seems to be a *hapax legomenon* that occurs only as a scribal correction in this particular copy of Cyprian.[19] It is not difficult to imagine a scribe coming up with a word to mean 'be removed from' if we assume that he no longer had his archetype available, but could see from the context that something like that was required. Since 'ex' can mean 'out of,' he might easily have started writing *ex-* then completed the word with the last part of 'separari.' 'Ex' might thus have imperfectly reminded him of the word he had omitted.

A lot more can be done with photo software to make readings clearer. Not only can letters be enhanced (as I have demonstrated above with the first four letters of HERETICOS); this technique of selecting an area bounded by similar colours and then filling the area with a uniform colour can also be applied to the areas surrounding letters, with dramatic results. To produce the image in Figure 8.10, for example, required some experimentation. It probably doesn't look much like the original manuscript, but the readings are clear. Another technique that may yield useful results is 'horizontal density slicing,' in which pixels are removed selectively over a specified area. For example, we can 'remove' the twelfth-century table of contents, and attempt to recover what was underneath. Of course the camera lens cannot look underneath layers of ink, so that much of what has been scraped off to make space for the table of contents must be reconstructed. It is also possible to change individual colours from one shade to another, and thereby lighten the background or intensify the letters, but this is a very slow process. Even grey-scaled images contain 255 unique shades ranging from white to black, and colour images have millions of possible combinations of red, blue, and green, making such manipulation prohibitively time consuming.

Anyone who has ever looked at a manuscript through a microscope knows that we are looking, not at a two-dimensional object, but at a three-dimensional one. Geologists regularly use stereoscopic photographs to achieve a kind of three-dimensional effect for examining landscapes. Stereoscopic photography may thus offer another avenue to explore in the study of manuscripts. In this process two images are taken from slightly different angles and then merged to form a single stereoscopic image. Although this entails considerable expense, the technology has been developed in three-dimensional mapping of geological features.[20] Libraries that own manuscripts that might most benefit from this kind of technology are understandably reluctant to allow whole-scale photography of this kind. Even the British Library, which has undertaken a massive digitization project (of which the *Electronic Beowulf* is one small part), is at present not allowing digital photography except under special conditions, in part because of potential copyright difficulties.[21] There is, moreover, a persistent rumour that once a manuscript has been digitized no one will be allowed to see it in person again. That this already seems to be the case with manuscripts such as the Très Riches Heures de Duc de Berri,[22] or virtually the case with the Lindisfarne Gospels or the Book of Kells, does not mean that in-person access to manuscripts must become a thing of the past, just because the past decade has witnessed advances in photographic and digital technology beyond our wildest dreams. But the refinement of the technology does mean that we can examine even our least readable manuscripts in ways that ten years ago would have been inconceivable, and that we can, moreover, uncover words we did not know existed, and make the 'illisible' 'lisible.'

NOTES

1 N.R. Ker, *Catalogue of Manuscripts Containing Anglo-Saxon* (Oxford: Clarendon Press, 1959), no. 41, pp. 60–4. Ker notes that the thirteenth-century table of contents is written on a leaf probably taken from the last quire of Part B of the manuscript (containing a bilingual copy of the Benedictine

Rule), but makes no mention of the list. See William Schipper, 'A Worksheet of the Worcester 'Tremulous' Glossator,' *Anglia* 105 (1987): 1–17, for a full discusion and edition of the list. On the work of the glossator himself, Christine Franzen's *The Tremulous Hand of Worcester: A Study of Old English in the Thirteenth Century* (Oxford: Clarendon Press, 1991) is indispensable.

2 Nineteenth-century description, with three plates, in New Palaeographical Society, *Facsimiles of Ancient Manuscripts, Second Series* (London: Oxford University Press, 1913–30), 2: plate 101. See also E.A. Lowe, ed. *Codices Latini Antiquiores*, vol. 2: *Great Britain and Ireland*, 2nd ed., with Virginia Brown (Oxford: Clarendon Press, 1972), no. 178.

3 G.F. Diercks, ed. *Sancti Cypriani Episcopi Epistularium* (*Sancti Cypriani Episcopi Opera*, Pars III,1), Corpus Christianorum, Series Latina, 3B–3D (Turnhout: Brepols, 1994–9): Ep. 55, pp. 256–95; Ep. 69, pp. 469–96; Ep. 74, pp. 563–80.

4 On the date see E.A. Lowe, 'More Facts about our Oldest Latin Manuscripts,' *Classical Quarterly* 22 (1928): 43–62 at pp. 48–9 (no. 92); reprint in E.A. Lowe, *Palaeographical Papers*, ed. Ludwig Bieler (Oxford: Clarendon Press, 1972), pp. 251–74 at pp. 258–9.

5 See William Schipper, 'Speaking from the Margins,' in *Reading on the Edge: Space, Text, and Margins in Medieval Manuscripts*, ed. Rolf Bremmer, Sarah L. Keefer, and W. Schipper (Groningen: Egbert Forsten; forthcoming 2004), for further discussion.

6 On Hadrian see Michael Lapidge and Bernard Bischoff, eds, *Biblical Commentaries from the Canterbury School of Theodore and Hadrian*, Cambridge Studies in Anglo-Saxon England 10 (Cambridge: Cambridge University Press, 1994), pp. 82–132. On Theodore, see ibid. pp. 5–81; see also M. Lapidge, 'The Career of Archbishop Theodore,' in *Archbishop Theodore: Commemorative Studies on his Life and Influence*, ed. Michael Lapidge, Cambridge Studies in Anglo-Saxon England 11 (Cambridge: Cambridge University Press, 1995), pp. 1–29. On book importation into England, see David Dumville, 'The Importation of Mediterranean Manuscripts into Theodore's England,' in *Archbishop Theodore*, pp. 96–119.

7 See Maurice Bévenot, 'The Oldest Surviving Manuscript of St Cyprian now in the British Library,' *Journal of Theological Studies* 31 (1980): 368–77.

8 Lowe, 'More Facts,' estimates each page to have measured about 330 × 225 mm (12 × 10 in.). When open it would have presented an area about 330 × 450 mm (12 × 20 in.), in some respects resembling a roll rather than a codex.

9 Diercks, *Sancti Cypriani Episcopi Epistularium*, pp.772 and 773.

10 I am deeply grateful to the staff of the Department of Manuscripts at the British Library for allowing extended access to MS Add 40165A, and to

David French, one of the conservators in the Library, for taking the detailed digital photographs used in this study.

11 For two early studies on the possibilities that digital photography may hold for deciphering erased or palimpsest texts, see John F. Benton, 'Nouvelles recherches sur le déchiffrement des textes effacés, grattés ou lavés,' *Académie des Inscriptions et Belles-Lettres: Comptes-rendus des séances de l'année 1978* (Paris: l'Académie des Inscriptions et Belles-Lettres, 1978–9), pp. 580–94; and John F. Benton, Alan Gillespie, and James Soha, 'Digital Image-Processing Applied to the Photography of Manuscripts, with Examples Drawn from the Pincus MS of Arnald of Villanova,' *Scriptorium* 3 (1979): 40–55, with plates 9–13.

12 The Kontron camera is an improved version of the one used by the British Library project that produced photographs for Kevin Kiernan and Andrew Prescott, eds, *The Electronic Beowulf*, 2nd ed. (London: The British Library, 2000).

13 Most of the modifications made for the original presentation, including not only enhancements, but also cropping details, enlarging, and so on, were made with Paint Shop Pro, a program that can be downloaded as shareware. Though not as robust as Photoshop, it has many of the same features and is much less expensive. The enhancements and modifications of the plates included in this version were made with Photoshop. There is other software available, some of it not too expensive.

14 I began the original public presentation of this paper by showing a mysterious looking image of a 'ghostly quod' on a brown field. This 'ghostly quod' occurs in the first line of Figure 8.3.

15 See Diercks, *Sancti Cypriani Episcopi Epistularium*, p. 573.

16 Diercks, *Sancti Cypriani Episcopi Epistularium*, p. 569, and the variant readings listed there. Diercks concludes that 'separari' 'fait défaut dans *el* où on lit: *a sancto spiritu diuidi potest*' [Diercks's MS *e* is London, British Library, MS Royal 6 B.xv; his MS *l* is London, Lambeth Palace, MS 106]. Some manuscripts omit part of the clause in which 'separari' normally occurs (that is, 'separari neque ab ecclesia' is omitted from 'quia separari neque ab ecclesia neque a sancto spiritu potest'), but that omission is the result of a scribe skipping to the second 'neque.' The omission of 'separari' is found only in a group of manuscripts from England, all of which are probably descended from the fragment under discussion. The editors of the New Palaeographical Society facsimile would have had Wilhelm Hartel's edition (*Sancti Thasci Caecili Cypriani Opera Omnia*, Corpus Scriptorum Ecclesiasticorum Latinorum 3 [Vienna: F. Tempsky, 1868–71]) at their disposal to guide them in their transcriptions.

17 See Charlton Lewis and Charles Short, *A Latin Dictionary* (Oxford: Clarendon Press, 1879; reprint 1969); Alexander Souter, ed., *A Glossary of Later Latin to 600 A.D.* (Oxford: Clarendon Press, 1949; reprint 1959); and Charles Dufresne, Sieur du Cange, *Glossarium ad scriptores mediae et infimae Latinitatis* (Paris: Charles Osmont, 1733–9).

18 Paul Tombeur, ed., *Library of Latin Texts, CLC-5* (Turnhout: Brepols, 2003).

19 It is surprising that no one has commented on this particular *hapax legomenon* in this context before, given how clear this photograph is, but this lack of comment may simply be the result of the photograph not having circulated widely, if at all.

20 I am grateful for some friendly advice on this topic from Andrew Hynes, Department of Geography, McGill University.

21 The effects of digital photography on the condition of manuscripts are not yet entirely clear. Most libraries are also concerned about copyright issues associated with digital images, and hence permit digital photography only under carefully controlled circumstances, usually for publication on CD-ROM. The British Library agreed to take digital photographs of the Cyprian manuscript needed for this study only because they were unable to find images that had been made in 1998.

22 Michael Camille, 'The Très Riches Heures: An Illuminated Manuscript in the Age of Mechanical Reproduction,' *Critical Inquiry* 17 (1990): 72–107.

9

Unbinding Lydgate's *Lives of Ss. Edmund and Fremund*

STEPHEN R. REIMER

I am engaged in an editing project that could be described as an attempt at a 'book unbound.' I am preparing a new edition of a fifteenth-century hagiographical poem, *The Lives of Ss. Edmund and Fremund* (*Index of Middle English Verse* [IMEV] no. 3440), by John Lydgate, monk of the abbey of Bury St. Edmunds in East Anglia. This is one of the only Lydgate texts that is not available in an Early English Text Society (EETS) or any other published modern edition, and it is a significant text both for its importance to Lydgate studies (through it Lydgate gained something of a reputation as a hagiographer, and obtained commissions for further hagiographical works – notably the *Lives of Ss. Alban and Amphibal* – because of its success) and for its historical and political importance, about which more will be said below.[1]

Figure 9.1 shows a page of the oldest manuscript of the work and a page of the 'editio princeps' of the poem prepared by Carl Horstmann and published in 1881.[2] The manuscript page includes one stanza of the poem. The bulk of the work is written in Chaucerian 'rhyme royal' stanzas of seven lines each, with some portions of the work in 'monk's' stanzas of eight lines; here is one of the eight-line stanzas, which reappears in printed form in the second column of the Horstmann page reproduced here (Prologue, ll. 73–80). Notice several things in this juxtaposition. Though its layout is somewhat cramped, the printed text does have an obvious advantage of clarity and ease of reading: no paleographical skill is required. There is also an economy in that the text of several manuscript pages is produced on a single page of the printed edition, though this contributes to its relatively 'cramped' appearance.

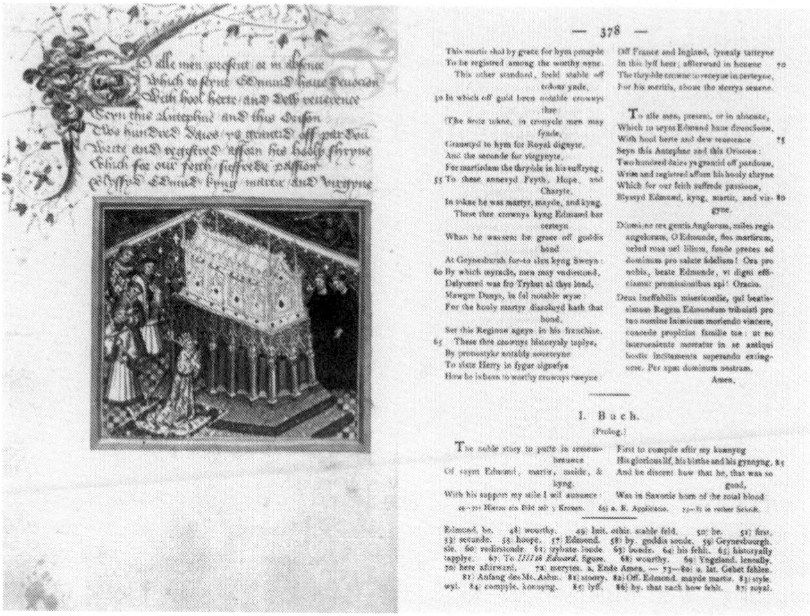

Figure 9.1 Left: British Library, MS Harley 2278, folio 4v (by permission of the British Library). Right: p. 378 of Horstmann's edition, including the text of the manuscript page on the left (ll. 73–80).

Further, there are line numbers to aid in referencing and cross-referencing, which suggests that the editor was offering an aid to scholarly study. Though intended for study, however, this edition has no commentary apart from a short introductory paragraph that identifies the base manuscript; while there are collation notes at the foot of the page, no other commentary is included. (This fact alone would justify the preparation of a new edition.) More generally, it is a commonplace that the evolution in European culture from manuscript to print has brought many advantages: it has fostered public education and an ideal (not yet fully realized) of universal literacy; printing has made reading affordable and 'easy.' But I hope, too, that this juxtaposition of two pages, one manuscript and one print, illustrates that the movement from manuscript to printed text has also involved some loss. Horstmann, working with the manuscript page shown here, produced the printed page reproduced next to it, and they are not the same; the latter is not equivalent to the former.

The digital revolution, like the printing revolution brought about by the invention of movable type in the fifteenth century (mere decades after the composition of Lydgate's work), takes us a further remove from the culture of manuscript production and dissemination in which Lydgate's manuscript was created and in which it had currency as cultural capital. Still, distant as hypertext is from medieval manuscript culture, the computer edition provides us with opportunities to present manuscript evidence and various relevant aspects of cultural context more fully and inclusively than the conventions of the printed edition have done.

The modern printed edition focuses exclusively on the words; all non-linguistic elements, here specifically the decoration and illustration, have been erased in the process. The printed edition reduces this complex 'multimedia' work to mere alphabetic characters. A kind of translation has taken place, and the edited text is not the same as the manuscript text, even if the words are the same. Further, Horstmann's edition includes no literary, historical, or other commentary; the text is treated merely as a linguistic artifact, useful as an example of the state of the English language in the early fifteenth century, but of no other interest. In the discipline of literary studies these days we talk a great deal about revisiting and recontextualizing, rehistoricizing ancient texts; I propose that a good place to start to recontextualize is to restore some of the non-textual context that appears in the manuscript.

There are a number of factors involved in the history of editing literary texts that I believe we need to rethink. First of all, as suggested, we as editors have been guilty of logocentrism in several senses, not least a tendency to isolate the textual and extract it from the stream of the reading experience, fetishizing the word while dismissing the pictures, the music, and other elements which may have been part of the original whole composition. Part of this is a matter of professionalism and the maintenance of academic disciplinarity: pictures or music belong to other people's departments. Another part is economics: the high cost of printing – even printing just words – sets severe limits on how much context can be included with a text. Yet another part is a matter of cultural value and priority: educated and cultivated people feel superior to children and other poor souls who desire pictures in their books.

While I am not one who imagines that anyone will, anytime soon, curl up with a good electronic book, or that the computer is about to do away with paper – indeed, the computerization of our offices has created the need for more paper, not less – nevertheless, the computer affords us opportunities to reconsider and re-evaluate our assumptions about the nature of the edited text, which is one of the main themes of this collection of papers. It is a fact of literary history that many of Lydgate's poems were intended to be accompanied by pictures: his poems appeared alongside paintings, stitched into wall-hangings, or, most famous of all, accompanying a large painting of the Dance of Death on the wall of the cloisters of Old St Paul's cathedral. Other of his works were written to be performed, either acted or sung. Yet, when we read Lydgate, when we read him at all, we read these texts in scholarly editions in which the works are stripped of performative contexts. Another fact of literary history is that Lydgate was tremendously popular in his own time but is not highly regarded or frequently read now, and it seems to me that this fact may have some connection with the former; our lack of taste for Lydgate may have to do, in part at least, with the nature of modern editions in which we find his texts reduced to mere words. One group of scholars has experimented with singing Lydgate, with good results;[3] one of my graduate students has declared that *The Fall of Princes* is quite a delightful story collection when read aloud. By restoring the pictures to the text of *Edmund and Fremund* – by recreating the manuscript, in some sense, in computerized form – I hope to prove, among other things, that Lydgate's works are not best assessed in typical scholarly editions; they may well appear to be much better poems when the pictures are restored.

Furthermore, I would argue that this is not simply a matter of aesthetics or personal taste, but that in this particular work these particular illustrations are vital to the work's signification. The oldest manuscript of Lydgate's *Edmund and Fremund* is preserved in the British Library as MS Harley 2278, and this manuscript is the source of the miniatures reproduced here. As can be seen, it is richly decorated and illustrated – there are 120 such miniatures among the pages of the manuscript – and because of this wealth of illustration, it is one of the great treasures of the British Library's extraordinary collections. Making this remarkable manuscript more accessible, both as a Lydgate text (which is not currently available in a modern edition) and as a treasure of fifteenth-century illustration, is part of the rationale for this hypertext edition. Further, Harley 2278 is almost certainly the manuscript prepared for (perhaps at) Lydgate's abbey for presentation to King Henry VI to commemorate his visit to Bury Abbey at Christmas of 1433; in Figure 9.2 the king can be seen kneeling at the shrine of St Edmund in the abbey church.

The manuscript, then, commemorates a particular occasion in a par-

Figure 9.2 British Library, MS Harley 2278, folio 4v: King Henry VI at Bury shrine (by permission of the British Library).

ticular place, and it was produced either in the scriptorium of Bury Abbey, or, more likely, under abbey direction in a nearby commercial atelier. Further, it is quite probable that Lydgate himself personally oversaw the production of the manuscript and gave instruction to the scribes and illuminators. Indeed, Lydgate's prologue to the poem is a verbal description of one of the pictures that accompany the poem: the text comments on the picture that was designed to accompany the text. The picture, then, was already conceived if not in fact executed when the prologue was composed, and this miniature (and I believe, by extension, the program of illustrations as a whole) is thus seen to be 'authorial.' Further, the picture is not only authorized but integral; the poem speaks to the pictures as the pictures visually represent the poem. Yet the published edition includes no illustrations – not even (with somewhat absurd effect) the picture that Lydgate describes in the prologue. I believe that this detracts from the experience of reading Lydgate's text; he conceived it not as words alone, but rather as words with accompanying illustrations.

These pictures, then, have considerable interest and value on their own as works of fifteenth-century illustration, while also contributing to the story which they illustrate. The text stripped of these pictures is a lesser thing. John Fleming, in an article on illustration in the manuscripts of Bonaventure, adapts the words of Malvolio to declare that some texts are born to have illustrations, some achieve illustrations, and some have illustrations thrust upon them;[4] this, I think, is a story which was born to have illustrations.

An analogous situation arises in literary departments concerning the way that we teach songs and ballads: our textbooks too often present the words stripped of music.[5] Moreover, in the modern academy, the same ballad will be studied differently in an English course and in a music course, but is it desirable to have one department study the words and another study the music, dividing what the original composition united? Imagine *Alice in Wonderland* without Tenniel's illustrations, or consider the different experiences of William Blake depending on whether one studies him in the Oxford Standard Authors edition with words alone, or in one of the lovely colour facsimile editions with the poet's original plates. I wish to suggest that, in a computer edition, we should no longer have to choose; the false dichotomy is resolved, the either/or becomes both/and. To continue with the example of William Blake, the computer has provided us with tremendous new opportunities, as is evident, for example, from the William Blake Archive Web site, which presents reproductions, made with meticulous attention to colour correctness and clarity, of many images from rare and otherwise inaccessible copies of Blake's works; further, these images are accompanied by commentary, and are being indexed so that particular subjects within the pictures can be found by keyword searching.[6] Colour imaging in a printed book is terribly expensive; colour imaging on the computer screen is not. The computer thus opens up new possibilities in reproduction.

I certainly do not wish to lose what we have gained in the evolution from manuscript to printed text, any more than I would wish a return to medieval medical practices, but I would like to restore to the modern edition some of the context that has been lost. With the advent of hypertext systems, one of the economic objections has been eliminated;

reproducing colour pictures in a printed book raises the price of a book prohibitively, but reproducing colour pictures on a computer screen costs practically nothing – ignoring for the moment the cost of computer hardware and questions of copyright and royalty payments. One can reproduce a CD-ROM containing hundreds of colour pictures for computer display at a cost of about $2.00 for the disk, which amounts to mere pennies per picture. Viewing a digitized picture on a computer screen, displaying it for a large audience via computer and digital projector, or publishing it even more widely through a Web site involves no printing presses (which must be maintained, staffed, and adjusted), no colour dyes, and no glossy paper; the reproduction of multiple copies of this picture (with no gradual loss of quality, as is common in analogue forms of reproduction) costs almost nothing, once the first copy is prepared. The computer offers us new opportunities in colour pictorial reproduction.

The question of copyright and royalty payments cannot be set aside for long, because it is a significant and difficult one; the desire of editors for easy access to archival materials seems to be increasingly bumping up against the desire of the owners of the archival materials for fair compensation. With the growth of information technology we have also witnessed the commodification of the information itself. We have seen commercial firms, for instance, produce databases of bibliographical information and then charge academic libraries phenomenal fees for access. Similarly, archives that hold manuscript materials find themselves with new opportunities – in part because well-financed commercial firms can offer substantial fees – and new political pressures from the sources of their funding to capitalize on their holdings. Thus even 'academic' use of archive materials now often carries 'commercial' fees for such things as reproduction rights, and some repositories further impose strict rules governing the quality and method of display of the images reproduced.[7] Thus while the technology theoretically improves accessibility, it has also brought a new potential for the commercial exploitation of information, and academic editors are rarely so well financed that such barriers can be overcome easily.

Still, though there are such difficulties, the technology has great potential for new kinds of editions. Besides restoring the pictures to the story, a hypertext edition of a work such as Lydgate's can offer other advantages. Of course, it is not particularly comfortable to read a book on the screen, and it will be a long while (if ever) before we will routinely curl up in an easy chair with a mystery novel in e-book format: the physical book still has a long life ahead. But for academics interested not only in reading a book but in studying it, electronic media permit one to do things with a text that cannot be done with a printed book, such as searching through the text for a particular passage, making a concordance of the entire text (in a matter of seconds), or doing computer-aided linguistic and stylistic analyses.

Here, too, there is a negative note to be sounded; one should not minimize the amount of non-editorial labour involved. Any computer edition, even a relatively 'simple' one encoded in HTML for use with common browser software (Murray McGillivray's edition of Chaucer's *Book of the Duchess*, for instance) involves a considerable amount of work in tagging and encoding.[8] Permitting the users of an edition to do things beyond the usual capabilities of the browser will require a certain amount of programming or 'Java-scripting.' Adding sophisticated search mechanisms, tools for linguistic or stylistic study, or the ability to highlight something in one window and have other windows automatically display commentary or glosses relevant to the highlighted item adds considerably to the complexity and labour of producing a hypertext edition; the increase in the capabilities of the edition carries a concomitant increase in the difficulty of producing it.

But while there are, admittedly, difficulties and significant amounts of labour involved in producing a hypertext edition, the rewards can nevertheless be substantial. Computer technology in its current form permits us, I suggest, to have our cake and eat it too: my hypertext edition of Lydgate's *Lives of Ss. Edmund and Fremund* will combine the clarity of modern typefaces with the capabilities of electronic text for computer-aided study of the work, and will also permit us to restore the pictures and other non-linguistic contexts which have been too expensive to include in most modern editions. The computer and hypertext technology, then, provide us with an opportunity quite literally to recontextualize that which has been stripped of its original context – that is, we can easily and inexpensively bring back something of the medieval manuscript in which this poem appeared – while also permitting us to do sophisticated things of which the scribes who made medieval manuscripts never dreamed.

My intention, then, is to prepare a text of the poem, together with several types of study aids, as part of a hypertext system, in part to explore the potential of the 'unbound' book. The poem will be presented in a modern typescript (no paleographical skills required), and the electronic text can be searched and analyzed. There will be a glossarial concordance keyed to the words in the text (click on a word, and the glossary window will skip to that entry in the glossary; click on a line number in the glossary, and the associated text will be displayed). The textual notes will be relatively few; this will be a conservative edition of a single manuscript rather than a full critical edition, so textual notes will be limited to explaining emendations and cruxes.[9] The commentary will, like the glossary, be keyed to each line (click on the line number, and the commentary window will skip to the corresponding annotation). It is my intention that all of the original 120 illustrations will be reproduced (provided that the necessary permission can be obtained from the British Library at an affordable fee) and restored to their original positions in the text, and these also will be accompanied by commentary.

Besides restoring Lydgate's pictures, I will also add many of my own, and this illustrates another kind of recontextualization. The introduction (portions of a draft of which can be found on my Web site) will include sections on the poet, on the manuscript, on the abbey of Bury St Edmunds, on the occasion of the poem (King Henry's visit to the abbey), and so forth.[10] The introduction will also include many photographs of the places mentioned: the ruins of the abbey, sites associated with the life of Edmund, and so on. While modern photographs do not tell us what these places looked like in Lydgate's time, they can help us to imagine, for instance, the size and splendour of the abbey church, which was larger than most surviving English cathedrals. The story of Edmund and the story of Lydgate both take place within the physical landscape of East Anglia, and I hope that a collection of photographs of the modern landscape may help readers to imagine the medieval landscape which is integral to the story and which would have been familiar to Lydgate's initial audience.

Furthermore, the legend of St Edmund continues to be very much a part of the landscape of East Anglia today; one of the contexts of Lydgate's poem which the computer can help us to restore is the sense of local legend attached to very real localities. I hope to use modern photographs to illustrate, in part, the overlaying of sacred geography onto the geo-political map of East Anglia, of legend onto landscape, which is central to Lydgate's work and Bury Abbey's sponsorship of it. St Edmund, as king of East Anglia in the 860s, had a physical presence in Norfolk and Suffolk, and the legend of his life and martyrdom is closely tied to features of the visible landscape of East Anglia, as I shall attempt to illustrate. Moreover, not only did Bury Abbey claim to have the uncorrupted body of St Edmund in its church, but the abbot was also a

Figure 9.3 St Edmund's Point, Hunstanton, Norfolk (photograph by S.R. Reimer, 1996).

landowner within Edmund's kingdom on a scale superior to that of the dukes of both Norfolk and Suffolk, and the abbots of Bury had a quasi-regal status (including full control of the local courts) within the 'Liberty of St Edmund' (being the abbey and town of Bury and its immediate vicinity). Lydgate's work, addressed to the young king on behalf of Bury Abbey, offers implicitly a hagiographical rationalization of Bury Abbey's economic and political role in the region, based upon a notion that the abbey represented the heavenly King Edmund, still powerful and influential on earth. Part of the message of Lydgate's text, made explicit, for instance, in its repeated emphasis on the terrible fate of King Sweyn who tried to tax Bury Abbey and died at the hands of the spirit of Edmund, is that kings or magnates who attempt to hinder or frustrate the Abbey can expect vengeance enacted by the Abbey's saintly patron.

The links of the legend to the landscape of Edmund's kingdom can be illustrated with a particular example, which will also demonstrate something of the role that modern photographs can play in a hypertext edition of such a work, the 'truth' of which is less a matter of historicity than of locality.

Figure 9.3 shows the cliffs of St Edmund's Point at Hunstanton, in

Figure 9.4 Ruins of St Edmund's chapel atop the cliffs (and near the lighthouse) at Hunstanton, Norfolk (photograph by S.R. Reimer).

north-west Norfolk (north of King's Lynn, at the top of The Wash). According to Lydgate's narrative, Edmund was born in Saxony in 841 and grew up in Nuremberg (note that Nuremberg is not, despite the Edmund legend, in Saxony), to which city King Offa of East Anglia (but note that no known king of East Anglia had that name) travelled on his way to Rome. Being himself childless, Offa chose the virtuous young Edmund to be his heir. Offa died while on his way back from Rome, and Edmund was summoned to East Anglia. Edmund arrived in his new kingdom in 854 at this spot, and he and his companions are said to have built the adjacent village of (Old) Hunstanton, which is also said to have been one of his favourite retreats throughout his reign.

In the later Middle Ages a chapel dedicated to St Edmund was built up on top of the cliffs to commemorate his landing here; the ruined chapel is shown in Figure 9.4. Furthermore, in the modern church in the new town (New Hunstanton was built in Victorian times as a seaside resort) there is a stained glass window showing Edmund's landing at Hunstanton. The ancient legend is remembered in modern East Anglia.

After Edmund's landing, he and his companions ascended the cliffs, and found themselves thirsty but could find no water. Edmund prayed,

Figure 9.5 British Library, MS Harley 2278, folio 28r, detail: St Edmund's springs (by permission of the British Library).

and God granted a miracle of springs of fresh water. Figure 9.5 shows the illustration of the miracle in Lydgate's manuscript; Figure 9.6 shows the springs, which can still be seen in Old Hunstanton and are pointed to by the local folk who tell the story of Edmund's miracle.

While obviously the medieval illuminator was not attempting to provide a realistic image of the site, as a photograph attempts to do, the modern photograph does help to remind the reader, I think, that the poet, his illuminator, his patron abbot, and his audience had a very specific place in mind, a real and visitable spring, which the miniature symbolically represented. (It may well not, however, be as easily visited by those who use the modern hypertext edition, so photographs are useful as something of a substitute.) The sacred narrative is offered, in the first instance, to King Henry and his court, in commemoration of a visit to Bury Abbey, and part of its message is that East Anglia is a sacred realm in which there are holy sites that could motivate pilgrimage.

Besides Hunstanton with its cliffs, in the extreme north-west of the Anglo-Saxon kingdom of East Anglia, the legend also describes King Edmund's coronation in Bures St Mary, on the border with Essex in the south. Bury St Edmunds, the place of his entombment, is about half-way in between; Thetford (the site of Edmund's failed stand against the Vikings) is just north of Bury, and Hoxne, the supposed site of his

Figure 9.6 Springs by St Mary's Church, Old Hunstanton, Norfolk (photograph by S.R. Reimer, 1998).

martyrdom, is some thirty miles to the east of Thetford (and of Bury). Other places mentioned in the legend include Attleborough, where Edmund spent a year before his coronation to learn English, and Caistor St Edmund, where Lydgate says that Edmund was residing when he heard of the arrival of the Danes (others say Framlingham). Though not mentioned by Lydgate, the village of Burgate explains its name as a shortened form of 'burial gate,' and refers to a local legend that St Edmund's body rested here when it was being translated from Hoxne to Bury St Edmunds. The legend of St Edmund, then, covers the length and breadth of the ancient kingdom of East Anglia, almost as if someone deliberately set out to make sure that every region of the kingdom was represented in the story, or every village in the region found it worthwhile to claim a piece of Edmund's story for themselves. East Anglia in the Middle Ages (and to some extent even now) was a sacred and legendary realm, a new holy land, with the shrine of St Edmund in Bury St Edmunds as the spiritual centre from which the region's significance flowed.

Thus, particular localities through the length and breadth of East Anglia play a role in the legend of this king; dozens of places across the whole of East Anglia claimed in medieval times, and still claim, some association with the life of St Edmund. However, the only fact that we know with any certainty about St Edmund, as recorded in the *Anglo-Saxon Chronicle*, is that he died at the time of a battle with the Danish invaders in the year 869. It is not even clear whether he fell in battle, which seems probable, or was captured and deliberately slain after the battle, as the legend claims, but I want to emphasize that everything except the fact of his death as a consequence of a lost battle is a product of later elaboration and fabrication. The official Vita, then, was developed out of an accumulation of local legendary associations which predate it, and Lydgate's text is informed by such local legends.

The details of St Edmund's martyrdom at the hands of the Danish victors were first recorded about 116 years after his death by Abbo, a monk of Fleury, who claimed to have the story from St Dunstan, who claimed to have heard it from an old warrior who had been present at Edmund's death. Abbo's truth claim is that his story is a third-generation eyewitness account.[11] Abbo's story focuses on the Danish invasion and Edmund's martyrdom, and says nothing about Edmund's early life or events during his reign. Abbo's account continued to be the official version of the death of Edmund throughout the Middle Ages, but because Abbo said nothing about Edmund's life, the story needed to be supplemented. Around 1150, three centuries after the fact, but during a period when the monks of St Edmund's Abbey at Bury were active in the promotion of the cult of St Edmund – including a relic tour of the continent with the establishment of altars to St Edmund in several continental cathedrals, even as far away as Italy – appeared Geoffrey of Wells's book of the *Infantia Eadmundi*, giving details of Edmund's birth and childhood, how he was adopted by the childless King Offa of East Anglia, and how he eventually succeeded to the throne of East Anglia.[12]

In his preface to the work, Geoffrey provides an intriguing glimpse into the process of its composition; he tells us that the monks of Bury met together to compare notes on the various local legends they had heard about Edmund's early life, from all different regions of the countryside, in an attempt to determine which of these various local traditions were worth preserving. In other words, the monks of Bury met together to *decide* on the contents of the *Infantia* and then hired a writer, Geoffrey of Wells (who already had an established reputation as a hagiographer), to compose the final version.[13]

Thus we know that oral tales and local legends preceded the written version, and that the literary work was intended both to record those oral tales – the various legends of Edmund that were associated with various localities – and to create from them a coherent and continuous narrative. Furthermore, on the one hand, the perceived need for a coherent narrative suggests that Geoffrey may have been permitted some literary licence to fill in gaps so as to make a continuous narrative. On the other hand, the need for a consistent narrative suggests that a process of selection would have been necessary: choices would have been made over competing versions, and some harmonization and adjudication of rival claims would have been necessary.

The fact that there were competing versions of Edmund's story current in medieval East Anglia is evident from the fact that some traces of such variant versions have survived despite the attempt by the cult centre in Bury to promote a single, coherent narrative. For instance, as noted above, the *Anglo-Saxon Chronicle* states that Edmund died fighting the Vikings, presumably having fallen in battle; the versions of the story promoted later by Bury Abbey, however, make Edmund into a pacifist who was martyred because he surrendered, declaring that he refused to be the cause of further bloodshed. One chronicle mentions that Edmund had a wife and son, but the official version promoted by Bury Abbey insists that the martyr was a 'clean virgin.' Indeed, the arms of Bury Abbey, which were said to have been the arms of the saintly king himself, display three crowns, which Lydgate explains as the crowns of East Anglia, of martyrdom, and of virginity.

It would seem probable, then, that if two localities both claimed to be the site of an event in Edmund's life, such as the place of his martyrdom, the monks at the cult centre who were responsible for disseminating the official Vita would make the choice: one particular locality's claim was accepted as consistent with what was known and believed, and therefore another locality's version of the story was rejected and denied. Such choices will certainly have reflected 'political' motivations. As David Rollason notes, particularly with respect to Durham and that monastery's tales of the various resting places of the uncorrupted body of St Cuthbert during their ten years of wandering, the identification of a particular locality as one of the resting places of St Cuthbert's body led to claims of proprietorship by the monastery over those localities;[14] more generally, translations of relics 'seem to have been linked with acquisitions of, or claims to, landed property.'[15] Hagiographical literature, then, can be studied, on one level at least, in terms of its use in the rationalization of property claims; the cult centre might well have used geographical references in the official Vita to justify existing – or to promote desirable – proprietorial and territorial claims. Because St Edmund was crowned in Bures St Mary, it therefore seems appropriate that the abbey should own land in Bures St Mary (as they did) and to exercise influence there through the Chapel of St Edmund, where they displayed some of Edmund's relics annually. Similarly, in Thetford, the site of Edmund's battle against the Danish invaders, Bury Abbey held both a parish church (dedicated to St Edmund) and a priory (dedicated to St George) in close proximity to one another, located in a part of the town which in the eighteenth century was identified as the actual battle site. (I have not found any confirmation from medieval sources, but the eighteenth-century legends may preserve a medieval tradition.)

Part of what I am working toward in my current research, then, is to explore in the case of St Edmund some of the implications of these ideas of the 'geography of power' represented in hagiographical literature such as Lydgate's life of Edmund. From Hunstanton in the northwest corner of Norfolk, to Bures St Mary on the Stour River, Bury Abbey was the single largest landowner in East Anglia, and the abbot of Bury was a magnate of the realm greater than the dukes of Norfolk and Suffolk in terms of the number of manors held. The Domesday Book lists some sixty manors belonging to Bury Abbey in Norfolk and Suffolk (the abbey also held a number of manors in Essex and in various other parts of England), and there are many more villages where the abbey held parcels of land or controlled fishing rights, or where men owed service to the abbey. There were also daughter houses of the abbey in various locations throughout East Anglia – including Thetford – and the abbey held many parish churches throughout East Anglia, including all the churches in the town of Bury and surrounding area. Bury Abbey was a centre of economic and political power in the region.

The abbey enjoyed royal favour through most of its history, from the time of Canute, who gave the shrine of St Edmund to the Benedictines and endowed the new abbey with many of the manors listed as 'Edmund's' in Domesday Book, to Henry VI, who stayed at Bury for Christmas and Easter of 1433 and held parliament at Bury Abbey in 1449. St Edmund, along with St Edward the Confessor, was patron of the royal family and came within a whisker of becoming the patron saint of England – until Edward III tipped the scales in favour of St George at the time of the founding of the Order of the Garter. Edward I marched under a banner of St Edmund, continuing his father's special devotion to Ss Edmund and Edward the Confessor, and came on pilgrimage to Bury Abbey to celebrate his victories. As mentioned above, within the Liberty of St Edmund, the abbot held quasi-regal status, answerable neither to sheriff nor bishop. The abbot of Bury was a friend and adviser to the king, as we know, for instance, from the Register of Abbot Curteys, which preserves some of his correspondence with Henry VI, including an exchange of letters while the King was planning the foundation of Eton College in Windsor and King's College in Cambridge. In the reign of King John, it was on the altar of Bury Abbey before the shrine of St Edmund that the barons of the realm swore that changes must be made, an oath which culminated in Magna Carta. In the fifteenth century, as mentioned above, Lydgate was both a monk of Bury and the court poet and chief apologist for the Lancastrian regime, perhaps in part because he was from Bury. Bury Abbey was the principal political centre in East Anglia, and one of the political centres of the realm, and the abbot of Bury was one of the great magnates – not by his own merits but because of the royal and national importance of the cult of St Edmund as embodied in Bury Abbey. Bury thus was one of the wealthiest institutions in England, a pilgrimage site of great significance (probably the greatest in England until overtaken by Canterbury's St Thomas), and favoured by king and court.

Sanctity is proven by miracles, and a pilgrimage site is maintained by accounts of the miracles performed. Claims of miracles associated with King Edmund begin with several at the end of Abbo's *Passio* (including the story that Edmund's severed head was guarded by a wolf until found by searchers, a legend that is the basis for one of the common iconographical presentations of Edmund). Miracle stories, growing steadily in number over time, were collected by the monks of Bury in the eleventh century in the *De miraculis sancti Eadmundi* by Hermann the Archdeacon.[16] This was revised and supplemented at various times during the later Middle Ages, and even Lydgate, in the fifteenth century, recorded three new miracles of St Edmund that occurred during his own lifetime; one of these took place in the abbey church and Lydgate certainly heard of it from eyewitnesses.[17]

It is of interest that many of the miracles of St Edmund, as indexed in Arnold's *Memorials*, are miracles of punishment (nearly equal in number to the miracles of healing), primarily for violations of property.[18] The most significant of these is the story, previously mentioned, of the death of King Sweyn, father of Canute, the abbey's great benefactor. Sweyn had demanded a payment of tribute by the keepers of St Edmund's shrine (at that time a college of secular priests). Sweyn's demand for tribute was resisted, and Sweyn died suddenly one night in his sleep; it was a significant part of Edmund's later legend – the story is referred to no less than three times in Lydgate's version of Edmund's life – that St Edmund visited Sweyn in a dream and ran a spear through his heart in vengeance for his actions against St Edmund's shrine.

Note that the abbey told the story in terms of a violation of the saint and his shrine, not of the keepers of the shrine; similarly Bury's land holdings are recorded in Domesday Book as St Edmund's land, not the abbey's land. Challenges to the abbot – such as the disputes with the various bishops of Norwich over the abbey's exemption from episcopal visitation and control – are described by Bury chroniclers as challenges to the saint. There is a passage in Abbot Curteys's Register (from Lydgate's time) in which a monkish chronicler of recent disputes with the then Bishop of Norwich declared these disputes to be like an ill wind coming out of the demon-infested north, which the Saint himself had turned back. The abbey's victories in property disputes are consistently described as the vengeance of an angered saint, and the records prove that St Edmund, in the form of his abbots, was a very litigious fellow in the later Middle Ages. It has been suggested by at least one historian that St Edmund appears to have been far more active and effective in protecting his territory after his death than he was while alive.[19] The legend of St Edmund is very much a local legend and is closely connected to questions of abbey property and privilege.

David Rollason declares that knowing where the saints are is as important an insight into the politics of early medieval England as is the question of where the kings and chieftains are to be found.[20] I am, therefore, pursuing questions of church dedications, holy wells, and local legends in an attempt to discover the intersections between political geography and sacred geography, and will present this material (including modern photographs by way of illustration) in the hypertext edition of Lydgate's version of Edmund's legend. I wish to suggest here that it is, at least in part, *because* these places have been sanctified by the footsteps of the sainted king, that even as late as the fifteenth century – even, though to a much lesser extent, in the twentieth century – they had a certain significance in the political geography of East Anglia, a claim to a certain status and privilege, and a claim to come under the notice and protection of Bury Abbey. The 'Liberty of St Edmund' is a physical and delimited territory including and surrounding Bury Abbey, but there was also a sense that the 'Liberty of St Edmund' was an extensible concept, that the abbey's sphere of influence could and should be no more circumscribed than the life and footsteps of St Edmund himself, from Hunstanton to Bures St Mary.

Here, again, the computer provides us an opportunity to contextualize our texts in ways that were previously cumbersome and expensive. Part of my point is that these legends still live as part of the local lore, as part of the culture, the sense of identity, and the inheritance of East Anglian villages and towns. Whether or not Edmund the King of East Anglia was ever in Hunstanton – whether or not he came from Nuremberg, landed at St Edmund's point, climbed the hill, prayed for water, and received the miracle of the springs – whether or not any of this is ninth-century fact, it is twentieth-century and was fifteenth-century fact that there are springs at Hunstanton to which people point and say, 'That's where St Edmund received his miracle of water.' The springs are there, and one purpose of local legends of this sort is to invest the landscape with significance, to give the geographical fact some religious or historical meaning. And such legends continue, in Lydgate's time and ours, to fulfill such a purpose, a purpose that is relevant to an understanding of Lydgate's work. Part of the context of Lydgate's *Lives of Ss. Edmund and Fremund* is the continued presence of St Edmund in the landscape of East Anglia.

Obviously such an emphasis, as I have outlined here, on the 'sacred geography' that informs the text reflects my personal sense of one of the ways in which this text signifies; other emphases are equally possible. For instance, my introduction to this edition, when complete, will also consider the manuscript (its production and history), the poem's language (again, one of my primary interests in this text is as evidence for Lydgate's style), and its themes and methods. The 'contexts' that I have highlighted for the sake of this paper are not to be taken as exclusive of others; I have foregrounded them here not least because of the way in which these particular aspects of the text and its contexts make a hypertext edition, rather than a traditional printed edition, seem an obvious choice. Working with this text has caused me to ponder the idea that traditional editions, bound books, have done little and can do little, given their boundaries and bindings, to contextualize the text with its local geographical and local cultural significance, just as they have stripped the text of its performative elements and accompanying illustrations. It seems to me that computer editions and hypertext systems offer us an opportunity to begin to restore such contexts to our texts, and to remove from the book some of the limitations that bind it.

NOTES

This article is a revised and expanded version of the paper presented at the 'Book Unbound' workshop in Vancouver, September 1999, which also incorporates portions of a second paper presented to the Northwest Conference on British Studies, held in Edmonton in October 1999.

1 My own primary interest in the text is stylistic, although I will not say more here about that aspect of it. I am engaged in a study of Lydgate's style, and have come to believe (for reasons that will become clear in the next few paragraphs) that the text of *The Lives of Ss. Edmund and Fremund* in its oldest surviving manuscript (British Library MS Harley 2278) is one step removed from a Lydgate 'autograph,' making this manuscript a key text for a stylistic study. The lack of a published modern edition that I could use in my stylistic study was the initial impetus for undertaking my own edition of the text.

2 Carl Horstmann, ed., *Altenglische Legenden: Neue Folge* (Heilbronn: Gebr. Henninger, 1881), 376–445, edited from London, British Library, MS Harley 2278. Another transcription of the Harley manuscript appears in Lord Francis Hervey, ed., *Corolla Sancti Eadmundi: The Garland of St Edmund, King and Martyr* (London: J. Murray, 1907), pp. 409–524, and there have been several editions in modern theses, most notably that by J.I. Miller (Harvard, 1967). The manuscript image here is from Harley 2278, fol. 4v.

3 Elza Tiner, Shirley Carnahan, and Anne Fjestad Peterson, '"Euer aftir to be rad & song": Lydgate's Texts in Performance' (2 parts), *Early Drama, Art and Music Review* 19.1 (1996): 41–52; 19.2 (1997): 85–93.

4 John V. Fleming, 'Obscure Images by Illustrious Hands,' in *Text and Image*, ed. David W. Burchmore, Acta 10 (Binghamton: Center for Medieval and Early Renaissance Studies, SUNY, 1986), p. 1.

5 Andrew Taylor's essay in this collection, for example, points out how common it is to ignore the musical aspects of medieval texts. Even a hypertext project that restores the pictures to a medieval text might well overlook sound.

6 The William Blake Archive can be found at http://www.blakearchive.org (URL verified 10 May 2003).

7 See William Schipper's comments about limits placed on digitization by research libraries in his essay in this collection.

8 *Geoffrey Chaucer's 'Book of the Duchess': A Hypertext Edition* [CD-ROM], ed. Murray McGillivray, 2nd ed. (Calgary: University of Calgary Press, 1999).

9 I have chosen to make this an edition of the one manuscript, rather than a critical edition collating all known manuscripts, because of the significance of this particular manuscript version, especially the probability that the

preparation of this manuscript was overseen by Lydgate himself, making this version of special significance for my stylistic studies.

10 URL: http://www.ualberta.ca/~sreimer/lydgate.htm.

11 The *Passio S. Eadmundi* by Abbo of Fleury (*Bibliotheca Hagiographica Latina* [BHL] no. 2392) is printed in E. Thomas Arnold, ed., *Memorials of St Edmund's Abbey*, Rolls Series 96 (London: HMSO, 1890–6), 3 vols, 1: 3–25; *Patrologia Latina* 139: 507–20; Hervey's *Corolla*, pp. 6–58; Michael Winterbottom, ed., *Three Lives of English Saints* (Toronto: Centre for Medieval Studies, 1972), pp. 67–87.

12 Geoffrey of Wells, *Liber de infantia S. Edmundi* (BHL 2393), is printed in Arnold's *Memorials*, 1: 93–103; also (ed. by R.M. Thomson) in *Analecta Bollandiana* 95 (1977): 25–42. The 'Wells' from which Geoffrey came is Wells-next-Sea in Norfolk, not Wells in Somerset: he was a 'local' writer from a village not far from Hunstanton, and was probably quite familiar with some of the local legends of St Edmund.

13 There is some discussion of the significance of the idea that there are oral traditions underlying Geoffrey's work in Cyril Ernest Wright, *The Cultivation of Saga in Anglo-Saxon England* (Edinburgh: Oliver and Boyd, 1939), pp. 62–4.

14 David Rollason, 'The Shrines of Saints in Later Anglo-Saxon England: Distribution and Significance,' in *The Anglo-Saxon Church: Papers on History, Architecture, and Archaeology in Honour of Dr. H.M. Taylor*, ed. L.A.S. Butler and R.K. Morris (Council for British Archaeology Research Report, 60; London, 1986), pp. 32–43 at 34.

15 Rollason, 'The Shrines of Saints,' p. 38.

16 BHL 2395, printed in Arnold, *Memorials*, 1: 26–50. A version with an alternative prologue (BHL 2395a) is excerpted in Hervey's *Corolla*, pp. 90–4. A later revision (BHL 2396) is printed in Arnold, *Memorials*, 1: 50–92. Later expanded versions attributed to Osbert of Clare and to Abbot Samson (BHL 2397, 2398, 2398a) are also reproduced and further supplemented in later versions of Edmund's *Vita et passio*, culminating in the version of the 'Vita, passio, et miracula' found in the late fourteenth-century compilation (used in the instruction of Bury novices at the time when Lydgate came to the abbey, and the immediate source for his *Lives of Ss. Edmund and Fremund*) in Oxford, Bodleian Library, MS Bodley 240 (BHL 2399), printed in Horstmann's *Nova Legenda Anglie*, 2: 575–688.

17 Lydgate's 'Miracles of St. Edmund' (IMEV no. 1843) is included by Horstmann as an addendum to his edition of the *Lives of Ss. Edmund and Fremund*, transcribing the version found in Oxford, Bodleian Library, MS Ashmole 46.

18 In the index to Vol. 2, 389–90.

19 Norman Scarfe, *Jocelin of Brakelond: The Life of a Monk and Chronicler of the Great Abbey of St Edmund* (Leominster: Gracewing, 1997), p. 10.

20 Rollason, 'The Shrines of Saints,' p. 32.

10

Server-Side Databases, the World Wide Web, and the Editing of Medieval Poetry: The Case of *La Belle dame qui eut mercy*

JOAN GRENIER-WINTHER

Editing medieval texts has always been about choices. Choices about which text to edit. Choices about which manuscript witness to name as the base manuscript for that text. Choices about whether to prepare a diplomatic or a critical edition. Choices about what information to include in the critical apparatus and in what order. Choices about which words to include in the glossary and how to present the glossary entries. Some choices were imposed by tradition. There was a certain taxonomy one followed if an edition was to be considered scholarly. Some choices were imposed by the delivery (publication) method. Publishers had to maintain a balance between the importance of printing and distributing a text and the costs involved in the enterprise. If the scale of an edition and the relative cost of production exceeded the market potential of the text, compromises had to be made in the amount of material to be presented, leaving editors with even more choices to make as the edition was pruned for harmony of length and marketability.

With the advent of electronic editions some of these choices have become moot, while others have surfaced. Increasing computer processor (CPU) speeds and decreasing costs for disk storage space are diminishing the constraints on the amount of textual information that can be stored and presented efficiently. Editors preparing text for electronic delivery are no longer confronted with the limitations and consequential choices imposed by traditional paper-based media. Effectively they are free to include as much access to the text as they see fit, even for works that would not have been considered 'marketable' in the print world. This may include diplomatic and critical transcriptions of all manuscript witnesses to a text, complete analyses and textual apparatus, multiple appendices, and an abundant glossary. This abundance of data presents a whole new set of choices to the editor regarding which aspects of the text and ancillary materials to present to readers, who undoubtedly have different purposes for viewing the text. Reproductions of manuscript folios may also be included, although decisions must be made regarding the best way to link transcriptions and facsimiles and about how to accommodate file size to bandwidth during transmission to readers with various modes of connection to the Internet and disc reader speeds. Audio and video components are another exciting possible feature of electronic editions, but they too force similar considerations of file size and bandwidth compatibility as well as copyright infringement. Finally, the medium for publication must be chosen. Disc (CD-ROM, DVD-ROM, or other current standard) or World Wide Web are the most common options today, although given the rapidity with which technological innovations occur, a new delivery standard is likely just over the horizon, bringing with it another set of enhancements *and* concerns.

The choices facing the editor in the electronic environment and the decisions she or he ultimately makes will have an impact on the relationship between editor and reader and on their respective locations on the intellectual continuum that is the scholarly edition of a text. In the past, the editor would have prepared and presented a single, 'definitive' version of a text using one or several manuscript witnesses, accompanied by a list of variant readings. With no other effective access to the text, a relatively passive readership had to accept the editorial product. Thus, the editor's control over the continuum extended far, and a reader gained entry to that continuum only at a point nearing its end, likely at the point of literary analysis.

In the new landscape of the electronic edition, which potentially includes full access to a text and its multiple witnesses in a variety of formats, readers will be allowed, if not encouraged, to enter the continuum at an earlier stage than before. No longer will editorial decisions relating to the transcription of a line or the choice between variant readings be made unilaterally by the editor, hidden from readers. Instead, when given access to facsimiles of all manuscript witnesses, readers will be able to verify editorial transcriptions and even propose alternative readings of a text. In addition, readers will no longer have to accept the editor's choice of a best text or base manuscript. Instead, when all of the manuscript witnesses are available for consideration in full text views (rather than being presented in a stark list of variants), readers will more easily be able to weigh the various merits of all witnesses and opt for any one or a combination as base text(s). In short, as readers of full-access electronic editions are empowered to delve into the text, to propose alternative readings of the scribal copy, to compare different versions of the text, to select the base text, and to propose alternative ways of punctuating, correcting, and emending the text, they ultimately enhance the level of their engagement in the text in meaningful ways.

Realistically speaking, however, even though the potential for full access to a text exists in an electronic format, there is a natural tradeoff between the amount of access desirable for the reader and the amount of work necessary by the editor to achieve that level of access.[1] Editors still need to make choices about exactly how much of the text they will present, the format in which the text will be presented, and the extent to which readers will be able to interact with the text. In other words, even in electronic editions of the type promoted here, editorial ideology still comes into play, as the editor determines the point along the editorial/textual continuum at which the reader may enter and the kinds of readers (scholarly and/or general) for whom the edition is created.

As the editor of a late medieval poem entitled *La Belle dame qui eut mercy* (or occasionally *La Belle dame a mercy*), I have been faced with choices similar to those mentioned above. This poem, written by an unidentified author, is found in at least sixteen different fifteenth- and sixteenth-century manuscript witnesses.[2] All of these manuscripts have been fully catalogued, and while several of the works found in these same manuscripts have already been edited, *La Belle dame qui eut mercy* has not. In a series of articles published in *Romania* between 1901 and 1905, entitled 'Les Imitations de *La Belle dame sans mercy*,' Arthur Piaget presented the more than one dozen works written on the same or similar themes as Alain Chartier's famous poem, *La Belle dame sans mercy*, documented the manuscripts he knew to contain these poems, and included partial editions of some of them. *La Belle dame qui eut mercy* was among those discussed, but Piaget did not include the text of the poem.[3] In the end, he summarily dismissed all of the poems as pale 'imitations' of Chartier's opus. Since that time, relatively little attention has been paid to the poems, undoubtedly due to the fact that they remain largely unavailable in any print edition and are accessible only in manuscript form, either *in situ* or on microfilm. As a result, Chartier's work still stands today as a unique and solitary fifteenth-century text about a merciless lady, rather than as only one example of a literary tradition attested by a corpus of contemporary works including *La Belle dame qui eut mercy*.

My decision, therefore, to prepare an edition of *La Belle dame qui eut mercy* was initially made because I felt that it was important that this poem, as well as others in the corpus, be made available so that scholars could situate Chartier's poem within the larger context of other contemporary poems written on a similar theme. It was important to me, as well, that full access to the text be opened up to the reader, from facsimile views of the original manuscript folios to diplomatic and critical transcriptions of each manuscript witness to the text. I also wanted to give readers in various interrelated fields of literary study the ability to conduct statistical and summary searches on the components of the poem according to their research interests. And although the scholarly edition has always been a tool for sophisticated readers in various branches of literary study, I considered it important to choose a publication format and variety of access levels for the poem that would reach and appeal to the broadest possible audience, including both scholarly and general readers.

Publication of the edition on the World Wide Web, combined with the use of a database application, most fully met the criteria of unrestricted scale, wide accessibility, and interactivity with the reader that I sought for my edition of the *Belle dame* poem(s). As mentioned above, the Web format presents no effective restrictions on the amount of material presented in an electronic edition, so I can include as many views of the text as I believe useful for potential readers. Documents published on the Web have a potentially global audience, being accessible to anyone with a computer, Web browsing software, and a connection to the Internet. And, although in the early years of its existence the Web was a medium for the static presentation of electronic texts and images, developments in Internet technologies have added the kinds of interactive capabilities to the Web that I have envisioned for the edition, with readers being able not only to view texts through their browsing software, but also to send predefined requests for information back to the Web server to be processed and responded to in some way. In particular, developments in the area of Web-based, server-side relational databases seemed to fit most closely with my desire to give readers the ability to interact with the text in ways that would be meaningful to them.

A data-driven approach seemed all the more appropriate when I considered how well poetry lends itself to management in a database. Poems, unlike more free-flowing prose, tend to be relatively compact and follow fixed stylistic patterns. Poems contain discrete, meaningful, and relatively manageable components that have historically been categorized as distinct entities: stanzas, lines, refrains, envois, etc. What is more, these categories have been determined to have the potential to possess specific characteristics not unlike the database concepts of entities and attributes. A three-line stanza, for example, can be classified as a tercet. A ten-syllable line can be classified as being decasyllabic. A word can be identified as a specific part of speech, such as a conjunction, an article, or the second person singular, future indicative of a verb. Words used at the rhyme with the ending 'esse' can be classified in early French poetry as being feminine and of 'léonine simple' rhyme quality.

Furthermore, the central components of a poem, the metric units (whether one considers these to be the line, the stanza, or the whole poem), have definable characteristics and may be related one to another, within a poem and between versions of a single poem, in significant ways. While analysis of a prose passage, sentence by sentence, is possible, there is no elaborate system of categorization like the system that exists for and that reflects the aesthetics of poetry. In short, the fairly complex, yet orderly, system of classification that exists around poetry makes it feasible to break poems up into logical components, and thus manage them within a database.

An even stronger argument in favor of a database treatment of poetry can be made for poems that have been preserved in multiple manuscript witnesses (as is often the case for ancient and medieval works) and thus require that the editor prepare and eventually compare multiple transcriptions of the same text. The example of *La Belle dame qui eut mercy*, a single poem of 378 lines found in sixteen manuscript witnesses – thus totaling over 6,000 lines – demonstrates how the number of entities (stanzas, lines, words) that an editor must manage can increase exponentially in a multi-version text and how a mechanism for sifting through this information would be of value.

Finally, management of the considerable meta-data that can be generated about the components of a poem also seems well suited to a database approach. At least initially, this meta-data might consist of information as straightforward as the part of speech of a word, or the gender of a word used at the rhyme. Later, an expanded set of meta-data fields might be added to the database so as to label more sophisticated elements of the poetry at the word or word-group level, including rhetorical figures, stylistic elements, and idiomatic expressions. One might expect that such textual data would be more broadly researched if it were maintained in a database and, therefore, more efficiently searchable.

After consideration of all these factors, the World Wide Web with its global availability and an Internet-accessible relational database server tuned to manage and deliver the content of the poem and meta-data on the poem seemed the most appropriate answer to the questions of how and where to publish *La Belle dame qui eut mercy*.

The decision to manage the edition in a relational database and to deliver its content and meta-data on the Web, however, brings with it two major areas for consideration: first, the selection, installation, and maintenance of software applications and hardware platforms in support of the project; and second, the design, implementation, and maintenance of both the database and the Web-based user interface through which data relating to the edition is extracted and presented to the reader.[4] Though the success of an electronic edition depends on effectively dealing with issues in both of these areas, in this paper I will limit my focus to design, implementation and maintenance issues relating to the database and the user interface, using the *Belle dame* edition as a case study. Throughout this discussion, it is vital to keep in mind that the database and Web development described here is essentially iterative and one's approach to it must reflect this fact. Designing, implementing, and maintaining tools with the understanding that re-evaluation and change are a part of the process will inform this work and, hopefully, extend the usefulness of the tools.

[NB: All italicized database-related terms used in the following pages are defined in the glossary in Appendix A.]

Preliminary Considerations in Database Design

The work of database design is, at its core, about understanding the purpose of the data, first in a general sense, and then with greater concern for the details. Broadly stated, the *Belle dame* project requires a database designed to deliver not only basically static data but also dynamically generated information about that data to end-users (readers) located anywhere on the Internet (that is, globally). Stated another way, the general purpose of this database is to offer broad access to relatively unchanging data and statistics about that data.

This broadly stated purpose of providing access to existing data brings with it design principles that will impact the structure of the database.

For example, a database to which *records* are not regularly added or in which records are not regularly updated (such as a database used for an edition, as opposed to one used for tracking inventory) does not demand strict adherence to the data *normalization* guidelines concerned with data *atomicity*, particularly if offering summarized data serves to speed up or simplify access to the data in valuable ways. At the same time, queries to this type of database will run more efficiently if some effort is made to reduce the occurrence of *null values* in the database. This is accomplished by converting the columns of a table that are not dependent on the table's *primary key* into new related tables. The reduction within the datebase of *many-to-many relationships* into *one-to-many relationships* (for example, one entity in a table, such as line content, is linked to the content of a line from each of multiple manuscripts) will also likely speed up access to the data. When this is coupled with the use of *views* to mask the resulting need for relatively complicated *join commands* or *join queries* to present the data, the benefits of faster access would seem to outweigh the drawbacks as regards query complexity. It is possible to make these kinds of relatively high-level assessments of database design only with an understanding of both the overarching purpose of the database and the data contained in that database. This general information alone, though, is not enough to guide the design of an electronic edition such as the *Belle dame* project. It is also necessary to gather more detailed information about the various uses that the database will be expected to support.

Gathering and interpreting information about the potential uses of a database requires special expertise in and sensitivity to the subject matter, since what grows out of this process will inform the design of the database tables and their relationships. This process is essentially about determining the most likely information analysis activities readers will engage in when using the edition. A good starting point for this process is the editor herself. As a kind of super-reader and as someone trained in paleography, codicology, and the language and literature of the period, the editor brings to this task a certain set of ideas about how readers may want to use the edition. From there, assessment of potential uses of such an edition can be accomplished by surveying representative readers and their research from the most likely fields, including linguistics, philology, and textual theory.[5] Examining existing editions may also be useful, as may considering the traditions that have evolved in textual criticism and the resulting expectations of scholars who make use of traditionally prepared manuscript editions. Awareness of the efforts of groups such as the TEI (Text Encoding Initiative) and MASTER (Manuscript Access through Standards for Electronic Records) at defining SGML tags for codifying descriptors of texts and manuscripts should also inform the design of the database.[6] Other techniques for understanding the kinds of information readers might want to access could include focus groups at professional conferences; the preparation of a Web site for presenting information regarding the use of databases in managing and presenting edited medieval poetry, with the possibility for feedback from visitors to the site; and the creation of a listserv dedicated to the discussion and dissemination of information related to building and using databases in the management and presentation of medieval poems.[7]

In the case of the *Belle dame* edition, four basic types of readers were identified. The first would be primarily interested in the text at the level at which literary analysis or interpretation is carried out. Such a reader might have a specific research question to answer: for example, 'What does the poet (poem) have to say about love and the role of women in the relationship?' To arrive at an answer, this reader might want to read the full poem in the critically edited version first, so as to identify the passages pertinent to the research question. She or he might then want to look simultaneously at specific passages, stanza by stanza, comparing the critical and the diplomatic (without editorial intervention) versions. In a poem with multiple manuscript witnesses, this access would be three-dimensional, so that the reader would be able to view the same lines or stanzas across multiple witnesses at the same time, in order to take into account the variant readings. For this kind of reader, access to the poem by line, by stanza, and ultimately by the poem as a whole, would probably be of greatest interest.[8]

The second type of reader of the *Belle dame* edition and database would be interested in viewing the poem at a more atomic level than stanza or line, which is to say their interest would be in a particular word or group of words. It is further expected that this type of reader would be interested in the word in terms of its relationship to other words (that is, in a particular context), as well as *meta-data* regarding its grammatical function or simple statistics concerning its frequency of usage or position within the metric unit. For example, a linguist studying the orthographical and dialectical characteristics of the sixteen different scribal versions of the *Belle dame* poem may wish to have access to all of the variant spellings of words used at the rhyme. Statistical data showing that words ending in 'eur' frequently rhymed with words ending in 'our' could provide him or her with valuable information concerning the date and provenance of the scribal copy, as well as on the pronunciation of certain spellings at a given time. This research need would entail requesting information regarding the intra-line position and spelling of particular words in the poem or one of its witnesses. Another example might be a philologist accessing the *Belle dame* edition to determine if this late medieval poem shows evidence of the evolution in the late Middle Ages of the gender of the definite article 'le' from feminine to masculine. The need to search the text for all collocates of this article to see the percentages of masculine or feminine nouns would argue in favour of being able to search the data by word groupings as well as by single words.

A third type of reader, a hybrid of the two described above, might be a scholar interested in line data that is identified by the position or existence of a particular word within the line. Someone studying the use of the rhetorical figure of anaphora, for example, might wish to see all contiguous lines in which a certain word or words are in the first position in the line. This type of reader would require access to both word and word meta-data in order to identify this specific line data.

Finally, a fourth type of reader, scholarly or general, might want to access the text through a particular translation only – say in the modern French or the English – for research purposes or for general interest.

Obviously there is no way to know absolutely all of the types of requests that scholars or readers might want to make of a edition managed in a database. Nevertheless, the editor must try to anticipate to the fullest the uses of the edition, through his or her own knowledge of the domain and through input from sources suggested above. Only in this way will the text of the edition be stored in the database in a manner complementary to the needs of the readers. An understanding of the uses that will be made of the edition will also help the editor to determine the database application tool that will be robust and versatile enough to render the desired functionality.

Designing the Database

The design or model that evolves out of the information discussed above is concerned with essentially three inter-related issues: first, what is the most efficient way to store the content of the edition in the database; second, what are the various logical divisions of the edition by which users will evaluate and analyze it; and third, how are these two sets of *entities* related. Considered as a whole, these issues are about understanding and evaluating (elaborating) the edition's entities and their relationships.

Storing the Poem

Deciding how to store the content of the edition involves determining which of the many possible *entities* of the edition represent its core components. For clarity and to indicate their special role, I will refer to these core components as *super-entities.* Determining super-entities requires consideration of readers' data uses (as I have described above) and optimizing overall data access and data storage. It is also important to consider the physical layout of the poem on the manuscript folios. Consideration of layout, along with use, access and storage, will help to ensure that the texts can be efficiently accessed and easily presented in a format similar to the original manuscript artifact.

For this edition, considering the data access needs of the readers, it seems that the poem, or its metric units, are most efficiently stored and retrieved by line of verse (hereafter referred to as 'line') or perhaps by stanza, while the components of metric unit (words or word phrases) are more efficiently retrieved by word. When considered in terms of their expected use by readers, the atomicity of these components seems sufficient, within their appointed realms, to allow detailed analysis. Opting to store the data essentially twice (in two tiers), first by word and then by line or stanza, seems to solve the problem of having the poem stored in components too small for quick and easy access to a metric unit or complete poem presentation of the data. Also, by storing the data at different levels of *granularity,* we are able to maintain quick and easy access to word level data, yet are not hampered in our ability to present an entire poem or metric unit efficiently. As I noted above, duplicating the data in the database, as I am proposing here, can be an effective way to enhance data access for a database with static content.

Of the higher-level candidates for classification as a super-entity, that is, line or stanza, LINE seems the more appropriate, since stanza can be easily decomposed to line and reconstructed from line when a reader's need demands such use. At the more granular level, WORD seems the obvious choice, since no strong alternatives present themselves and a number of expected reader uses focus directly on word data. Though it is different in significant ways (in terms of both use and storage), a possible third level of super-entity would be the folio image of the manuscript. Though this is not 'data' in the sense of the two levels of super-entities already mentioned, it nonetheless could be beneficial to the reader in that it would allow images of the original manuscripts to be related to the other super-entities and entities in the database. Relating these images to specific metric or lexical units (line or word) enhances the utility of the images in content analysis by making them more readily accessible to the reader.

To get a sense of the access and storage optimization qualities of the proposed super-entities, we can look at how well their size and data-types are balanced against the processing time necessary to retrieve them or their most commonly requested related entities (for example, stanza or poem). As concerns the WORD super-entity, there seems to be little reason to go into great detail, as there are no apparent alternatives to the use of WORD as the super-entity at this lower level. Roots of words could be considered, but for all intents and purposes, this level of granularity seems unncessary. At the higher-level super-entity, LINE presents an interesting, and I think, clear-cut choice. Due to the structure of poetry, particularly medieval poetry, where content is often sub-divided into metric units, we can consider these units as potential units of storage. Furthermore, since LINE is a relatively short *character string* and thus will fit into a *varchar data-type field definition* (wherein the length of any value can be between 0 and 255 characters), we can reap access and storage benefits if we choose this as our super-entity. This is, in fact, the main reason from a data access and storage optimization perspective for selecting LINE over STANZA as our higher-level super-entity. Selecting STANZA would require the use of a data-type often referred to as text. *Text data-type field definitions* are quite different from varchar data-types in that, because they may contain an unlimited number of characters (that is, more than 255), they are stored, less efficiently, outside the database application itself, in the file system (although still managed by the database application), and consequently require more processing time to retrieve. It seems clear from a data access and storage perspective that LINE and WORD are the preferred super-entities.

As noted above, there are also good reasons for storing folio images of the manuscript, since they would provide an additional and interesting dimension to the reader's view of the text. Unfortunately, a discussion of the issues surrounding the storage and retrieval of image data must remain outside the scope of this article.

As is suggested by the mention of folio images, however, the physical look and layout of a manuscript can play an important role in holistically understanding and valuing the variant manuscript witnesses of a poem.

To this end, I believe that considering the general physical layout of the poem witnesses is useful in assessing proposed super-entities and super-entity *attributes*. This is particularly true with the higher-level LINE super-entity, since it is LINE that will be used to re-compose the variant readings of the poem as found in these manuscript witnesses (that is, to recreate the look of the poem to as great an extent as possible using the attributes of the super-entity). Reviewing the physical layout of the poem witnesses in this manner allows one to get a sense of how best to construct super-entity attributes so as to enable as realistic a representation as possible of the physical divisions of the poem. This consideration grows in importance as one realizes that the dimension of a line, the example of our super-entity, contains not only the simple poetic content of that line but may also include abbreviations, decorative elements, scribal corrections and additions, folio and/or page numbers, and marginalia. Obviously, these are components of the line that must be dealt with, both from the perspective of how best to represent them in the database for efficiency of re-composition (that is, display) and for purposes of comparative analysis.[9] Reviewing the physical layout of the manuscript witnesses, as indicated above, is, I believe, an effective way to affirm and/or enlighten the determination of super-entity attributes that will become the building blocks of the electronic edition. I have set out the super-entities and their attributes and domains as they were selected for the *Belle dame* project in Appendix B.

As we move on to a discussion of entities, it is worth repeating that the super-entities proposed above (excluding the folio image super-entity) encompass the components with which all other database entities will be displayed and identified. Stated in another way, this means that all analytical entities must be identified in terms of their relationship to one or both of these super-entities and their attributes or components.

Defining Analytical Entities

Analytical entities are the logical divisions by which the data of a poem can be broken down for analytical and descriptive purposes. The reason for tracking entities as separate units of analysis is so that we can have ready access to data about these divisions. I will call this data the meta-data, since it represents data about the poem and not the poem content itself. In understanding entities, it is also important to realize that meta-data describing a specific entity is referred to as an *attribute* of that entity. So while the term meta-data describes the type of data (that is, data about the poem), the term attribute describes the data's (or in this case the meta-data's) relationship to the entity. Another way of saying this is that an entity's attributes describe that entity and establish its characteristics. In a traditional edition, one would find meta-data in the critical apparatus or perhaps in footnotes to the poem. As concerns entities and attributes, a common example of an entity is WORD (for us this is also a super-entity) and a common attribute for WORD is its definition. In a traditional edition, this entity with this particular attribute would be displayed in the glossary. Another term which is useful in describing an entity's attributes is *domain.* Domain represents the possible values that an attribute may utilize in describing an entity. In some cases, domain is very broad, such as in the example above, 'WORD-definition.' In other cases, domain can be much more limited; for example, the attribute 'WORD-type' would have a limited domain including noun, pronoun, verb, adjective, adverb, article, etc.

For the *Belle dame* project, I have focused on developing analytical entities and attributes that correspond to the traditional divisions of a manuscript edition, including manuscript descriptions, poem witness information, metric unit information, and word description. This is by no means an exhaustive list, though the work involved in preparing even such a relatively short list of entities is considerable. As was noted above, analytical entities are inextricably linked to the super-entities since they, in fact, represent different groupings of these super-entities and meta-data about these groupings. As with all relational database tools, the relationships of these entities are represented through the use of primary keys and/or other unique keys. Using keys and the relational logic of the SQL join command, it is possible to connect these separate entities to express unique views or line/word groupings of one or many of the poem witnesses.

Once the database structure is in place, it is necessary to load text into a database table – also known as populating a database. These tables are the very entities we have been carefully constructing; their attributes have become the database table columns. By populating the table columns, we will be creating rows of data. The charts in Appendix B name some of the *Belle dame* tables, their columns, and the types and domains of data that they will hold.

Populating a database requires some prior text processing. For example, let us consider the LINE table. According to the structure displayed in Appendix B, this table incorporates the following columns:

line_id	a unique line identifier that numbers not only lines of verse but also elements such as rubrics, subtitles, and spaces. (This identifier is different from numbers of lines that are used to identify a specific line of verse in different manuscript witnesses.)
line_type	domain may include rubric, subtitle, line of verse, refrain, envoi, explicit, or empty space
line_no	line number, reflecting poetic unit across manuscript witnesses
line	poetic line content
folio_id	folio or page identifier
marginalia	content of any marginal notations
text_id	variant reading identifier defined by different manuscript witnesses
placement_id	line placement, used in layout to order both lines with content and those without (for example, empty lines that serve as spaces between stanzas)

To load data into these columns and, thereby, to create rows, we must produce or acquire a flat ASCII-based digital file of the poem in which each component of text is contained on its own line. To this file, we would then add a unique item number (line_id) to identify each line of text, whether it be a line of verse, a heading, an explicit, or any other element occupying the line. Each of these unique item numbers would be separated from the remaining content of the same line with a standard separator character (often a TAB or a comma). This same method would be used to add values for all of the remaining columns, being careful to order the columns exactly as they are ordered in the LINE table. In preparing texts for loading into a table, I have found text editors with relatively robust 'search and replace' features or spreadsheet applications that allow for text file manipulation by column to be the most useful tools.

Generally text file manipulation in preparation for data loading is done in stages, with subsequent stages building on prior data manipulations. Due to this fact, it is wise to consider and plan the stages of changes or additions to the text file(s) before actually completing them; in this way, one is less likely to neglect an important addition or change which, if not performed at the correct stage, can result in significantly more work to manipulate appropriately. Thorough initial planning can, in general, save significant time. In like manner, it is wise to begin the data manipulation process with a careful examination of the text file input requirements of the database application that will be used for data storage and manipulation.

Once the database has been designed, built, and populated, data can be extracted and presented to readers. Presentation of data to the reader requires the development of a user interface and the selection of a method of distribution. As we have noted above, the evolutionary path of the Web, along with the standardized and universally available tools used for accessing it, have led to certain choices regarding the user interface and the delivery mechanism for the *Belle dame* edition. These will be discussed next.

Preliminary Considerations in User Interface Design

A number of relatively recent but crucial advances in database and Internet applications have made possible the on-line publication of database-driven editions such as the *Belle dame* edition. Of particular interest are advances in HTML semantics and the development and continuing enhancement of web-based scripting languages, sophisticated web server and browser applications, and database interface applications such as ODBC. A brief discussion of each of these developments will serve to frame the subsequent description of the design chosen for the *Belle dame* user interface.

Evolution of HTML Semantics

Hypertext Markup Language (HTML) is a markup language made up of a set of pre-determined code words, appearing within 'tags' or delimiters (angle brackets <...>) that are embedded into a text to describe the 'look' of a page destined for on-line delivery.[10] Features such as font size, alignment of text and graphics, foreign characters and symbols, background color and texture, multimedia components, and hyperlinks to other pages on the Web or to email forms, are all given specific HTML tags. HTML semantics allow the reader's Web browsing software to determine how to display a Web page on the reader's computer from among a set number of stylistic variations.

Second-generation innovations within HTML, including formatting features such as TABLES and FRAMES, allow information to be presented in more sophisticated ways. Designers now have more control over the layout of information on the page using the tables feature (with borders of varying thickness or completely hidden from the viewer) and can have information displayed in multiple, independently scrollable windows or frames on the screen. Both of these tagging features are used in the *Belle dame* project where poem witnesses are displayed in separate scrollable frames, while within each frame, line components are displayed in invisible table cells. This approach allows the reader to select and view multiple poem witnesses simultaneously for purposes of comparative reading.

Another important HTML development, as regards this project, was the creation of the FORM element within the HTML tag set. This tag allows the editor to configure screens wherein the reader can select different pre-defined options from a menu of choices, or input text into a form to be transmitted back to the site server. When the site server queries the database server for specific information requested in a query, the information is retrieved from the database server and then formatted to display properly in the reader's browser. This feature, which gives the reader the ability to send information from her or his browser back to the site server to have a report containing the specific information requested created 'on the fly,' opens up the possibility for significant interaction between the edition (the web site) and the reader, a primary goal in the *Belle dame* edition.

This type of interactivity is possible primarily because of the FORM element in HTML, but is also due to the availability of scripting language enhancements to HTML.

Development and Evolution of Scripting Languages

Scripting languages such as Javascript and VBScript allow for greater sophistication in the processing of text and images on both browsers and servers. On the client or browser side, they offer a way to pre-process user input (collected via the FORM tag) on the user's own computer, before the input is sent to the Web server, in order to ensure that the input has been entered in the correct format. This pre-processing can provide faster local data type verification and total processing speed than if incorrectly formatted input must be sent out to the Web server and then returned for reformatting. Client-side scripting can also provide for a more visually sophisticated user interface. One example of this that has relevance for the scholarly edition is 'mouse over' activity. As a reader runs the mouse over a highlighted word or image, for example, a text box pops up containing information of some kind. An editor might consider using this application to embed glossary items into the text, with the text boxes containing word definitions. Notes that would traditionally be found as footnotes or endnotes might also be deployed in this way.

On the server side, scripting languages have provided for much greater flexibility in processing and preparing text for formatting in HTML prior to transmission from the Web server back to the browser. When using server-side scripts, the Web server reads the request made from the client's (reader's) browser and finds the requested Web page from among the pages stored there. Any requests for data from the database are passed from the Web server to the database server using a scripting language. After the data is extracted, the Web server executes all commands provided in the scripting language for presenting the data. In this way, data output is tailored specifically to meet the needs or instructions of the client. The Web server then converts the results into plain HTML and sends the formatted page back across the Internet to the client's browser, with the server-side code regarding the data request already executed. Server-side scripting can be used together with regular HTML formatting, text and/or multimedia components, and even client-side scripts (such as the data type verification function described above) to create truly dynamic and customized pages. For the *Belle dame* project, server side scripting plays a critically important role in preparing the data requested from the database for customized and readable display on the client (reader's) browser.

These enhancements in HTML semantics and in scripting languages are also closely linked to the development of more robust Web servers and browsers that are able to manipulate the FORM data and maintain server knowledge on the browser.

Web Server and Browser Application Advancements – Cookies

Advancements in Web server and browser software that take advantage of the interactive features made possible with the FORM tag and the universal availability of relatively sophisticated scripting languages (to enhance the functionality of HTML) have led the way toward the use of Web browsers as universal data access front-end applications. These evolving server and client applications allow for the kind of text manipulation necessary for efficiently retrieving and presenting poem witnesses and meta-data in sites such as the *Belle dame* edition.

One feature of particular importance in this evolution is the interactive maintenance of server knowledge on the browser. These knowledge modules are often referred to as *cookies.* A cookie is a very small text file placed on the user's hard drive by a Web page server when a site is visited. This file identifies the user's particular machine to the Web server, allowing the server to maintain 'state.' Another way of explaining state is to say that the Web server recognizes where the user (the user's machine) has been in an application, because the cookie passes on information to the server indicating what part of the site the user has visited.[11]

Cookies are important because, before their development, Web servers had only ephemeral knowledge of the user requesting a site. Requests for Web pages were independent one from another, and Web servers maintained no memory of what had been sent to a user or what were the preferences of that user. Once the page was sent to the user's machine, the server no longer maintained state with that user. Cookies allow the generally stateless environment of the Web to support state-like features that are common in database application front-ends. When a user makes multiple requests, or refines and resubmits a request, the server does not have to re-identify the user each time; instead, the server uses the cookie to recognize the origin of the request, thus permitting far greater efficiency in handling data queries. Cookies, together with the availability of data interface applications such as ODBC, which will be discussed next, are essential to the presentation of electronic poem editions as described in this paper.

Data Interface Applications – ODBC

The development of interface applications such as ODBC (Open Database Connectivity) has allowed database applications and Web servers to easily interact and exchange data. ODBC is a Microsoft-defined application program interface (API), widely accepted within the database applications industry, for accessing a database.[12] Using the ODBC interface, SQL-like database commands and the resulting data sets can be passed in a *platform-independent* way between Web server applications and database applications. This is possible because ODBC allows programs to use SQL requests to access databases without having to know the proprietary interfaces to those databases. This linkage essentially allows relatively simple Web browsers to access data managed in a variety of potentially sophisticated server-side database applications. Such linkage is an essential feature in the use of database technology to manage the texts of the variant manuscript witnesses, as well as the meta-data about those texts, and thus to create an interactive electronic edition.

Taken together, the evolution of the ODBC interface, the creation of more sophisticated scripting languages, the advancements in browser applications such as the development of cookies, and the extensions to the HTML semantics have all made it possible to conceive of and to develop an interactive, data-driven Web-based edition like the one presented here. They have also had, and will continue to have, a significant impact on the user interface for the edition. In the final section of this essay, I will briefly discuss some of the design features chosen or planned for the *Belle dame* edition.

Designing the User Interface

As with the design of the database, it is critical that the design of the user interface reflect the overarching goal(s) of the editor in preparing the edition and the uses that the editor anticipates being made of the edition, in order to enhance reader satisfaction with the edition. Simply stated, my goal in creating the *Belle dame* edition is to give broad and interactive access to a work that has significant literary interest.

Given this goal, it was natural to consider basing the design of the user interface for the *Belle dame* edition on a Web-defined networking standard and utilizing access tools known as Web browsers, because the Web environment offers several distinct advantages over paper or disc publication.[13] These advantages include the relatively unlimited scale of the edition, the organic nature of the display, the relatively universal and immediate access given to all iterations of the edition, as well as the possibility for interactivity with the reader. The term 'unlimited scale' means that as many views of the textual material can be given as the editor determines desirable, including diplomatic and critical transcriptions of all manuscript witnesses, folio images, glossary, and indices. This type of edition is considered organic because addition of new materials and updates or changes can be integrated continuously into the site, as they become ready for publication. A Web-based edition is universal, because, as long as connectivity to the Internet is not an issue for readers (a complex and contentious issue well beyond the scope of this paper), the work of the editor is universally available once it is placed on-line. Access to the edition is immediate, because all additions, emendations, or corrections to the edition are universally available at the moment they are posted to the site, rather than being tied to a print publication schedule. Finally, such editions have the potential to be interactive, because readers may be given the ability to participate in threaded and archived discussion lists linked to the edition, to make data requests and have reports returned to them, and even to contribute material to the edition itself.

Among the points of access that have been (or may be) developed in response to the anticipated uses of the *Belle dame* edition are:

- An archaeological or diplomatic transcription of each manuscript witness to the text, with punctuation, abbreviations, spelling, and word division appearing exactly as in the original manuscripts.
- The ability to compare variant readings of the text by simultaneously displaying on the computer screen all versions of a single line or stanza as they appear in each manuscript witness.
- A critical edition of each text, with documented editorial emendations and corrections as judged necessary for reader comprehension.
- The identification of an 'Editor's Choice' text, reminiscent of the 'single best text' or 'base manuscript' chosen by editors of print editions. This 'Editor's Choice' text is presented in such a way, however, that the reader can view it at the same time as each one of the other manuscript witnesses.
- The ability for the reader to choose any text as a 'base manuscript,' a kind of floating 'Reader's Choice' text, against which she or he has the ability to display the text of each of the other manuscript witnesses.
- Digitized images of the manuscript folios, allowing readers to view the layout of the text on the folio as well as details such as decoration, marginalia, and intra-linear notations.
- Multimedia components such as audio recordings or video clips of performances of the work (if such are available and copyright permissions can be obtained).
- All manner of analytical searches of the data contained in the database, such as ones to reveal rhyme schemes, grammatical structures, orthographical and dialectal patterns, and so on. The exact nature of these queries will be pre-determined by the editor, but may be modified or augmented if the database design permits.
- The ability to download the raw text of a witness so that individuals with knowledge of SQL and access to other analytical tools can write their own queries of the data.
- Feeder databases where scholars could be invited to add meta-data to

entities in the database not already given attributes by the editor. These would be reviewed by the editor for eventual inclusion in the master database.
- Additional hyperlinks to other electronic literary, historical, philosophical, scientific, and legal documents on the World Wide Web, thereby weaving a broader context in which to situate Chartier's poem of the merciless lady and other poems in the cycle, and thus reifying the intertextual connection between nodes on the Web.
- Discussion lists or subscription forms for listservs to allow readers to discuss various aspects of the text on-line.
- Translations of the 'Editor's Choice' text into modern French and English.

The decision to present this amount of material, however, brings with it the necessity to build an interface that will take into account basic Web design principles having to do with clarity in the presentation of content and user options, with ease of navigation, and with overall attractiveness. A helpful step in the early design stage is to survey similar, text-based Web pages to see what features or techniques can be put to good use to create an aesthetically pleasing, user-friendly, and compelling site for the edition. Feedback from initial users of the edition can also inform the ongoing development of the site, as can awareness of proprietary and non-proprietary innovations in user interface design applications and other Internet technologies.

Consideration of the layout and design features for a Web-delivered, database-managed edition might also take into account the traditional reading experience most people will bring to an on-line edition. In a paper-based edition, access is essentially linear; one progresses from the introduction to a line by line reading of the text, occasionally jumping to the glossary or to a footnote or endnote for supplementary information. While the basic units of text in the edition I am proposing follow the traditional divisions of line, stanza, and poem, access to these units can be either linear (reading the text from start to finish, line by line in a scrollable page or in a linked set of pages) or non-linear (with readers creating customized pages 'on the fly' according to their requests to view specific lines or stanzas). Access can be one-dimensional (a view of a single line or stanza or the entire poem from one manuscript witness) or multi-dimensional (a single line or stanza which is displayed simultaneously as it appears in all manuscript witnesses, so that readers can compare the variant readings). In a sense, the traditional paper-based edition is a sub-set of the new multi-dimensional Web- and database-managed edition. This relationship may be instructive as the editor makes decisions regarding the imposition of the edition on the computer screen and the ways in which readers will be able to interact with the text.

In the current iteration of the *Belle dame* edition, I have chosen to present access options to readers from a table of contents (which appears not only on its own page immediately after the title page but also in abbreviated form in a top border on every page) and from a main text grid (which is an item in the Table of Contents). Sections which include static (non-interactive) commentary on the poem (general introduction, notes on the author and date of the poem, establishment of the text, analysis of the text, plus sections on elements such as the poem's versification, grammar, orthography, and morphology) are hyperlinked options from the Table of Contents. All the manifestations of the poem itself, as well as data on the manuscript witnesses, are accessible from the 'Manuscript and Text' grid.

The columns of this grid contain four headings: Editor's Choice Text, Siglum and Notice, Location and Diplomatic Transcription, and Facsimile. There are sixteen rows in the grid, one row for each of the sixteen manuscript witnesses. One of these manuscript witnesses has a hyperlinked symbol in Column One, which indicates that it is the Editor's Choice Text. When a reader clicks on this link, a critically edited version of that manuscript appears in a scrollable window on the left of the computer screen. At the top of this window, there is a pull-down menu listing all sixteen manuscript witnesses (in their diplomatically transcribed form, including that of the Editor's Choice manuscript), plus an English translation of the poem based on the Editor's Choice Text. When a reader chooses one of these items, it appears in an adjacent scrollable window on the right. In this way, diplomatic transcriptions of any of the sixteen manuscript witnesses can be compared to the critically edited one. In addition, each line number of the Editor's Choice Text is hyperlinked. If a reader clicks on any one of them, the same line in the diplomatic transcription of each of the sixteen manuscripts will appear in the frame to the right, thus allowing the reader to compare the editor's transcription and correction of lines in the Editor's Choice version with variants found in all manuscript witnesses. Forms for searching for specific words or word groupings are also provided. Finally, running the mouse over highlighted words in the Editor's Choice version of the text will trigger the appearance of glossary definitions in a text box (currently under development).

Column Two, 'Siglum and Notice,' lists the two-letter siglum given to each manuscript,[14] which, when clicked, gives a full description of the manuscript and details of its contents. Column Three, 'Location and Diplomatic Transcription,' identifies the library or archive that houses each manuscript and that codex's most recent call number. Clicking on an item in this column reveals a diplomatic (sometimes called archeological) transcription of each manuscript witness, minus editorial intervention. Column Four, the 'Facsimile' column, gives readers access to facsimiles of the original manuscript folios for each manuscript witness.

A full description of the kind of options built into or under consideration or construction in the *Belle dame* interface far exceeds the scope of this article. Suffice it to say that the current interface design for the *Belle dame* edition provides the reader with a level of interactive access to the poem hardly possible in a print edition. Nevertheless, the degree of access is, as stated earlier, dependent on how the editor has structured both the database and the forms for extracting data contained in that database.

If we build the edition around a relational database and have ODBC handle the SQL request made to the database, however, the user interface has the potential to include open access to the data itself. Today, relational databases can often understand ODBC. This makes them compatible with the majority of evolving Web server software tools on the market. In addition, with the ODBC interface, one is no longer limited to using HTML-based Web browsers on the front-end (that is, the client/reader side). The possibility exists now of building more sophisticated front-end applications (user interfaces) that speak directly to the database server, rather than having to go through the intermediary of a Web server. In this environment, an editor can consider giving readers network-based access to specific views of the data content of the edition(s). Readers with a knowledge of SQL could download the raw data and utilize any of a number of commercially available query and reporting tools that employ ODBC to write and run sophisticated data queries tailored precisely to their research interests. This flexibility would be especially useful if a reader's specific interest in the text was not met by the types of queries built into the user interface of the Web-based edition by the editor.

By the time this essay appears, several other new possibilities for dealing with the presentation of the edition to the reader may have been developed. The rapidity of developments in user interface design represents both the promise and the challenge of on-line publication as it is evolving today.

Conclusion

The World Wide Web is quickly becoming the preferred medium of communication for a growing percentage of the world's population, and using databases to store and manage data and information to be displayed on the Web is becoming more commonplace with each passing day and in a wide variety of fields. By adopting an Internet-based means of publication for textual editions, editors are gaining access to the kinds of innovations in user interface applications that have become the trademark of the Internet. This will, I believe, help to ensure and even broaden the readership for these texts.

For the purpose of archiving and preserving works such as *La Belle dame qui eut mercy*, however, it is important that the textual data be stored accurately and systematically, with thorough documentation, so as to facilitate smooth migration into future generations of data storage systems. It is also important that the work be consonant with other major editorial and preservation efforts within the field of textual criticism. The very legitimate work of cataloguing and describing texts and manuscripts that is being conducted by the TEI and MASTER groups is one example. Decisions regarding the design of data entities and attributes (particularly meta-data attributes) in a database-driven edition should reflect the TEI/MASTER divisions (to the extent that they are known and are felt to be applicable) so that it will be possible, at some later date, to write a procedure for generating a version of the poems marked up with the SGML tags used by the TEI or the MASTER initiatives. Incorporating the ability to generate each poem as a complete flat text file that can be transmitted by email might perhaps also be useful to scholars wishing to use one of a variety of textbase-type analytical tools, such as TACT, the University of Toronto–supported, COCOA-standard tool.[15]

Consideration of such efforts as these, as well as careful attention to the design, development, and implementation of database managed scholarly editions, will help to ensure that future readers will have full and open access to important literary texts such as *La Belle dame qui eut mercy*. Our challenge as editors is to continue to make the kinds of choices that will support that goal.

Appendix A: Glossary of Database-Related Terms

Atomicity. The smallest level(s) at which data is broken down for maximum utility; related to the determination of super-entities in the design of the *Belle dame* edition (see below).

Attribute. A descriptor for an entity (for example, line number is an attribute of the line entity, word definition is an attribute of word) which can be used to relate entities; constitutes meta-data about the entity.

Character string. A series of letters and symbols.

Cookies. Small pieces of information sent by a Web server to a Web browser for storage there, so that they can later be read back from the browser, enabling the browser to remember specific information about the user (the user's computer).

Domain. The possible values that an attribute may give to describe an entity (for example, the domain for the rhyme gender attribute would consist of 'masculine' and 'feminine').

Entity. A component of the data which becomes a table in the database (that is, a line is an entity; attributes of that entity are defined and added into the database table).

Granularity. Refers to how fine or detailed the data is.

Join command (query). In SQL programming, join commands or queries are used in normalized databases during a database query to link tables that have related data.

Many-to-many relationship. A type of relationship that enables one to relate (in an unwieldy manner) many rows in one table to many rows in another table. A many-to-many relationship could be created between the line numbers and the line content; however, creating a one-to-many relationship from either table would incorrectly assume that a line can appear in only one manuscript or that one manuscript contains only one line.

Meta-data. Information about data, as separate from the data itself (for example, definition and part of speech represent meta-data on a word).

Normalization. Structuring a database so as to avoid data duplication, often by breaking the database into several narrow tables, rather than fewer wider ones. Normalization is generally recommended to optimize data processing time, since wider tables tend to contain more records with null values. When a request for data is made, all records in the table must be checked, even those with null values, which negatively impacts processing speed.

Null values. In database fields that can have a value or not, these records have been determined to have no value (that is, the database registers them as null), as opposed to a blank space (see 'normalization').

One-to-many relationship. The preferred relationship in normalized databases; one entity in a table (such as line content) is linked to the matching field or fields of many records (such as the actual content of a line from each of the individual manuscript witnesses) in a related table.

Platform independence. Having no barrier due to the operating system on the user's computer (Windows, Mac, Unix, or other).

Primary key. The entity that links one table to another.

Record. Individual piece of data stored within a single cell in a database table. For the *Belle dame* edition, records will contain such data as line number, line content, and individual words.

Super-entity. The core components of the data set; these mark the level at which the data will be stored into tables.

Text data-type field definition. A character field of unlimited length that can contain letters, symbols, and numbers.

Varchar data-type field definition. A character field of variable length that can contain up to 255 elements (letters, symbols, or numbers), but can be set or defined at any logical figure between 0 and 255. Numbers may be included in a varchar data-type field – for example, the year '1492' – but they are treated as characters and cannot have calculations performed on them.

View. A way to only give access to a limited number of columns in a database table; used when making join commands.

Appendix B: Database Super-Entities

In the tables below, I have outlined a sample set of super-entities that I think would be useful to include in the Belle Dame database. The tables show sample entities (WORD and LINE), their attributes, and attribute domains. This is not intended to be a complete list.

Table 1.

Entity: WORD	**Entity Description**: Poem data by word	
Attributes (including data-type)	**Domains**	**Narrative Description**
word_id (integer)	unique numerical identifier (**Primary Key**)	unique number assigned to each word in database as found in all ms. witnesses
word_no (integer)	no greater than the total words in line	the word's numerical placement in the line in which it appears
line_no (integer)	no greater than the total lines in poem	the line's numerical placement in the poem
text_id (integer)	no greater than the total number of variant poems	the number given each manuscript witness to distinguish it from others
folio_id (integer)	no greater than the total number of folios	the folio's numerical placement in the manuscript in which it appears
word (varchar)	must be composed of alphanumeric characters	the word itself
marginalia (logical)	true or false	determination if the word is found in margins or not
word_definition (varchar)	must be composed of alphanumeric characters	concise glossary-type definition
word_type (varchar)	must be composed of alphanumeric characters	determination of the word's part of speech (noun, verb, etc.)

Table 2.

Entity: LINE	**Desc**: Poem Data by line	
Attribute (including data-type)	**Domain**	**Narrative Description**
line_id (integer)	unique identifier – primary key	unique number assigned to each line in database as found in all manuscript witnesses
line_no (integer)	no greater than the total lines of text in poem	the line's numerical placement in the poem in which it appears
line (varchar)	must be composed of alphanumeric characters	the content of the line itself
line_type (varchar)	must be composed of alphanumeric characters	the type of text found in line (including line of poetry, title, rubric, subtitle, refrain, envoi, empty space, explicit, etc.)
marginalia (varchar)	must be composed of alphanumeric characters	the content of the marginalia
text_id (integer)	no greater than the total number of variant poems	the number given each manuscript witness to distinguish it from others
folio_id (integer)	no greater than the total number of folios	the folio's numerical placement in the manuscript in which it appears
placement_id (integer)	no greater than the total lines in poem (with text and without)	a numerical value given each successive line-like space in poem (including line of poetry, title, rubric, subtitle, refrain, envoi, empty space, explicit, etc.)

NOTES

1 In his essay in this collection, for example, Stephen Reimer remarks that even a relatively simple browser-based hypertext involves a fair amount of labour in markup.

2 Several of these manuscripts attribute the poem to Alain Chartier, author of the more famous and long-since edited *La Belle dame sans mercy* (*The Beautiful Lady without Mercy*), a fifteenth-century work about a lady who steadfastly refuses a suitor's request for her love. The fact that the two works are often found together, in the same manuscripts, makes this attribution tempting. Modern scholars, however, have pointed instead to Oton de Granson, the fourteenth-century knight-poet, author of numerous poems on the Saint Valentine's Day theme and on unrequited love. Neither attribution, however, can be confirmed with any certainty.

3 In total, there are almost twenty poems on the same and the contrasting theme of the *La Belle dame sans mercy*, that is, ladies without and with mercy toward a lover's advances. Certain of these poems may even pre-date Chartier's poem. Achille Caulier's *L'Ospital d'amour* and *La Cruelle femme en amour*, and Baudet Herenc's *Le Parlement d'amour*, along with several other anonymous works, make up a corpus that I have called 'the cycle of *La Belle dame sans mercy*.' Those that have so far been identified range in length from 300 to 1400 lines, and are found in at least thirty-eight manuscripts and twelve incunabulae, with many poems found in up to ten manuscripts each, totaling over eighty manuscript witnesses and 3,500 manuscript folios containing the poetry. Cf. Arthur Piaget, 'Les Imitations de *La Belle dame sans mercy*,' *Romania* 30 (1901): 22–48, 317–35; 31 (1902): 315–49; 33 (1904): 179–208; 34 (1905): 375–428, 559–97. Most of these poems are unedited. One notable exception is the Web-based edition undertaken by Jesse Hurlbut of Brigham Young University of Caulier's *L'Ospital d'amour* (cf. http://www.byu.edu/~hurlbut/ospital/toc.html). My larger project is to eventually edit and/or link all of these poems together. The current URL for the *Belle dame qui eut mercy* site is: http://www.innoved.org/belledame.asp.

4 Admittedly, the required expertise for such a project is not inconsequential. In addition to the skills in paleography, codicology, philology, and literary analysis required of an editor of a scholarly edition, such a project requires of the editor, or the technician working with the editor, skills in database design and construction; data transformation, manipulation, and loading skills; database maintenance skills; database querying skills (generally SQL programming); knowledge of HTML and/or additional scripting or software programs; and user interface design skills.

5 Interestingly, the realms of literary study and textual criticism have both traditionally been characterized by the solitary nature of the work involved. This 'go-it-alone' attitude common in both domains can make the editor's task of determining the data needs of end-users most difficult.

6 SGML (Standard Generalized Markup Language) is defined by ISO 8879 and has been the standard, non-proprietary way to maintain print repositories of structured documentation since the 1980s. SGML is a huge meta-language used to mark up, and thus standardize, the printing of thousands of types of documents that must retain all the formatting of the original document and yet be fully platform-independent. If a document has been marked up in SGML, anyone working on any kind of computer system running any kind of operating system and word processing software can have access to the same identically formatted document. Documents tagged in SGML are often technical, containing field-specific notations, symbols, and page imposition, and are found primarily in the government and business sectors. Increasingly, however, documents as diverse as those containing musical scores, vector graphics, mathematical equations, medical records, and catalog entries for medieval manuscripts are being written with SGML to ensure consistent, platform-independent viewing of the printed documents. For more information on SGML, see http://www.oasis-open.org/cover/general.html. The Web site addresses of TEI and MASTER are respectively http://etext.virginia.edu/TEI.html and http://www.cta.dmu.ac.uk/projects/master/.

7 Once a model for the uses of the database has been elaborated, a final review of this model may be sought by presenting it to representative readers or to focus groups from the scholarly community as a whole, to determine whether or not they see it as reflecting their own needs or the needs of their field. Modification of the design may be required at this point, in order to reflect the feedback, and testing may be repeated. While revision to the database design may be frustrating, it is less disruptive than trying to modify the database once it has been developed or implemented.

8 It is perhaps worth noting here that such access could be further enhanced by inclusion of facsimiles of the manuscript folios. This type of reader may want a way to compare the transcription of a particular line, stanza, etc. with how it appears in the original manuscript. However, images that are to be correlated with components of the text can impact the overall database design and must be considered carefully by the editor during the database design phase.

9 Another area of concern regarding the physical layout of the witnesses that should be noted, though it has less to do with determining entity attributes, is the issue of the non-standard letters, characters, and abbreviation sym-

bols that are necessary to represent electronically in the diplomatic transcription of witnesses to the poem. A significant number of these characters or symbols are not readily available for computer generation and consequently require that the editor consider alternative approaches for their representation without detracting from the readability of the text. In this regard, editors must consider the limitations of character sets and the issues such limitations present in electronic editions.

10 HTML tags are a sub-set of the much larger set of tags making up SGML (see note 6 above).

11 For more information on cookies, see http://www.microsoft.com/info/cookies.htm or http://www.cookiecentral.com/cm002.htm

12 ODBC was developed by the SQL Access Group and first released in September 1992. Versions of ODBC now exist for UNIX, OS/2, and Macintosh platforms, as well as for Windows. General information on ODBC can be found at http://searchvb.techtarget.com/sDefinition/0,,sid8_gci214133,00.html.

13 A disc format (CD-ROM or DVD-ROM) was not chosen for this edition because of its inorganic nature. As regards production and distribution, a disc is similar to the traditional hardcover format: the data content of the disk is frozen at the moment of production, and no additional changes or additions can be incorporated unless a new production run is made. Also, distribution of a disc still requires the post office and the expense of postage, plus a considerable effort on the part of the individual wishing to receive the product (given the obscurity of most works of this nature). Though there are other concerns surrounding distribution on the Web, once the potential reader is 'connected' to the medium (the Internet), accessing a site such as the one proposed here is no more difficult that accessing any other site. Furthermore, the marginal cost of this access, considered from the perspective of either the client or the Web server, is not substantial. Finally, it is not currently possible with a disc format to include interactivity with the readership, a feature that was considered to be an important factor in the overall conception of the edition.

14 The system of sigla used in this edition is based on that used by J. C. Laidlaw in his edition of the works of Alain Chartier, because almost all of the *Belle dame* manuscripts are included therein. Where a *Belle dame* manuscript was not included by Laidlaw, a siglum was added following Laidlaw's system as closely as possible. See J.C. Laidlaw, *The Poetic Works of Alain Chartier* (London; New York: Cambridge University Press, 1974).

15 For more information on TACT, see http://www.chass.utoronto.ca/cch/tact.html.

Contributors

Peter Diehl is Associate Professor of History at Western Washington University. He co-edited *Christendom and Its Discontents: Exclusion, Persecution, and Rebellion 1000–1500* (1996) and has written a number of articles on medieval heresy.

Siân Echard is Associate Professor of English and Distinguished University Scholar at the University of British Columbia. She has published widely on the manuscript and print history of John Gower, and recently edited *A Companion to Gower* (2004). Other books include *Arthurian Narrative in the Latin Tradition* (1998).

Joan Grenier-Winther is Associate Professor of French, Washington State University. She has prepared editions of the works of Jean de Werchin and Oton de Granson, and has given numerous talks on computer-based editing.

Anne Klinck is Professor of English at the University of New Brunswick. Her editorial work includes *The Old English Elegies* (1992) and the Middle English *Cursor Mundi,* volume 5 of which, co-edited with Laurence Eldredge, was recently published.

Julia Marvin is Assistant Professor in the Program of Liberal Studies at the University of Notre Dame. She has recently completed an edition and translation of the oldest version of the Anglo-Norman prose *Brut* chronicle.

Stephen Partridge is Assistant Professor of English at the University of British Columbia. He was a contributor to *The Wife of Bath's Prologue on CD-ROM* and has also published elsewhere on the manuscripts and texts of Chaucer's works.

Stephen Reimer is Associate Professor of English at the University of Alberta. His work on the editing of John Lydgate has appeared in such journals as *Notes and Queries*, *Textual Studies in Canada*, and *English Language Notes*. He has recently completed a study of British Library MS Harley 2255.

William Robins is Associate Professor of English and Medieval Studies at the University of Toronto. He has published on Latin and English medieval romance, and on fourteenth-century Italian popular poetry. He is currently preparing an edition of Antonio *Pucci's Cantari della Reina d'Oriente.*

Meg Roland recently completed a PhD in English literature at the University of Washington, and is a faculty member at Marylhurst University. Her interest in the editing of Malory has already led to an essay on the Roman war episode in *The Malory Debate: Essays on the Texts of Le Morte Darthur* (2000). She has also published on textual theory.

William Schipper is Associate Professor of English at Memorial University. His articles on various aspects of Anglo-Saxon manuscripts have appeared in *Anglia* and *The British Library Journal*, and as contributions to books. Most recently he has published a study of vernacular layout style in *Anglo-Saxon Styles* (2003). He is editing Hrabanus Maurus's encyclopedia *De rerum naturis*, and is working on a book on Hrabanus Maurus.

Carol Symes is Assistant Professor of History at the University of Illinois at Urbana-Champaign. She is the author of numerous articles on the manuscript transmission of medieval plays, and is currently at work on *A Medieval Theatre: Plays and Public Life in Thirteenth-Century Arras*, a book examining the historical circumstances that produced the earliest surviving vernacular plays of medieval Europe, and developing a new methodology for studying the impact and importance of pre-modern theatrical media.

Andrew Taylor is Associate Professor of English at the University of Ottawa. He has published numerous articles on reading practice and manuscript studies, and is the author of *Textual Situations: Three Medieval Manuscripts and Their Readers* (2002). He is also co-editor of *The Idea of the Vernacular* (1999), and *The Tongue of the Fathers* (1998).

Index of Manuscripts

Index of Names and Subjects

STUDIES IN BOOK AND PRINT CULTURE

General editor: Leslie Howsam

Bill Bell, et al., *Where Is Book History? Essays in the Emergence of a Discipline*

Hazel Bell, *Indexes and Indexing in Fact and Fiction*

Heather Murray, *Come, bright Improvement! The Literary Societies of Nineteenth-Century Ontario*

Joseph A. Dane, *The Myth of Print Culture: Essays on Evidence, Textuality, and Bibliographical Method*

William A. Johnson, *Bookrolls and Scribes in Oxyrhynchus*

Christopher J. Knight, *Uncommon Readers: Denis Donoghue, Frank Kermode, George Steiner, and the Tradition of the Common Reader*

Eva Hemmungs Wirtén, *No Trespassing: Authorship, Intellectual Property Rights, and the Boundaries of Globalization*

Siân Echard and Stephen Partridge, eds, *The Book Unbound: Editing and Reading Medieval Manuscripts and Texts*